1992–93
14th Edition

ALASKA'S
INSIDE
PASSAGE
TRAVELER

See More, Spend Less!

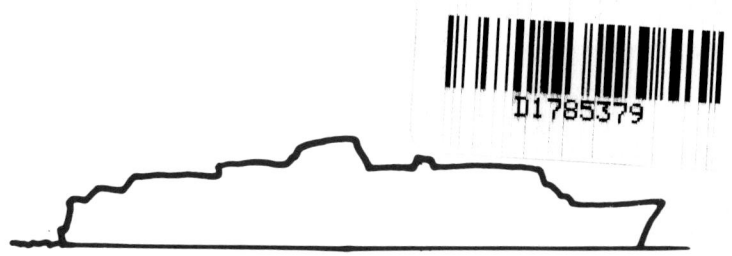

By: Ellen Searby

Windham Bay Press
Occidental, California

Also from Windham Bay Press:

Vancouver Island Traveler by Linda Daniel
The Costa Rica Traveler by Ellen Searby

Alaska's Inside Passage traveler : see more, spend less! / by Ellen
Searby. Occidental, California: Windham Bay Press
   v. : ill., maps ; 22 cm.
   Annual

   ISSN: 1046-5871 0736-9298
   Inside Passage traveler
   Description based on: 14th ed. (1992-1993).
   Continues: Inside Passage traveler 0736-9298 (DLC)sn 83001988
(OCoLC)8469819

   1. Alaska--Description and travel--1959---Guide-books. 2. Inside
Passage--Description and travel--1959---Guide-books.   I. Searby,
Ellen. II. Title: III. Title: Inside passage traveler.

Front Cover: *M/V Taku* approaches dock at Haines.

Back Cover: The Mendenhall Glacier and Mendenhall Towers rise behind Juneau
International Airport and its floatplane pond.

Photos by Ellen Searby unless otherwise noted.
Maps by Ellen Searby and Henry Jori.

Windham Bay Press
Box 1198, Occidental, California 95465

Foreword For 1992-93

After three summers as a U. S. Forest Service shipboard naturalist, answering (or trying to answer) all the questions that more than 30,000 people aboard the Alaska ferries could ask, I thought it would be worthwhile to put the information into book form. Many questions concerned not forest and wildlife, but towns, routes and ferries.

I hope that knowing what is in Southeastern Alaska, how the ferry system works, and how you can make best use of it will help you to have a really great trip.

In this fourteenth edition of the book, I have used the information and suggestions some of you have provided, what I learned as a member of the ferry crew from 1978 to 1990, and current information collected in research. Henry Jori, my husband, has redrawn and improved most street maps of the towns. Please note that all prices are the anticipated 1992 summer rates, except as noted.

As you may know, 1992 is the fiftieth anniversary of the construction of the Alaska Highway. With an all-out push during World War II, thousar.ds of men and machines graded and bridged miles of wilderness in eight months. Today, as you rock over the occasional frost heave in the shortened and improved highway, look at the scenery on either side to appreciate what those recent pioneers faced. Even the smallest villages are celebrating in 1992 and you are invited to join in.

Please send suggestions and information you think others would find useful to Windham Bay Press, Box 1198, Occidental, California 95465. I apologize for having very little time to answer questions (and no time to plan readers' trips), but a 24 hour day isn't long enough.

Many thanks again to all the nice people in towns, visitors' bureaus, the ferry system, and passengers on the ships who helped gather and update the current information we all need.

Have a wonderful time! I hope the sun shines for you.

Ellen Searby

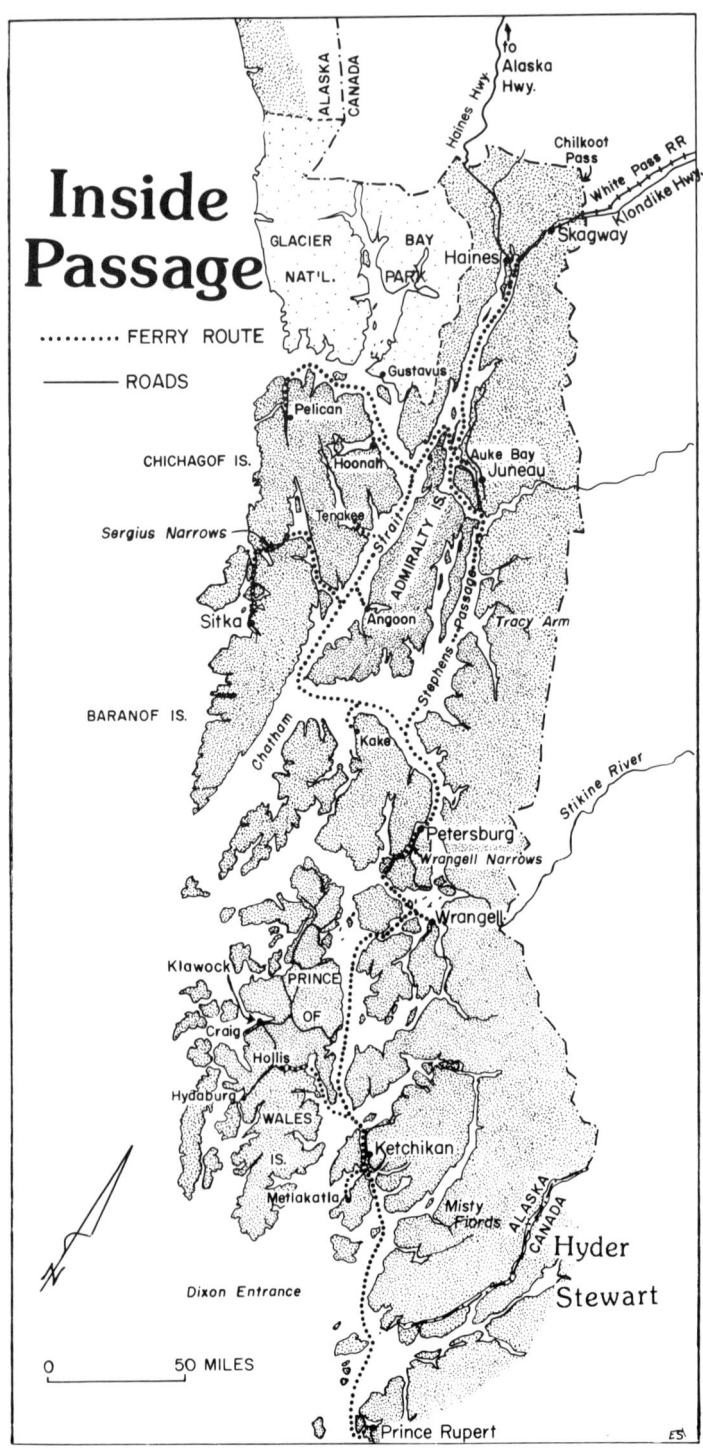

Inside Passage

········· FERRY ROUTE

——— ROADS

ALASKA / CANADA

to Alaska Hwy.

Haines Hwy

Chilkoot Pass

White Pass RR

Klondike Hwy.

Skagway

GLACIER BAY

NAT'L. PARK

Haines

Gustavus

Pelican

CHICHAGOF IS.

Hoonah

Auke Bay

Juneau

Tenakee

Sergius Narrows

Strait

ADMIRALTY IS.

Stephens Passage

Sitka

Angoon

Tracy Arm

BARANOF IS.

Chatham

Kake

Stikine River

Petersburg

Wrangell Narrows

Wrangell

Klawock

PRINCE

OF

Craig

Hollis

Hydaburg

WALES

IS.

Ketchikan

Metlakatla

Misty Fiords

ALASKA / CANADA

Hyder

Stewart

Dixon Entrance

N

0   50 MILES

ES

Prince Rupert

TABLE OF CONTENTS

MAPS AND TABLES

TABLE 1

AVERAGE PRECIPITATION BY MONTH
(in inches)

	KETCHIKAN	JUNEAU
January	12.79	4.94
February	13.35	7.10
March	13.46	6.17
April	13.15	6.43
May	9.70	6.23
June	7.74	3.58
July	7.50	5.34
August	12.17	7.58
September	12.84	9.59
October	24.96	13.01
November	17.90	10.02
December	18.83	10.11
Annual	164.39" (over 13 ft!)	90.10"

AVERAGE TEMPERATURE BY MONTH
(Degrees Fahrenheit)

	KETCHIKAN	JUNEAU
January	34.0	25.8
February	36.5	30.9
March	37.7	33.9
April	43.4	41.0
May	50.3	48.9
June	54.7	55.4
July	58.7	58.9
August	58.7	57.0
September	54.4	51.8
October	47.3	47.3
November	40.7	37.3
December	37.2	32.1

Good luck picking the weather for your trip!

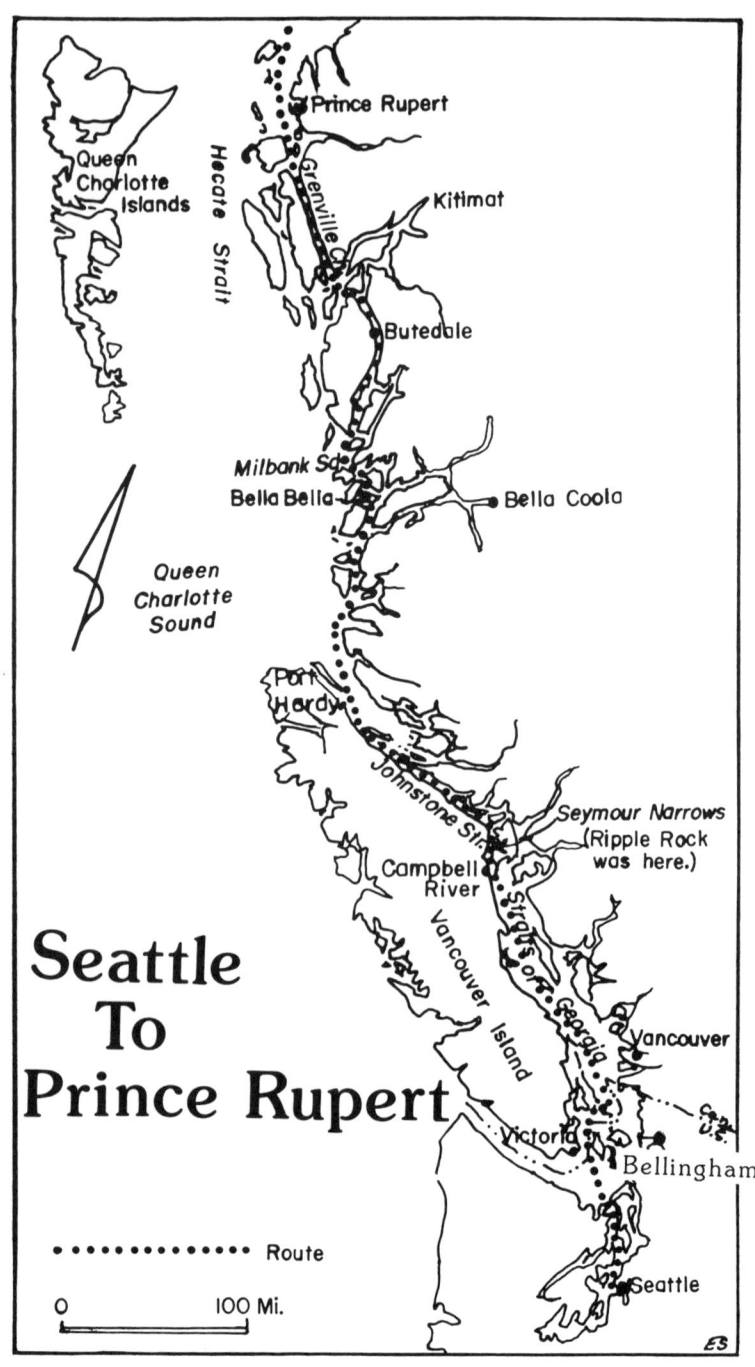

Queen
Charlotte
Islands

Hecate Strait

Prince Rupert

Grenville Ch.

Kitimat

Butedale

Milbank Sd.
Bella Bella

Bella Coola

Queen
Charlotte
Sound

Port
Hardy

Johnstone Str.

Seymour Narrows
(Ripple Rock
was here.)

Campbell
River

Seattle
To
Prince Rupert

Vancouver Island

Strait of Georgia

Vancouver

Victoria

Bellingham

•••••••••••••• Route

0   100 Mi.

Seattle

ES

Bear Glacier "calves" ice into its lake beside the Stewart-Hyder road.

SOUTHEAST ALASKA

Welcome to Southeast Alaska, the northern Inside Passage, the Alaska Marine Highway, and the Tongass National Forest. Here are hundreds of miles of sheltered waterways, islands, mountains, glaciers, fiords, and thick spruce/hemlock forests, with all the wildlife that can live on land and sea. Scattered throughout an area larger than Massachusetts, there are just seven towns and a dozen villages, with fewer than 60,000 people. That leaves a lot of uncrowded country and clean air!

The scenery and climate are comparable to the coast of Norway, but much closer to home. The Inside Passage is one of few places on earth where you can be among mountains and glaciers with no physical exertion, keeping your cardiovascular system at sea level, and without even getting seasick. For the athletic, there are waterways to kayak, mountains to climb, and the Chilkoot Trail to hike.

There are two kinds of weather here: the one that makes the area what it is, and the one you hoped it would be. Rain and clouds are common, but the climate gets drier as you head north. The sunny days are worth it all. June and July are the driest months, while October is the wettest. Do bring rain gear so you can get out and explore, no matter what the weather. For city streets and organized tours, a raincoat, a hat, and waterproof shoes or rainboots are enough. For trail or cross-country hiking,

9

see our Chilkoot Pass and Off the Beaten Track sections.

Most towns in Southeast Alaska are on islands, with water that is often 1000 feet deep between them. There are no roads connecting the main towns, as the expense per capita is simply too great. Water can be an obstacle, or it can be a well-marked freeway, built by nature and maintained at small cost by tides and the Coast Guard.

Alaska has used her natural waterways to provide a transportation system among the people of "Southeastern," as it's often called (and you thought this was the northwest!), and to link Alaska with the "Lower 48"states. Using ships instead of buses and trucks, Alaska has developed the most enjoyable public transit system in the world—the Alaska Marine Highway.

Fishing for salmon and Dolly Varden in Chilkoot Lake near Haines.

The *Malaspina* near Sitka.

THE ALASKA MARINE HIGHWAY

What It Is

The Alaska Marine Highway is Alaska's answer to surface transportation for people and vehicles on the Southeast Alaska coast. People traveling in Southeast Alaska drive, but between its towns they ride the ferries. Your fellow passengers may include the circus, the carnival, Scout troops, and Little League teams.

Sailing the world's longest ferry route, 1060 statute miles in Southeast Alaska, Canada, and Puget Sound, the Marine Highway System began service in 1963 with three new ships named for Alaskan glaciers: *Malaspina,Taku,* and*Matanuska*. The *Columbia,* largest and fastest of the fleet, was added for the Seattle run in 1974. Ferries sail from Bellingham, Washington, and Prince Rupert, B. C., north to Skagway several times weekly, stopping at Ketchikan, Wrangell, Petersburg, Sitka, Juneau, and Haines.

The *LeConte* and *Aurora*, smaller ferries, provide local service to Hoonah, Pelican, Tenakee Springs, Angoon, Kake, Hollis, Metlakatla, and Hyder, as well as to several mainline ports.

Serving most towns and villages in Southeast Alaska, these ferries run through narrow passages close to shore. In Wrangell Narrows and Peril Strait, passengers are near enough to see bald eagles on their nests and sometimes bear and deer on shore. The ferries run all year, though they

11

make fewer trips in winter as ships take turns in the shipyard for annual maintenance.

Two additional ships, the *Tustamena* and *Bartlett*, also are operated by the Alaska Marine Highway. They serve South Central and Southwest Alaska, including Kodiak Island and the Aleutian Chain. Their routes don't connect with those of the Southeast ships, except for several winter runs of the *Tustamena* between Seward and Juneau. These ships and their routes are discussed briefly in the Southwestern section of this book.

Malaspina Campground—the solarium in summer.

The Ships

The gleaming blue and white ships of the Alaska fleet may change your image of a "ferry". Despite running continuously, they are nearly spotless, thanks to the stewards and deck crew.

On the four mainline ships you will find cabins with two or four berths (some with three and five berths on the *Matanuska*), a cafeteria, cocktail lounge, gift shop, and a forward observation lounge. All have closed-circuit TV on which documentary films are played. There is a recliner lounge with airline-type chairs for sleeping if you don't have a cabin, plus free showers and baggage lockers. You can bring your own or rent towels, pillows, and blankets (with a deposit). The *Taku* has the fewest staterooms but has several lounges with tables for writing or cards and it provides plenty of seating even in summer.

The *Columbia* leaves Haines for Skagway, threadding her way between fishing boats.

The car deck holds more than 100 standard-size cars, or their equivalent in vans and campers. You may go to your vehicle while the ferry is in port, or with a crew escort during car deck calls, but Coast Guard regulations do **not** allow you to stay on the car deck while the ship is underway. If you really need something from your vehicle which can't wait until the next port or car deck call, you can ask at the purser's counter for an escort to the car deck. Pets must remain on the car deck in vehicles or in secure containers provided by their owners.

All Southeastern ferries have glassed solariums astern of the bridge on the top deck. These are roofed, somewhat heated, and open to the rear for a clear view of scenery and wildlife. The clean Alaskan air is a real treat. You can lounge in the solarium, and even sleep there in dry comfort if you bring a good sleeping bag, a plastic sheet or tarp, and perhaps a foam pad. A limited number of chaise lounges are provided. On warm days passengers sun-bathe and sometimes even fly kites.

The *Columbia, Matanuska, Taku,* and*Malaspina* have passenger elevators. All are located forward on the car deck. Motorized chairs assist handicapped passengers upstairs on the *LeConte* and *Aurora*. A powered baggage cart hauls baggage between the car deck and the terminal building. Passengers are responsible for all other handling of their baggage. It is convenient to have what you will need enroute packed separately to

13

The *LeConte* approaches the Sitka dock.

bring to upper decks (including medicines, cameras, film, binoculars, etc.) so you can leave the rest in your vehicle. Baggage should not be left on the cart unless you are getting off at the next port. There is space on the car deck to stow it (ask the crew).

Many passenger bring snack food with them, and there are several places on the ships where brown-bagging is allowed, including the solarium. Fire regulations do not allow cooking aboard ship except in the galley. The steward's department will heat baby bottles and fill thermoses, if you bring them, so you can have hot coffee in your cabin. They will also heat special diet foods you bring, but are not equipped to provide them. Prescription medicines such as insulin, which need refrigeration, can be stored in the galley, but food and fish cannot.

Cooks prepare at least three entrees for each lunch and dinner as well as fresh salads, sandwiches and soup. Seafood is featured at each meal, often locally caught salmon or halibut. The *Columbia* offers seated dining service in the dining room, and also has a snack bar serving hamburgers, salads, etc. The other ships have cafeterias.

If you need any help or information, you can ask those incredibly patient pursers (on the cabin deck forward), the watchmen and other crew members, and, in summer, the U.S. Forest Service interpreter.

The *LeConte* and *Aurora* have no cabins,as these ships usually serve shorter distances between ports. However it's possible to ride the *LeConte*

Passengers enjoy a sunny afternoon on the *Aurora's* stern cruising the Portland Canal.

from Skagway to Petersburg via Sitka and other stops, and the *Aurora* from Prince Rupert to Hollis on Thursdays. Both ships do have free showers (bring your own towel), solariums, small cafeterias, and cocktail lounges. They are really just miniatures of the big ships.

How The Ferry System Works

The Alaska Marine Highway is a public transit system (think of a marine bus), not a cruise ship fleet. Its routine is designed to provide the best possible service to an otherwise inaccessible area, which just happens to have fantastic scenery and wildlife. The terminals usually are not downtown, and may even be several miles away. The location of each terminal, and what is within walking distance from it, will be discussed separately for each port.

A ferry may dock at a civilized hour, allowing you to see the town and its surroundings, or it may dock and depart in the middle of the night. This you can discover from the ferry schedule. Stopovers are the solution to untimely landings in towns you want to explore, and will be discussed in the next section. Ferry schedules for summer are available the preceding autumn, and for winter, by the end of August. Early reservations (December) are advised for summer vehicle and cabin space.

The Marine Highway is not quite as predictable as the Los Angeles

15

Freeway. Fog may slow ferries, and reliable as they are, ships do occasionally need repair. When there is a capacity load on the car deck, loading takes longer, and sometimes a ship misses the tide. This doesn't happen often, but you will be more relaxed if you don't plan tight air or rail connections, especially at Prince Rupert and Ketchikan, where the airports are on other islands that must be reached by boat. As there are several areas of tide constraint on the Bellingham run, it's best to allow at least 8 hours for southbound air and rail connections in Bellingham. If you allow 6 to 12 hours at the Skagway end, you will have time to see the town and not miss a bus if the ship is late.

Tides may have more than 20 feet of range between high and low here. Your ship requires at least 5 feet of water under her keel in Wrangell Narrows, and slack water at the tide change when she goes through Sergius Narrows near Sitka. The captain will adjust the schedule as needed for these conditions, borrowing time from port stops to get back on the printed schedule. Occasionally these adjustments allow enough time at an otherwise short stop, like Wrangell or Petersburg, for a walk to town or a visit to a museum. Making up time from port stops may leave no time for exploring some towns, especially in summer when loading the car deck takes longer. If you really want to see a town, plan a stopover.

Because most ferry docks are out of town and the ships often arrive outside open hours, shopping en route can be difficult. In Ketchikan there is a shopping center 1/4 mile north of the dock, with a 24 hour grocery store. This is the easiest port on the whole route to resupply with ice if you need it in your RV. The Sitka stop is long enough, but shopping may mean not going on the sightseeing tour. The gift shops on the larger ships have some supplies and toiletries, as do coin-operated vending machines on board. It's wise to bring what you will need en route, including supplies for children's activities when traveling with children.

Young bald eagle doesn't yet have the white headof a mature one.

The *Matanuska* at the Sitka dock with Mt. Edgecumbe in the distance.

RESERVATIONS AND PEAK SEASONS

In summer the cabins and car decks are full, requiring either reservations or considerable flexibility in your schedule. Reservations are advisable **any** time. For summer travel you should make these reservations by December 10 to be sure of getting your choice of sailing.

Being "on standby" with a vehicle can mean getting up at 3 a.m. to see if you're going to get dropped off at a port to wait for the next day's ship. Standby vehicles usually have to unload at each port and remain in the terminal area for reloading during the port stop. Walk-on passengers without vehicles or staterooms usually don't need reservations between Southeast Alaskan ports though you should have them on the Bellingham run. Even in peak season there often is car space north of Ketchikan as far as Juneau, though not always between Juneau and Haines.

The staterooms are often fully reserved, though there may be some no-shows. If you don't have a room but want one, sign the purser's wait list as soon as you board the ship. In Bellingham the list is available in the terminal. After the ship sails, any available rooms are sold in order from the list. The ferry system now has "dormitory rooms", separate 4 berth rooms for men and women on each of the mainliners where you pay for a bunk instead of the whole room, and share the room with others. No children under 18 or smoking allowed. Reservations are accepted for space in these rooms.

The ferry system accepts applications for reservations any time they are sent in, acting on them in the order received starting the first working day of December. For example, in May 1992 you could apply for ferry reservations for July 1993, and yours would be held until December 1992, but would be acted on before those received in November 1992. Note: at the same time a full staff of phone operators starts taking reservations, putting them on the same computer. Very shortly some sailings from Bellingham have all staterooms booked. If you have only one or two available dates, you may want to write in early but also call on that first working morning in December if you can get a line. Know anyone with an automatic redialing phone? (800) 642-0066.

Your reservation request should include your ports of embarkation and debarkation, names of all members of your party, ages of children under 12 years at time of trip, stopovers if known ahead, width, height, and length **including** bumper and hitch of vehicle, mailing address and telephone number, alternate dates if cabin or vehicle space isn't available, date you will leave home. Fare must be paid at least 45 days before sailing or the reservation will be cancelled.

A toll-free reservation phone system has been installed in Juneau with additional agents for reservations and information, (800) 642-0066 from inside and outside Alaska. The system operates 10–12 hours a day in heavy demand times, so you may get through outside normal working hours in winter. Alaska time is 1 hour west of Pacific time, whether standard or daylight.

Demand for ferry transportation to and from Bellingham greatly exceeds the capacity of the ferry system, especially during peak season. Without building additional ships that aren't needed much of the year, the system can't provide all the staterooms and vehicle space people want. There is some luck as well as early action required in getting those reservations. The alternative, and the pleasure of riding less crowded ships, is finding another way to or from Prince Rupert, British Columbia, using highway, rail, air, or British Columbia ferries, or driving to Hyder, Alaska for the Saturday sailings of the *Aurora*. These are discussed under Prince Rupert and "Driving the Alaska Marine Highway Your Way", the next section. All passengers, including walk-ons, do need reservations to or from Bellingham.

Traffic flow during summer varies as follows, though the trend is for a longer heavy flow in the fall each year:

Northbound: Increasing traffic through June, peaking in mid-July, then tapering off.

Backing a fifth wheel trailer onto the ship with the help of a sailor alongside.

Southbound: Traffic increasing the second week of July and remaining heavy until Labor Day, when it drops off rapidly.

Recently there have been two additional peak periods, at the beginning and end of the winter off-season rates when the car deck may be full in both directions: October 1–20 and April 15–30.

Many people avoid crowded ferries and improve their chances of getting cabin and vehicle reservations, even in summer, by going north in May or early June, returning south in late June or early July. Others go north in August and return after Labor Day.

19

May usually offers **much** better weather than late September or October as well as longer daylight hours. Some tourist activities such as Glacier Bay tour boat and lodge dates and community summer plays are geared to a mid-May to mid-September season. Ferry service increases in frequency during May as ships end winter layup. Life aboard ship is more relaxed with seats available and no lines in cafeterias during spring.

Even in summer, the smaller ferries, *LeConte* and *Aurora*, are generally less crowded than the mainliners.

The weekends of the Little Norway Festival in Petersburg, May 15–17, 1992, and of the Southeast Alaska Fair in Haines, August 12–16, 1992, fill the ships between Petersburg, Juneau, and Haines even for walk-on passengers (reservations advised). If you plan around the foreseeable peak periods, you will find the ships less crowded and more relaxing. A fringe benefit: more of the passengers will be Alaskans, with lots to tell about their home.

Rates for passengers and vehicles, though not for staterooms, are lower between October 1 and April 30, when the driver is included in the fare for the vehicle.

During peak season, you and your fellow passengers will appreciate courtesy in using seats, especially near windows. There are no reserved seats on the ships, so they cannot be held while you eat or sleep somewhere else. You may want to bring a foam or air cushion for sitting on deck on nice days. If you smoke, please observe the smoking areas and think twice before lighting a pipe or cigar in enclosed parts of the ship.

Some passengers use freestanding tents on the stern decks. It's no problem when the solarium isn't crowded, but in summer can take more than one or two people's share of the space and block others' view of the scenery everyone came to see. The Coast Guard prohibits cooking, including inside tents, anywhere on the ship except by the crew in the galley.

Sometimes an all-out effort by the crew in Bellingham or Prince Rupert is needed to fit in all cars. That may mean that it isn't possible to park all vehicles according to their destinations. You may then have to drive off in Ketchikan (and stay with your car during the port stop) so vehicles can be reloaded in the order they will unload farther on.

TABLE 2
MILEAGE AND SAILING TIME ON THE ALASKA
MARINE HIGHWAY FROM BELLINGHAM

Ports	Travel Times at 17 knots	Nautical Miles
Bellingham to Ketchikan	36 Hours	594
Prince Rupert to Ketchikan	6 Hours	92
Ketchikan to Wrangell	5 hours 35 Min.	88
Wrangell to Petersburg	3 Hours	40
Petersburg to Auke Bay	7 Hours 30 Min.	128
Auke Bay to Haines	4 Hours 15 Min.	68
Haines to Skagway	1 Hour	14
Auke Bay to Sitka	8 Hours 45 Min.	131
Sitka to Petersburg	9 Hours 45 Min.	151
Bellingham to Skagway "direct"		934
Bellingham to Skagway via Sitka		1086
Prince Rupert to Skagway "direct"		430
Prince Rupert to Skagway via Sitka		584

Highway—Land Miles	
Haines to Valdez	702
Haines to Fairbanks	653
Haines to Anchorage	775
Skagway to Whitehorse	108
Skagway to Fairbanks	710
Skagway to Anchorage	832

A nautical mile is 1.15 statute miles. A knot is 1 nautical mile per hour. The *Columbia* is faster than the times shown. However all ferries reduce speed in narrows and congested areas and to reach narrows at a chosen time of the tide. Ships on the Bellingham run do not stop at Prince Rupert.

Time

North of the Alaska–Canada border in Dixon Entrance, your route is in the Alaska Time Zone, one hour west of the Pacific Time Zone. Blessed with a state government which doesn't believe in longitude, Alaska in 1983 persuaded the federal government to reduce its four time zones to two. The state is on Daylight Savings when the rest of the nation is.

All ferries operate on Alaska Time even when in Canada or Washington. You change time zones (set your watch back 1 hour) when you board the ship at Pier 48 or Prince Rupert. From there you have a leisurely few days to get over jet lag!

During May, June, and July Southeast Alaska has very long hours of daylight though not the midnight sun that shines farther north. There is nearly an hour more daylight at the north end of Southeastern Alaska than at the south during these months. The situation is reversed in winter as daylight in Juneau is about seven hours a day. In summer the sun is up over 19 hours a day and much of the night is twilight.

Location	Date	Sunrise	Sunset	Daylight Hours
Juneau	June 20	3:51 a.m.	10:09 p.m.	18
	Aug. 20	5:30 a.m.	8:31 p.m.	15
	Dec. 20	8:46 a.m.	3:07 p.m.	6
Prince Rupert	June 20	4:30 a.m.	9:30 p.m.	17
	Aug. 20	6:00 a.m.	8:00 p.m.	14
Seattle	June 20	5:00 a.m.	9:00 p.m.	16
	Aug. 20	6:15 a.m.	7:20 p.m.	13

Approximate times of sunset and sunrise with hours of daylight.

TABLE 3

RATES ON THE ALASKA MARINE HIGHWAY

May 1 to September 30, 1992. Reprinted from the ferry system's full rate schedule.

Staterooms are available on the four major vessels, but not on *Aurora* and *LeConte*. All staterooms have shower, toilet and basin. Two berth cabins are hardest to reserve in peak season. Berths are upper with ladder, and lower. "Outside" rooms have window.

	Bellingham to Skagway	Prince Rupert to Skagway
Passengers, 12 years & older	$ 236	$ 118
Vehicle 15' to 19' long	672	331
Vehicle 25' to 28' long	1420	699
Motorcycle	262	130
Bicycle, Kayak	38	21
Children under 6, free.		
Children 6 to 11, approximately 1/2.		
Pet (free between Alaskan ports)	10	5
2 berth cabins, all ships, outside	228	108
2 berth cabins, all ships, inside	196	93
4 berth cabins, all ships, outside	313	145
4 berth cabins, all ships inside	270	125
3 berth cabin, *Matanuska, Columbia* & *Malaspina*	254	113
4 berth with sitting room, outside *Columbia, Malaspina*	339	156
Dormitory room, per bunk, no children under 18, male or female room,	98	47

Matanuska, running between Prince Rupert and Skagway, also has 5 berth combinations, of 2 and 3 berth cabins.

For rates between other ports or for larger vehicles, see complete schedule. Meals are additional. Rates for passengers and vehicles are lower from October 1 through April 30, and the driver is included then. No out-of-state personal checks are accepted. However Visa, MasterCard, American Express and Diners Club are accepted by phone (800) 642-0066 and (907) 465-3941 and at terminals. Payment must be made at least 45 days before sailing to hold reservations. Lower rates apply to vehicles to 10 feet long (same as motorcycle rate), and subcompacts 10 to 15 feet long. Cancellation fees apply to any cancellation or change made within 14 days of sailing that results in a reduction of fare.

Reservations are strongly advised for cabins and vehicles. Fares are paid separately for each segment if you plan stopovers. Walk-on passengers boarding in Bellingham or sailing to Bellingham need reservations.

At all terminals passengers with reserved vehicles must check in with terminal *before* lining up in parking lot. Check-in times are 3 hours before departure at Bellingham and Prince Rupert, 2 hours at Ketchikan, Juneau, Haines, Skagway, Kodiak, Seward and Homer, and 1 hour at all other ports. Checking in late with a vehicle can result in losing your reservation and going on standby. Anyone cancelling anywhere on the route is encouraged to call the terminal or ferry office so others can plan on the space.

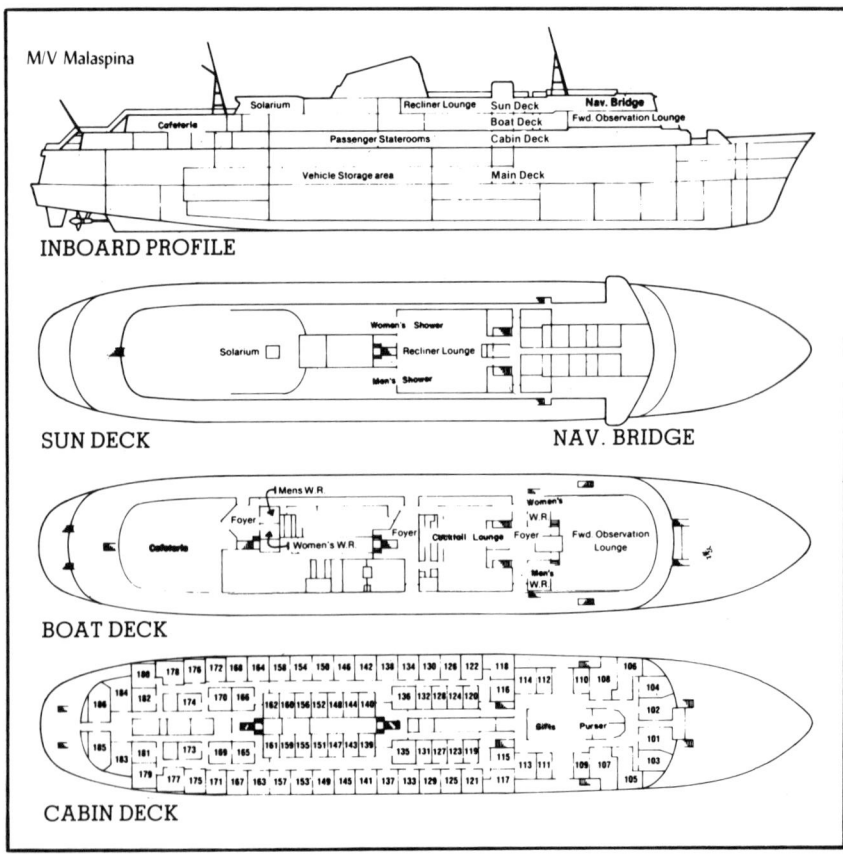

M/V Malaspina

INBOARD PROFILE

SUN DECK   NAV. BRIDGE

BOAT DECK

CABIN DECK

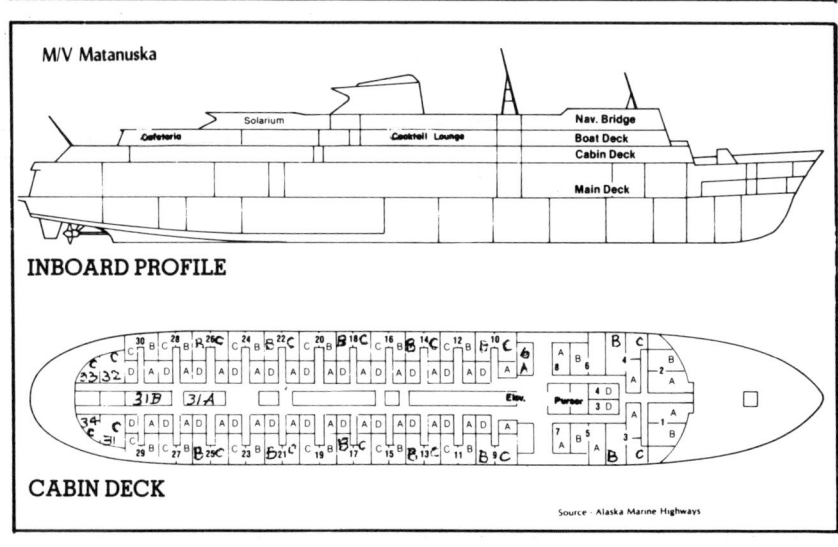

M/V Columbia

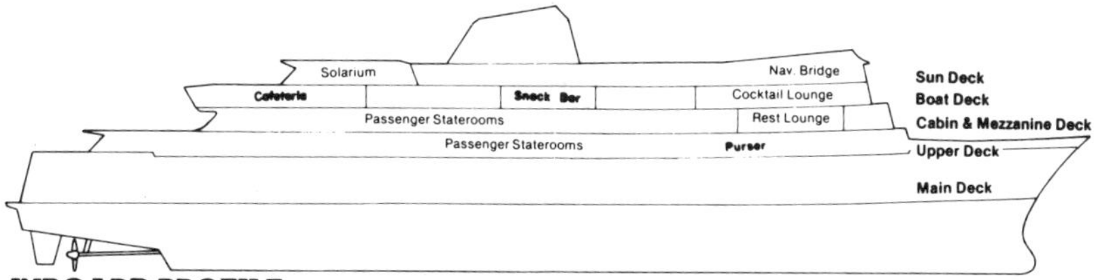

Solarium · Nav. Bridge — Sun Deck
Cafeteria · Snack Bar · Cocktail Lounge — Boat Deck
Passenger Staterooms · Rest Lounge — Cabin & Mezzanine Deck
Passenger Staterooms · Purser — Upper Deck
— Main Deck

INBOARD PROFILE

Cafeteria · Snack Bar · Mens W.R. · Women's W.R. · Elev. · Cocktail & Observation Lounge

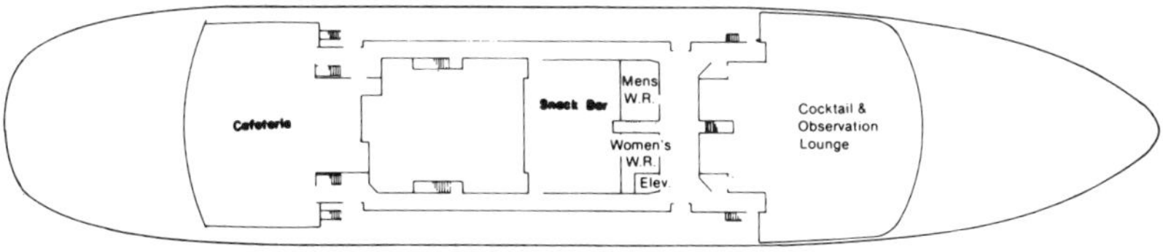

BOAT DECK Cafeteria, cocktail lounge

Camping OK · Women's Shower · Men's Shower · Women's W.R. · Gifts · Women's W.R. · Mens W.R. · Elev. · Forest Serv. · Rest Lounge

238 236 234 232 230 228 226 224 222 220 218 216 214 212 210 208 206 204 202 200
239 237 235 233 231 229 227 225 223 221 219 217 215 213 211 209 207 205 203 201

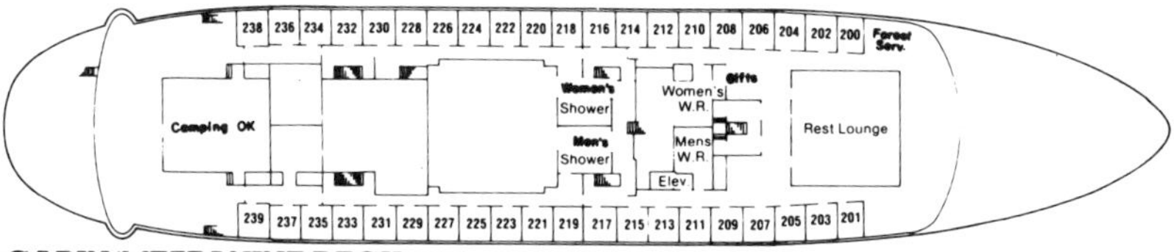

CABIN/MEZZANINE DECK 200-series staterooms

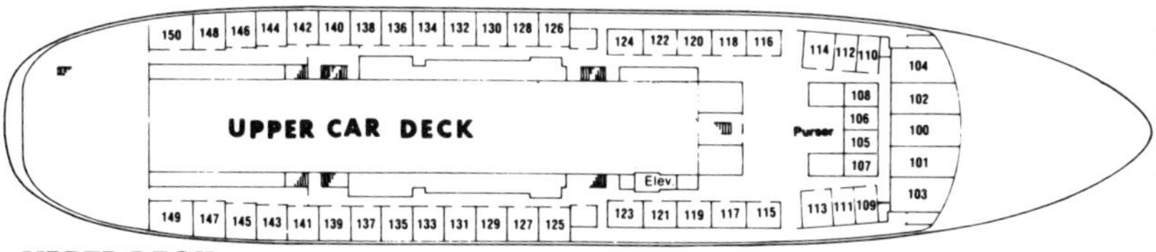

150 148 146 144 142 140 138 136 134 132 130 128 126 · 124 122 120 118 116 · 114 112 110 · 104
108 102
106 105 · 100
Purser
107 · 101
UPPER CAR DECK
Elev. · 103
149 147 145 143 141 139 137 135 133 131 129 127 125 · 123 121 119 117 115 · 113 111 109

UPPER DECK 100-series staterooms

M/V Matanuska

Solarium · Nav. Bridge
Cafeteria · Cocktail Lounge · Boat Deck
Cabin Deck
Main Deck

INBOARD PROFILE

CABIN DECK

Source - Alaska Marine Highways

RV's and travel styles vary widely! On arrival at Haines, some relax and enjoy the scenery and fishing while others seem ready to take on back roads and wilderness. Alaska and Canada are big enough for all.

A trio of orcas or killer whales surfaces beside the ferry. Some alert passengers took memorable home videos.

1992 SEASON

Most staterooms to and from Bellingham are booked early in the preceding December from June 1 through August, though there is usually some car deck space left. At presstime, 1992, the ferry system reports that staterooms throughout the system are booked and car deck space is filling fast, but there is space for walk-on passengers even out of Bellingham. While there are some no-shows and it's worth signing the purser's wait list as early as possible, you can't count on it. In Bellingham the purser's list is in the terminal. For all other ports it is at the purser's office aboard ship.

From Prince Rupert car and stateroom space is limited until May when the *Malaspina* and *Matanuska* come back on that run. For the remainder of the summer this port offers the most car deck and stateroom space as there are 4 mainline vessel sailings per week, plus the *Aurora* on Wednesdays and Fridays. Alternatives are traveling southbound during early summer, traveling earlier or later, or flying to one of the Southeast Alaska ports and riding ferries around their route from there. From Prince Rupert the *Matanuska* has the most staterooms, the *Malaspina* has them, but the *Aurora* does not.

Sailing times from Prince Rupert vary with tides to avoid having two ships using docks at the same time, particularly at Sitka. In-port times at Wrangell and Petersburg have been lengthened, allowing time for a walk ashore on many sailings, though often at unlikely hours. Most Skagway

27

stops are 1 to 3 hours long, though the *Malaspina* on Thursdays, are usually there for several hours, making a good excursion from Juneau or Haines.

Sailings To And From Bellingham

Columbia: Friday evenings, starting May 1, 1992. Has 91 staterooms and room for 140 cars, though some is taken by freight vans. Sailings are at 6-9 p.m. Reserved vehicles must check in before 3 p.m. or risk cancellation. Foot passengers usually start loading about 4 p.m. Southbound Bellingham arrivals are Friday mornings. Stopping at Sitka southbound, the *Columbia* leaves Skagway on Monday afternoons.

Note: In summer 1992, the *Columbia* will make one extra round trip between Juneau and Skagway per month, in late May and in mid-June, July, and August (during the Haines Fair). Check the schedule for exact dates. When she does this, the usual 6 hour layover in Skagway from mid-morning Monday to afternoon will not apply. Some through passengers may want to schedule to avoid a delay, while others could take advantage of a half-day stopover in Juneau or a round trip excursion from Juneau to Skagway or Haines.

In winter and early spring either the *Matanuska* or *Malaspina* leaves Bellingham on Friday evenings.

Taku : Tuesday evenings starting May 12 to mid-September. Smaller but very comfortable ship has 44 staterooms and room for 90 cars. With all its lounge space compared to staterooms and vehicles carried, the *Taku* always has seating even in peak season. Some lounges have tables for writing or playing cards. Will stop at Sitka northbound on Friday mornings and stop 3-4 hours at Skagway, mid-morning on Saturdays.

Sailings To And From Prince Rupert

Matanuska: Tuesday and Saturday mornings. Has 112 staterooms, mostly 2 and 3 berth, and room for 105 cars. Tuesday sailing stops in Sitka mid-afternoon on Wednesday, has 3-4 hour stop at Skagway on Thursday afternoon.

Malaspina: Monday and Thursday mornings. Has 86 staterooms and room for 105 cars. Most outside rooms are 4 berth and most inside rooms are 2 berth. Stops at Sitka southbound Saturday about midnight, and has 3-4 hour layover at Skagway late Friday night.

Aurora: Wednesday and Friday mornings. Has no staterooms. Takes cars as far as Ketchikan and Hollis. Also sails from Hyder (Stewart, B.C.) on Saturday afternoons in summer, connecting with the *Columbia* in Ketchikan.

Northern Panhandle

LeConte: Has no staterooms. Takes cars and vans. Leaves Petersburg Monday evenings and continues to Skagway via Kake, Sitka, Angoon, Tenakee, Hoonah, Juneau, and Haines. Has several runs to Sitka per week with stops at most of the villages listed above.

She goes to Pelican at least once a month all year, but more frequently in summer, usually twice a month, May through September. For additional information, see the section on Pelican. With a 1–2 hour layover at Pelican, this is a scenic, enjoyable excursion from Juneau.

The *Queen of the North* loads vehicles at Port Hardy for the run to Prince Rupert.

British Columbia Ferries
Port Hardy to Prince Rupert

The British Columbia ferry, *Queen of The North*, sails between Port Hardy on northern Vancouver Island and Prince Rupert.

In summer 1992 it is running all-daylight 15 hour cruises between Port Hardy and Prince Rupert, with all departures at 7:30 a.m. and all arrivals about 10:30 p.m. There is a short stop at Bella Bella. Note that a shipload of passengers can fill accommodations in Port Hardy the night before and the night of the ferry's arrival. We have listed motels in the section on Port Hardy and advise making reservations. Port McNeil, a few miles farther south, also has several motels.

B.C. Ferries

Schedule:	Lv Port Hardy	Lv Prince Rupert
June	odd dates	even dates
July	odd dates	even dates
August	even dates	odd dates
September	odd dates	even dates

The *Queen of the North* has food and drink service, elevators, day rooms for one-way travelers and staterooms on the boat deck which may be reserved for round trips, including 4 equipped for wheelchairs.

1992 Summer Fares, Port Hardy to Prince Rupert (lower in winter), Canadian $, driver included

Passenger, 12 years & older	$ 85
Vehicle to 7' high, 20' long	175
Vehicle over 7' high	300

Surcharge for vehicles over 20' long, $8.75–14.96 per ft. over 20', depending on whether vehicle is under or over height. *Note the saving* if you take off any cartop baggage or boat you can while riding the B.C. ferries, if it will allow you to stay at standard height! Dayrooms, 2 and 4 berth. Prices vary with deck.

While the B.C. ferry dock in Prince Rupert adjacent to the Alaska ferry dock allows ships of both lines to be docked at the same time, if the southbound Alaska ferry is late, you may not be able to make same day connections there as the B. C. ferry sails promptly at 7:30 and you have to unload and clear Canadian Customs with a shipload of passengers. If you can spend a day in Prince Rupert and reserve accordingly, it will be a surer thing, especially with a vehicle. Northbound passengers arrive on the B.C. ferry the night before so the connection is easy, though you will have to stay ashore that night.

British Columbia Ferry Corporation, 1112 Fort St., Victoria, B. C., Canada V8V 4V2. Phones:

Vancouver	(604) 669-1211
Victoria	(604) 386-3431
Fax:	(604) 381-5452
Port Hardy	(604) 949-6722
Prince Rupert	(604) 624-9627
Bellingham	(206) 676-8445

Sitka Run in 1992

On most ship arrivals in Sitka there is only one ship scheduled to use the dock which usually means a bus tour of town is possible. Bus tours are available for arrivals after 5 a.m. until late September with the museum open and coffee waiting! Sitka really does welcome you!

In 1992 most ship arrivals are scheduled for mid-day or early evening, except for the *Malaspina* on Saturday nights, and some *Columbia* sailings. I've noted the days each ship goes to Sitka in the earlier section on sailings from Bellingham and Prince Rupert. The smaller *LeConte* sails to Sitka several times a week and lays over there most of the day on Saturday on a round trip from Juneau, a good weekend excursion.

Information, Reservations

For reservations, schedules, and information: **Alaska Marine Highway**, P.O. Box 25535, Juneau, Alaska 99802. (907) 465-3941 or (800) 642-0066, anywhere in the U.S. including Alaska. In Anchorage, (907) 272-7116.

Important! If you're meeting an arriving ferry to get on or pick up a passenger, it's wise *always* to call the terminal an hour ahead of its scheduled arrival to see what time it is actually arriving. There's a phone number with a recording during closed hours in each town. Scheduled arrivals are given for a day or two ahead on the phone and on a notice board at each terminal.

Alaska Division of Tourism, P.O. Box E, Juneau, Alaska 99811. (907) 465-2010.

TravAlaska Tours, 555 Fourth & Battery Bldg., Seattle, WA 98121, (206) 682-4101 and **AlaskaBound**, 207 Main St., Ketchikan, AK 99901, (907)225-6131 have computer terminals on the ferry reservation system. They sell package tours which include additional services. Sometimes they have ferry staterooms available in spring after the ferry system is booked up.

AlaskaPass, Box 897, Haines, AK 99827. (800) 248-7598. (907) 766-3145 from Canada and locally. Offers transportation passes good in both Alaska and Canada for buses, trains, B.C. and Alaska ferries, for 8, 15, 22, and 30 day trips Between May 31 and September 15. If you're going to be on the move for most of the trip, these can save over $100 per person.

Great Alaska Highway Society, P.O. Box 74250, Fairbanks, AK 99707. (907) 452-8000. Call or write for information on 1992 celebrations of the Alaska Highway construction 50th anniversary.

DRIVING THE ALASKA MARINE HIGHWAY—
YOUR WAY

The Marine Highway is a well-designed system with thoroughly competent, experienced crews, running along an incredibly beautiful route. If you simply get on at one end and ride to the other, you will have a memorable trip. I you want to experience more of Southeastern Alaska, here is how you can do it:

Getting to the Ferry

From outside of Southeastern Alaska, you can reach the ferries at the following locations.

BELLINGHAM, Washington: 90 miles north of Seattle on I-5. Airlines to Bellingham and via Bellingham Airporter from SeaTac. Highway connections with bus service. Ferry sailings weekly, all year.

PRINCE RUPERT, B.C.: Airline, rail, and highway connections from interior Canada; airline from Vancouver; and B.C. ferry from Port Hardy on Vancouver Island. Ferries sail every other day in summer, less often in winter. In winter the ferry runs from Tsawwassen near Vancouver to Prince Rupert so one can choose whether or not to drive to Port Hardy. For accommodations in summer, especially at Port Hardy, be sure to get reservations in advance. (Note that we publish a guidebook to Vancouver Island,*Vancouver Island Traveler*, by Linda Daniel. To make the most of your time on the Island, with all its choices for adventure, see information on the last page of this book.)

From Horseshoe Bay near Vancouver, you can take the B.C. ferry, with or without your car, to Nanaimo near Victoria. You can then drive up Vancouver Island or ride the bus, **Pacific Coach Lines**, 710 Douglas St., Victoria, B.C., Canada. Phone (604) 287-7151 to Port Hardy at the north end. It's a 7 hour bus ride. For additional information, **British Columbia Ferry Corporation**, 1112 Fort St., Victoria, B.C., Canada V8V 4V2. Phones: Prince Rupert, (604) 624-9627, Port Hardy (604) 949-6722 Vancouver (604) 669-1211, Victoria (604) 386-3431. Schedule and fares are given in 1992 season section. Reservations are a must in summer, especially if you bring a car. Rail information is in the Prince Rupert section.

STEWART/HYDER: Highway. Ferry *Aurora* meets the highway here on Fridays in summer at the head of the Portland Canal, most scenic route into or out of southern Southeast Alaska. Reservations for vehicles are a must as ship is small and doesn't came back until the next week!

Forested islands and inlets line the Inside Passage.

HAINES, ALASKA: Haines Highway, connecting with the Alaska Highway, and bus service. Motorcoaches, bus: **Alaskon Express**, mid-May to mid-September. (800) 544-2206. **Alaska-Denali Transit**, alternative style, inexpensive bus, year around. (907) 273-3331.

SKAGWAY, ALASKA: Highway and bus to Whitehorse, Yukon. White Pass and Yukon Railroad runs excursions only from Skagway to Fraser, just over White Pass summit in Canada in summer, and has small rail cars serving Chilkoot hikers from Bennett to the highway. The Klondike Highway connection to the Alaska Highway southeast of Whitehorse is open all year.

Some mines have reopened and the ore is being hauled from Whitehorse to Skagway on truck-trailer rigs over 80 feet long. Do not try to pass them going up hill or down! They will pull over at pull-outs to let you by.

Airlines: Ketchikan, Wrangell, Petersburg, Sitka, Juneau and Gustavus in Southeastern Alaska have jet service with **Alaska Airlines**. **Delta Airlines** serves Juneau from Seattle and Fairbanks. Smaller air taxi services make connections to other towns.

Alaska Airlines toll free (800) 426-0333.

Delta Airlines toll free (800) 221-1212. Delta has announced it will cease operations in Southeast Alaska September 11, 1992, though rumors fly that it will be back in summer 1993.

Unlike flights on more competitive routes in the Lower 48 states and even the route from Setttle to Anchorage, the flights serving Southeast Alaska from Seattle and Anchorage feature some of the *highest* seat/mile costs in the country. There are discounted fares, especially during the off-season. Senior fares are slightly lower than super-savers and can be used for one-way flights. They don't have to be bought weeks ahead. It's well worth planning your trip to use any of these you can. (Markair flew through Southeast for a few months in 1992 but left in May.)

Alaska Airlines and **Delta Airlines** offer seniors 62 and over a coupon book of 4 or 8 coupons which must be used within a year. It takes 2 coupons to get from anywhere in the Lower 48 to or from Alaska ($568 for the round trip at presstime). The rate is very low if you're coming from farther away than Seattle, much less than super or ultra saver fares. You are limited to certain days of the week and can only reserve space 6 days ahead of the flight. Presently a 4 coupon book would cover a round trip from as far away as Miami, obviously subject to change without notice. Note that **Delta** stops only in Juneau between Fairbanks and Seattle, one flight north and south daily.

Many people fly to Juneau and use ferries for excursions throughout Southeast. *Suggestion:* for a very enjoyable week, you could fly from Seattle to Ketchikan, and ride the ferry to Skagway and back to Ketchikan in just over two days going direct both ways, or in three days if you go to Sitka on one leg. This would allow several days for stopovers in your choice of towns.

Alaska Airlines and the ferry system sometimes have a package fare allowing you to fly one way and ride the ferry the other.

AlaskaPass, Box 897, Haines, AK 99827. (800) 248-7598. (907) 766-3145 from Canada and locally. New in 1990. Offers transportation passes good in both Alaska and Canada for buses, trains, B.C. and Alaska ferries, for 8, 15, 22, and 30 day trips between May 31 and September 15. If you're going to be on the move for most of the trip, these can save over $100 per person.

Ferry stopovers at ports along the way usually cost only $4 to $8, equal to the difference between a through fare and separate tickets between the ports where you plan stops. Check the schedule when you are planning this to see which ferry you want to catch for the next leg. Make reservations (cabin or vehicle) before you leave the terminal if you have not done so already.

Walk-on passengers: It is easier to be flexible if you don't have a vehicle or a cabin, as there is usually space available on any of the ships for

Park Avenue Campground in Prince Rupert is near the ferry terminals (Alaska and B.C.).

walk-on passengers. Get a reservation to or from Bellingham, perhaps in Juneau and Haines during fair weekend in the third week of August, and between Juneau and Petersburg on the weekend nearest May 17, the Little Norway Festival. You may weigh this convenience against the use you could make of a camper ashore. In general, there are few roads to drive on out of town, and these are short. Drivers may spend time that they would prefer to spend sightseeing at ports in vehicle line-ups waiting to load or reload.

Vehicles: Leaving your vehicle in Bellingham (next section) or Prince Rupert is one solution. Bringing a bicycle, very inexpensively, on the ferry, is another. Many people travel without vehicles, saving considerable cost on the ferry, and rent a car as needed in ports where they stop over.

If you are traveling with a vehicle, you can plan stopovers ahead and reserve vehicle space for those segments of your trip. Once the cars are loaded on the car deck according to the ports where they will be unloaded, it is too late to change your mind. Note the required check-in times for vehicles at each port. Late arrival during loading can cost you your car deck reservation, putting your vehicle at the end of the standby line.

U.S. licensed vehicles may be left in Canada for as long as 45 days without a permit. In Prince Rupert they must be left in an authorized parking lot or with a private home where they can be parked off the street. They must be reported to the Inspector of Customs, either at his office in the Federal Building (Post Office at 2nd Avenue and 2nd street), to the right of the 2nd Ave. entrance or at the Alaska ferry office at the ferry dock before departure.

Note that Alaska has a child restraint law for children under 12 in vehicles. They must be in approved child seats if too small to use seat belts. Canada has a similar law and requires all passengers to buckle up.

Recreational Vehicles

With increasing hotel rates, many people planning leisurely tours and stopovers bring camping vehicles or trailers. All campgrounds in Southeast Alaska will accommodate vehicles up to 24 feet in length, with some having room for longer ones. Most spaces are not drive-through so you will have to maneuver. U.S. Forest Service and state campgrounds do not have hookups while most private trailer parks do. These are listed with the communities. Dump stations and sources for ice, propane and diesel are also listed.

During peak season, vehicle reservations to or from Bellingham require early (January) applications and some luck. Reservations to or from Prince Rupert, B.C. are much easier to get. You can drive to Prince Rupert through interior Canada on paved roads, camping along the way, or ride the British Columbia ferry from Port Hardy at the end of Vancouver Island.

The cost of carrying a vehicles on the ferry increases rapidly with length over 19 feet. Check the ferry schedule for details. The length is the total length of deck space covered, including trailer hitch, bumper, trail-bike carried on the back, etc. The B.C. ferry has a hefty surcharge for vehicles over 20' long or over 7' high. There is a surcharge for vehicles over 8' wide on the Alaska ferry.

You will need to be able to back and maneuver the vehicle accurately. Seamen on the car deck will direct you, but you'll enjoy the trip more if you can do it easily. The length of overhang at the rear of the vehicle is important. While loading ramps are two-stage and can be adjusted, the change from horizontal car deck to steep ramp at low tide is considerable. If you have more than a 2 foot overhang behind your rear wheels, you may want to have a protective bar added there. If you have a motion sensor or burglar alarm on the vehicle, you should deactivate it as the ship's motion may set it off.

You'll want to be sure your water and holding tanks seal tightly and check them regularly during the trip to be sure that recent travel on rough roads haven't started leaks. Propane tanks will be inspected and

The *Columbia* enters Wrangell Narrows.

sealed by ferry terminal staff before you board the ferry. Any spare fuel cans will be stored in the paint locker on the car deck after you board. Don't forget to pick them up when you leave.

If you carry perishables, including fish, on longer trips, it's best to plan ahead. A propane refrigerator will be off as the tank will be sealed. An electric one is OK if you have it on a separate battery so that running it won't make your RV battery too weak to start the vehicle. You will not be able to run the engine while it's parked on the car deck to recharge nor will you be able to plug into the ship's power. For short trips, the refrigerator will hold its temperature. For longer trips, you may want to put a chunk of ice in it. The Ketchikan shopping center two blocks from the ferry is a good place to get more if your vehicle remains on the ship. Note that it's 36 hours non-stop from Ketchikan to Bellingham.

If you fill your gas tank just before getting on the ferry, any increase in temperature may make it overflow onto the car deck, creating a fire hazard. To avoid delay, you should be sure your vehicle is in good enough condition to get on and off the ship unassisted. Be sure all switches are off before you leave your vehicle.

Remember that Coast Guard regulations will not allow you to stay in your vehicle on the car deck when the ship is underway and you will not be able to cook in it even when the ship is docked. You will be able to go to the vehicle whenever the ship is in port and at scheduled car deck calls when it is more than 8 hours between ports. If you run out of medicine, diapers, etc., and can't wait until the next port or car deck call to go to your vehicle, you can ask at the purser's counter for an escort. It's easier to plan ahead and bring what you'll need when you leave the vehicle.

On The Car Deck

A glance will tell you that the car deck is a working space, an equipment loading area. Eighteen wheel truck-van units maneuver in the small area along with cars, trailers, and RV's with blind spots from the driver's view. In summer when the crew is trying not to leave stand-bys behind at ports, you'll think they deserve a Golden Shoe Horn Award for fitting the last few in.

Foot passengers leaving the ship may go to the car deck as the vessel approaches the dock and the purser announces it. As the baggage cart is usually first off, that's your chance to put your gear on it for the ride up the ramp. Another choice is to take your bags down to the cart at the port before the one where you're getting off(just before the ferry leaves). Then you'll be ready to get off before the cars move.

If vehicles are moving when you're walking on or off, it's important to follow the crew's directions to get across the car deck and stay on the walkway of the loading ramp without stopping unnecessarily. Farewells and picture-taking are best done on the upper decks. If you're standing by your vehicle to see if you have to get off, the safest way is to sit in it. Standing where vehicles are unloading is dangerous for you and delays the unloading. When you drive a car off, the crew and your fellow passengers will appreciate your not starting it until a crew member tells you to, to avoid unnecessary exhaust fumes on the car deck. If you will need help loading or unloading, you should ask the purser.

Staterooms

Staterooms are paid for separately from passage tickets. You can buy a passage and vehicle ticket for the whole distance that you will travel and then reserve cabin space, if it is available, for those segments on which you will need it. Four-berth cabins are generally easier to reserve than two-berth. Four-berth rooms have two lower and two upper bunks. The *Matanuska* has more two-berth cabins than the other ships. See deck diagrams at the back of this book for cabin layouts. Outside rooms face the outside of the ship and have windows, for slightly higher charge. The *Taku* has two staterooms with bathrooms designed for wheelchair use and all the other ships have at least one.

Each mainliner has separate dormitory rooms designated for male and female passengers, allowing you to pay for one bunk instead of the whole

Group of traveling seniors enjoys a day side trip near Haines.

room. You must be willing to share the room. Smoking and children under 18 are not allowed in these rooms.

For passengers on a hurried trip, staterooms offer a welcome rest. All cabins on the *Malaspina, Matanuska, Taku,* and *Columbia* have washbasin, shower, and toilet. All electric current is standard household, 110 volt. There is a closet and a ladder for reaching the upper bunk. Rooms are cleaned and made up before you enter, but cannot be remade daily by the stewards. You may request extra blankets and towel changes at the purser's counter.

Remember the alternatives to cabins: the recliner and forward lounges, and using your sleeping bag in the solarium. A suggestion based on personal experience: being able to stretch out full length is more comfortable for a whole night than recliner chairs which don't recline very far. With a foam pad or air mattress and sleeping bag, sleeping on the deck, inside or out (if it's not raining or you're in the solarium) is comfortable. Except for the Bellingham-to-Ketchikan run, the time between adjacent ports is 10 hours or less.

Baggage

A powered baggage cart will haul your baggage between the car deck and the terminal on shore. You are responsible for all other handling of it. If you are riding beyond the next port, you should remove your baggage from the cart on the ship, for its safety at port stops and to leave space for others. While there is no limit on the amount of baggage you can bring in a vehicle, the baggage cart is for hand luggage only (not to exceed 100 pounds)—not for freight, household moving, boats or rafts (even disassembled). Clearly anyone who can paddle a boat or raft is more able to pack it onto the ship by hand than the arthritic oldster who has to carry his suitcase because the baggage cart is full. The crew will show you where to put canoes or kayaks safely. I recommend you pack only the amount you can easily carry at one time. You don't need many extra clothes—Alaskan living is simple. But don't forget raingear.

A reminder: the baggage cart is usually the first off and last on at ports. If you're leaving the ship and want your baggage carried up to the terminal, you should go to the car deck to load the cart as soon as the purser says the car deck is open.

Binoculars are helpful for close-up looks at eagles and other wildlife. These, and anything else you will need en route, including medicines, cameras and film, should be brought to the upper decks before the ship leaves the dock.

Children

As on any long trip, people traveling with children on the ferry should plan for their interests and safety. The trip can seem long for them, especially between Bellingham and Ketchikan where there is a day when the ship doesn't stop. There is no place on the ship to run that is not on someone else's ceiling. Quiet on the cabin deck is important to fellow passengers who may be trying to rest. The Forest Service naturalist may have some children's programs planned north of Prince Rupert. Walking ashore at stops helps. Games, books, coloring materials, sewing, knitting, according to age and interests would be worth bringing. One of those big doodle posters should last the whole trip. Older children might enjoy being provided with a simple camera and film to make the trip really "theirs." Climbing on the ship's rail is **dangerous** as the water is very cold and a child might fall overboard without being seen. For their safety you should know where your children are all the time they are aboard. They can find the trip a real adventure if you explore the ship and scenery with them as well as providing other diversions.

A play area for small children has been added to the aft lounge of the *Taku* on the cabin deck. The *Columbia*, *Matanuska*, and *Malaspina* have smaller play areas.

Peaks and glaciers are on both sides of Lynn Canal north of Juneau.

Seniors

The Alaska ferry system offers standby passage for a $5 boarding fee (each ticket) to seniors 65 and older between Alaska ports on the smaller ferries, the *LeConte, Aurora, Bartlett,* and *Tustamena,* except for sailings between Whittier and Valdez or Seward and Valdez, May 1 though September 30. This rate covers passage only and does not include meals, rooms, or vehicle. From October 1 through April 30, seniors may travel on all the ferries at 50% of the adult fare and may reserve vehicle and stateroom space. If you will use one of the senior fares, carry your Medicare card and plan to get the senior ticket for the portions of the trip where you will use it. Refunds aren't given for the reduced rate after you have traveled on a regular adult ticket.

You might book passage on the ferry from Bellingham to an Alaska port and then plan to use the smaller ferries for some trip segments or excursions.

Throughout Southeast Alaska many admission fares and some campground fees are reduced. For reductions at Forest Service campgrounds you need a Golden Age card. Most senior rates in British Columbia apply to B. C. senior residents only.

Alaska and **Delta Airlines** both have Senior fares similar to supersavers. Anyone over 62 is eligible. **Delta's** coupon book, with some conditions, is the lowest fare applying in Southeastern Alaska, but only gets you to or from Juneau.

Elderhostel offers programs during winter and spring on many round trips from Bellingham featuring staterooms, instruction by specialists who travel with the group, and tours ashore in several places—all at very reasonable rates. The groups I've seen on the ferry seem to be having a wonderful time. These are open to people over 60 and the spouse or companion of a participant, regardless of age. There are some Elderhostel programs given in summer that are shore-based, sometimes in Juneau and Sitka. For information, check the Elderhostel catalog in your local library or write **Elderhostel**, 80 Boylston Street, Suite 400, Boston, MA 02116-4899.

The following information applies to both senior citizens and handicapped individuals of any age. The pass privilege rate between Alaska ports on a stand-by basis has been extended to all year on the smaller ships only, the *LeConte, Aurora, Bartlett*, and *Tustamena*. Note that the first three of these don't have elevators or staterooms. Free travel is **not** allowed between May 1 and September 30 on the *Bartlett* or *Tustamena* between Whittier and Valdez or between Seward and Valdez. On the Tustamena's runs out the Aleutian Chain, I recommend buying a ticket rather than using the pass on a stand-by basis.

Handicapped

People of any age who have a certifiable physical or mental disability of 70% or more,, may apply to the ferry system for a $10 two year pass enabling them to travel free, space available, between Alaska ports from October 1 to May 15 on all the ships and all year on the smaller ones. This covers basic passenger fare but not stateroom, vehicle or food. The ferry system furnishes an application form which requires a physician's statement. The completed form is reviewed by the ferry system to see if it complies with the resolution passed by the Alaska legislature, and if so, a pass is issued. One should allow a month for this though the process generally takes less time.

Facilities for the handicapped are being added as the ships are renovated. Presently the *Taku* is the most completely equipped, with paraplegic staterooms (you should request one when making reservations), a restroom built for wheelchair use, and a ramp into the forward observation lounge. All four mainliners have elevators. On the other ships the crew will assist those who need help to the upper decks. Motorized rising chairs carry wheelchair passengers to the upper deck on the *LeConte* and *Aurora*. The *Matanuska* and *Malaspina* have ramps into their forward lounges and they and the *Columbia* now have staterooms adapted for wheelchairs. You should request these if you need them when making reservations..

Special diets are not provided on board though they can be heated in the microwaves on all vessels if you bring them. The stewards will refrigerate insulin if you request it.

The Reluctant Traveler.

Pets

Pets must remain on the car deck in vehicles or in strong containers, which must be provided by the owners. There is a surcharge of $5 for taking pets between Prince Rupert and any Alaskan port, and $10 between Bellingham and Alaska. At stops you may walk your pets ashore. Most travel times between ports are less than 8 hours, but Bellingham to Ketchikan can take over 36 hours and Petersburg to Sitka about 10 hours. Scheduled car deck calls will allow you to walk your pet on the car deck. Passengers are responsible for clean up, and a scooper is recommended. Tranquilizers may be advisable for nervous pets for their comfort and to avoid barking, which carries widely through the ship. Dogs really appreciate being walked at every port no matter what the hour.

Riding the ferry can be great fun for you, but probably isn't enjoyable for animals. In World War II we were supposed to ask ourselves "Is this trip necessary?" to save gas. You might well ask yourself the same for the pet. If he must travel, plan for his comfort with adequate space, water, ventilation, and his usual food. Even if he doesn't really need to go ashore, he'd certainly appreciate a pat and some encouragement at every car deck call or port—and you'll have a chance to spot any problem early. For its own safety, a pet should be leashed any time it's out on the car deck or ramp. If you have a bird in a cage, ask the purser for instructions.

Tlingit dancers from Hoonah perform on the dock at Tenakee while the LeConte is in port.

Arts on The Ferries

While the ferries don't specialize in entertainment like cruise ships, sometimes entertainers, musicians, and artists perform on board, particularly during winter. Upcoming performances are listed in the ferry terminals. Call (800) 642-0066 for a schedule. Enjoy when they're aboard!

Sitka Run

Each of the larger ships, northbound or southbound, goes to Sitka once a week. The *LeConte* also sails there several times a week. It costs no more to go the extra distance when you are riding between Petersburg and Juneau, but it does take almost a day longer. The time will be well spent even if you don't stop off in Sitka, because of the narrow passages, great scenery and wildlife. To be sure of being on that run, check the schedule. The ship passes through Peril Strait, Sergius Narrows (where you can

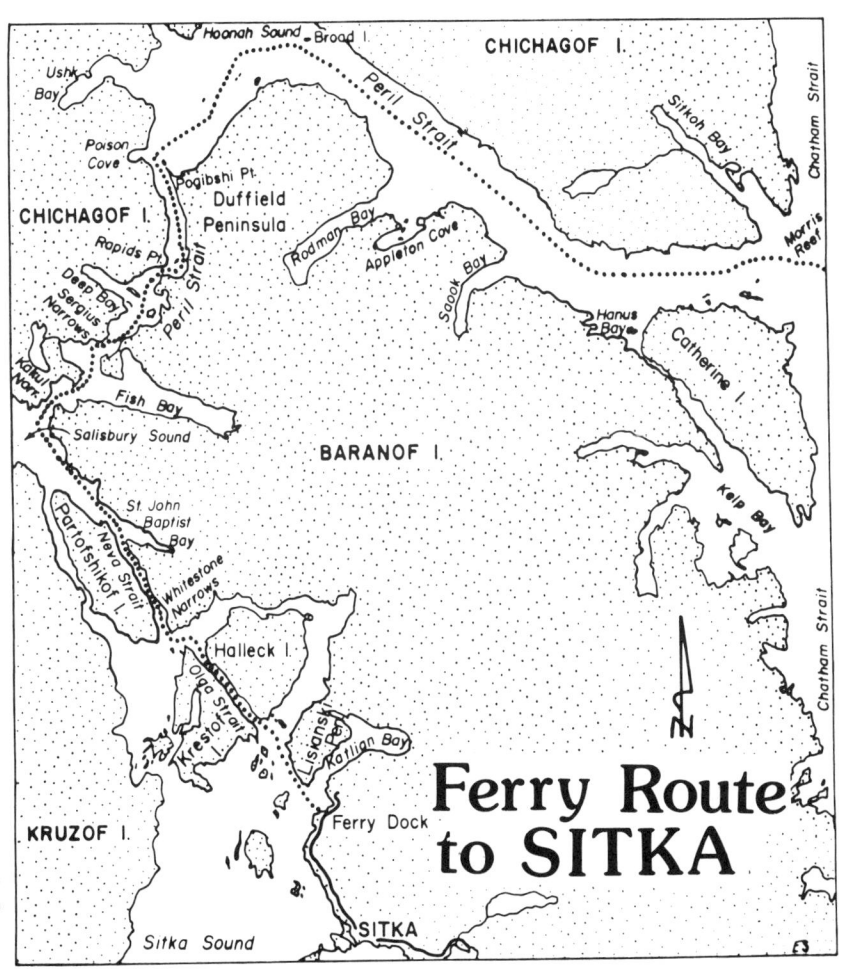

Ferry Route to SITKA

almost pick branches from the trees as you go by), and Olga and Neva straits. Leaving Sitka you follow the same route back out to Chatham Strait. Since the ship must wait 6 hours for slack tide at Sergius Narrows, you may have as much as 3 hours to spend in Sitka. The dock is 7 miles from town, but there usually is time for an optional bus tour or a trip downtown if it is daytime and there are no other ferries using the dock. When the captain schedules departure time, the purser will announce if a bus tour is possible.

The bus tour passes all the Russian buildings in town, and stops at Sitka National Historic Park and Sheldon Jackson Museum (good Russian and Indian artifacts). A longer tour is given for people staying in

In Sergius Narrows passengers enjoy a close-up view of the forest. The ship's wake shows how close we really are!

Sitka.

To be sure of seeing the town, and of having more time to enjoy the museums and Russian buildings, you may want to stop over. Note that both the tour bus and the bus to town leave very shortly after docking, so board the buses quickly or you'll miss them.

Smaller Ferries

You can see more of Southeastern Alaska by riding the *LeConte* and *Aurora* on their local routes. Based in Juneau, the *LeConte* serves the Tlingit villages of Hoonah, Angoon, and Kake, the fishing port of Pelican and Tenakee Springs on Chichagof Island, in addition to mainline ports.

Most passengers on these ships ride their marine bus regularly to shop in Juneau, Sitka, Petersburg, or Ketchikan. Some schedules allow them to come into town, shop for 4 or 5 hours, and return home. Before Christmas it's like being on Santa's sled without the reindeer!

In summer these ships are generally less crowded and have a more relaxed, local atmosphere than the mainliners. If you have time and don't need a stateroom, the *LeConte's* run from Juneau to Petersburg via Hoonah, Tenakee Springs, Angoon, Sitka and Kake, will add another dimension to your trip. The villages all have at least one hotel if you want to stop over. Reservations advised.

Pelican is an attractive fishing village beside scenic Lisianski Inlet on Chichagof Island, a one-day round trip from Juneau. In 1992 the *LeConte* will go twice a month in summer. The ship stays for an hour or more, allowing time to walk uptown on the boardwalk main street. En route scenery and usually whales make this a fine excursion from Juneau.

The *Aurora*, based in Ketchikan, goes to Hollis on Prince of Wales Island, connected by roads with Craig, Klawock, and some fine fishing and hunting areas. Prince of Wales Island has the most extensive road system within Southeast Alaska and lots to explore. There are no facilities except a waiting room at Hollis, but there is shuttle service to Craig and Klawock. Vehicles should have reservations.

The *Aurora* also goes weekly in summer to Hyder, actually docking at Stewart, B. C., where she can load vehicles up to 25 feet long. She stays about 6 hours, time enough to explore. The 9-hour trip up the scenic Portland Canal is a fine excursion. She leaves Thursday evening and arrives in Stewart Friday morning. She leaves Stewart Friday afternoon and arrives back in Ketchikan about midnight Friday.

The *Aurora* also goes from Ketchikan to the Tshimshian village of Metlakatla on Annette Island. On Saturdays in 1992 you can go from

Ketchikan to Metlakatla in the morning and return in the evening. On other days you may be able to reserve space in the only motel in Metlakatla to stay over. Metlakatla would be fun to explore. I'd bring a bike to ride the flat road out to Pt. Davidson.

The *LeConte* and *Aurora* have snack bars, and both ferries can carry limited numbers of cars. Several of their trips make good 1 or 2 day outings, even if you are not staying over.

Photography

The Inside Passage is a great place for photography, whether you are professional or simply want a few nice shots to show friends back home. If this is your first trip here, the following suggestions, based on what works for me, may help. The frequent rain and fog plus the ship's vibration make planning worthwhile. On any trip you'll improve your odds for good pictures by being very familiar with the camera, including loading film and rewinding, before you leave home. It's also well to bring all the film you think you'll need, plus a bit more. Shops along the way may be out of the film you use. If your camera is electronic, bring at least one set of spare batteries.

For color slides I use Kodachrome 64 under almost all conditions. I usually use a skylight filter, sometimes a polaroid. Particularly in summer, daylight hours are long enough so you rarely have to shoot in twilight. For black and white photos in this book I used Tri-X shot at 300 or 400. Most of the time I used a yellow filter, though some were shot with a polaroid filter. For bright days, especially in British Columbia where there's a greater variety of trees, a green filter would be good for black and white film to show the different tree species.

My cameras are two Pentax ME bodies (and a Pentax K-1000 for durable back-up), one with black and white and the other with color film. I use a Pentax 50 mm lens and a Vivitar 70-210 macro zoom lens, switching them between the identical camera bodies—and usually remembering to change the filters unless I'm using polaroid. The zoom is a marvel for photography from a ship where one can't control the distance to a boat or glacier. Unless you're going to use incredibly fast film, 300 mm is probably as much as you can hold steady on a moving ship. On shore, and sometimes when the engines are shut down at a dock, I use a Tokina 400 mm for wildlife. I use a Tokina 28 mm wide angle lens for deck shots, sea to mountaintop scenery, and in towns. On trips I take a changing bag for removing jammed film without losing the whole roll—rarely used but sometimes useful.

Keeping camera and film dry is all-important. Damp film jams easily in a camera. A rubber lens hood will keep raindrops off the lens or filter if it's not windy. In windy conditions with a telephoto lens, the hood may catch so much wind you have to remove it to hold the camera steady. I was able to keep working during an entire rainy afternoon in Petersburg by using a lens hood and tucking the camera in my rain parka whenever I wasn't shooting. I used a yellow filter to increase contrast. A good camera bag plus plastic bags helped.

On the ship, it's worth stepping out on deck for any picture you really want instead of shooting through windows. I dress warmly for the Narrows and stay out on deck (hypothermia in December!). The stern decks and several spots along the side decks on each ship are sheltered from the wind. From the stern you can photograph whatever comes up on either side, but there is more engine vibration. The side decks forward have far less vibration, important if you're using a telephoto. Photos used in this book were taken from both areas. Some spots on the stern decks have more vibration than others. I try not to let my camera or any part of my upper body touch the ship while shooting. Tripods are great on shore but they pick up engine vibration you can't even feel.

Some of these suggestions also apply to VCRs. You'll want a wind shield to avoid noise on your microphone if you use it outside.

Good luck with your pictures and the weather!

Exercise

For those who want to do more in fresh air than simply enjoy the scenery, you plan brisk walking laps around the ships on deck, adding flights of outside ladders (stairs, to the non-sailor) where the open deck doesn't go all the way around. If you run on these, or play hacky-sack, it will be disturbing on someone's cabin or dining room ceiling—about 5 on the Richter scale. The cabin deck stern (lowest deck) on all the ships is above the car deck. Running in place here is OK. Jumping would probably bother the people in the nearest cabins.

The ship offers many opportunities—but don't climb anything. The deck rails are about the height of a ballet barre. With the ship's wake, luminous at night, rushing by, you won't even miss the music if you're doing stretching exercises at the rail or on deck.

For hard core runners, planning a long run the day before and after the ferry trip may help, especially on the Bellingham-Ketchikan section where the ship doesn't stop. At most port stops there is a road leading away from town for good running if time permits. You should be back aboard the ship at least 15 minutes before announced departure as the ramp goes up *before* the departure moment. Otherwise you may share the feeling I had once, hundreds of miles from home in a sweaty T-shirt and running shorts, watching my ship pull out.

The Narrows

The high points of any ferry trip are the narrows. Wrangell Narrows—the 21 miles just south of Petersburg, is a 46-turn slalom course for ships. In several places the channel is only 300 feet wide and 19 feet deep. Watching the precision and seamanship of your captain and crew is a thrill, night or day. At night the channel and range markers flash in red, green and white. Near Blind Slough, you can see 16 markers ahead, and it looks as if you are winding through a Christmas tree. In daylight, Wrangell Narrows and Sergius Narrows, near Sitka, offer your best chances of seeing wildlife up close. These are eagle nesting areas where sometimes you'll also see deer or bears on the beach. Seals and sea lions haul out on some rocky islands. All the larger cruise ships miss these channels, going around the islands instead.

A humpback whale surfaces here only enough to clear its blowhole for a breath.

Whales

You may spot whales, especially humpback and killer whales, at any time. Sometimes the mate on watch announces them on the ship's speaker, though the mates are often shy about doing this because the whales sometimes dive soon after they are sighted. From the solarium, you may see whales come up behind the ship. Humpback whales tend to congregate in May and June near Juneau, Auke Bay, and the south end of Douglas Island. They usually can be seen July through September in Lower

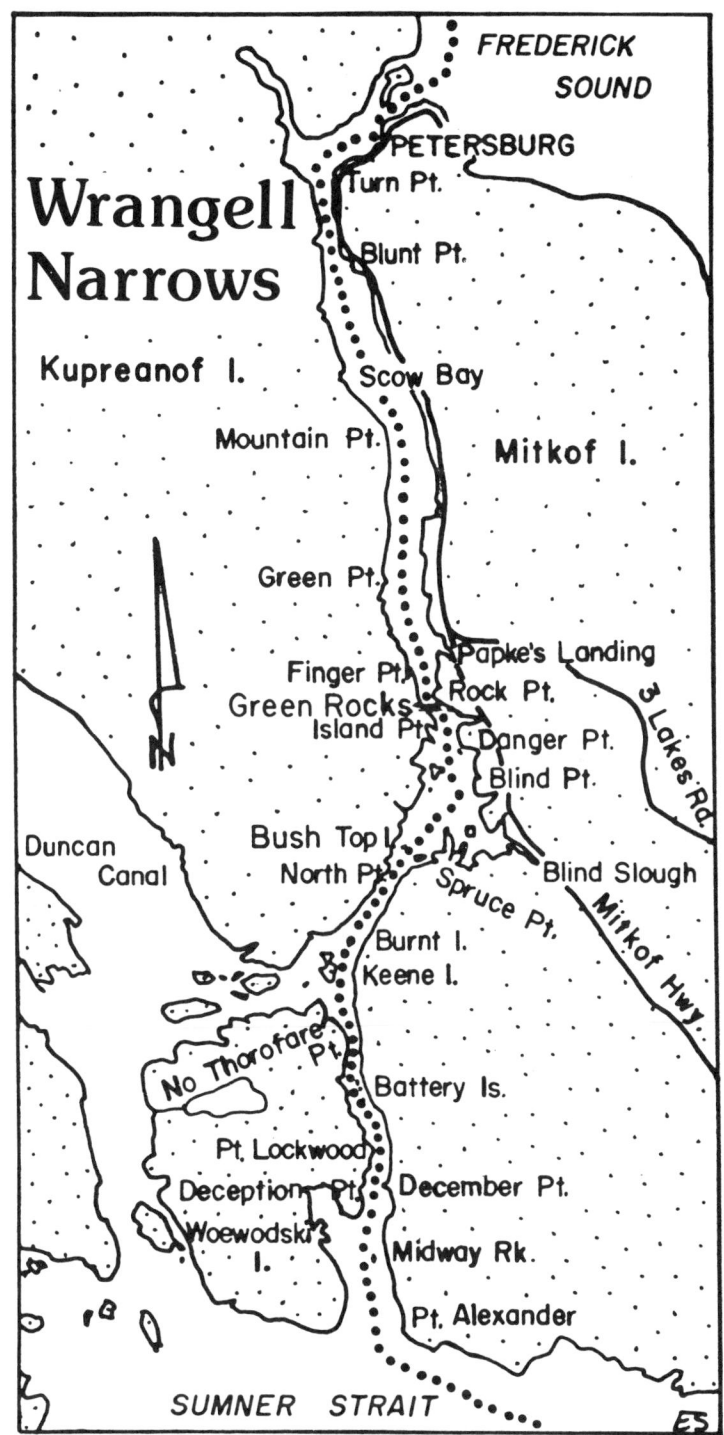

Wrangell Narrows

FREDERICK SOUND

PETERSBURG

Turn Pt.

Blunt Pt.

Kupreanof I.

Scow Bay

Mountain Pt.

Mitkof I.

Green Pt.

Papke's Landing

Finger Pt.

Rock Pt.

Green Rocks

Island Pt.

Danger Pt.

Blind Pt.

3 Lakes Rd.

Duncan Canal

Bush Top I.

North Pt.

Spruce Pt.

Blind Slough

Mitkof Hwy.

Burnt I.

Keene I.

No Thorofare Pt.

Battery Is.

Pt. Lockwood

Deception Pt.

December Pt.

Woewodski I.

Midway Rk.

Pt. Alexander

SUMNER STRAIT

N

ES

Stephens Passage, about 1.5 hours north of Petersburg. Passengers traveling through these areas in daylight may see as many as 40 whales, often very close to the ship. On trips to Pelican with the *LeConte*, you'll nearly always see whales near Hoonah.

Bears

Brown bears, the same species and irritability (caution!) as grizzly bears, live on Admiralty, Baranof, and Chichagof islands, as well as on the mainland. Black bears live on other islands, especially Prince of Wales, and on the mainland. You may see bears along the shore, particularly in spring, near skunk cabbage patches and stream mouths. Watching such spots from the ferry in the narrows, or even when docked at quiet places like Angoon, may let you see one safely. Fish streams and berry patches in season also attract bears. These can be hard places to see bears before you get too close. While you may like surprises, bears generally don't.

Most Alaska brown bear pictures are taken at McNeill River on the Alaska Peninsula or at Denali National Park. In Southeast Alaska tideflats and stream mouths almost anywhere on Admiralty, Baranof and Chichagof Islands during fish season offer the possibility if you're lucky and your lens is *long*. Brown bears are sometimes seen along fishing streams north of Juneau during salmon runs. The bears in and very near Juneau are black bears and their rare subspecies, the blue or glacier bear.

Pack Creek on northern Admiralty Island (reached by boat or plane) is famous for its bears although the ones there are usually females and cubs rather than big males. To protect the bears and avoid personal injury, the Forest Service has made some restrictions on where people may go, time of day, where food is allowed, etc. Peak season varies, but is usually July 10-August 20, when permits may be hard to reserve. The weeks just before or after that may have fewer people and just as many bears.

A viewing tower is planned to replace an old one built by the CCC. Until the tower is usable, visitors are kept 150 yards from bears fishing in the main creek unless a bear chooses to walk closer. You'll want binoculars and at least a 400 mm lens. Consideration for the bears and your fellow visitors will be appreciated. For current information, and to get a visiting permit, call the Admiralty National Monument office in Juneau, 789-3111 or 586-8790.

More information on encounters with bears is in our Having Fun in the Back Country chapter later in this book. The Forest Service has an excellent brochure on the subject.

A mature bald eagle shows the piercing eye that can see perhaps as well as we can using binoculars!

Bald Eagles

Southeastern Alaska has the largest remaining U.S. population of bald eagles, some 15,000 birds. The majority of them live along the coast most of the year. They nest beside the ferry route, and you can easily see them on their nests along the narrows in early summer. Between mid-July and September, you will see some eagles, but fewer than at other times of the year, as they go up streams to follow spawning salmon. In fall and winter, thousands of them feed on the Chilkat River flats beside Haines Highway, Mile 19. You will often see them swooping down for fish near the ferry in the Narrows, especially in early evening. Docked at Prince Rupert, Ketchikan, and Petersburg, I've watched them in the harbor. Notice the difference in fishing skill and precision (also success) between mature eagles with white heads and younger eagles.

Birding

Besides bald eagles there are hundreds of species of birds to watch, especially during spring and fall migration. Many ducks, geese and swans fly through to nesting areas farther north. Petersburg harbor usually has a variety of waterfowl due to fish processing waste in the water. Here even birds you know from elsewhere may look different in their summer breeding plumage. Besides ducks and gulls, loons and great blue herons are common. A walk around the deck while the ship is docked may be the most rewarding bird walk of your trip! Channel markers here may be perches for 4-8 cormorants drying their feathers.

In winter, Blind Slough south of Petersburg, is home to swans and geese. There is a viewing blind. In both Petersburg and Wrangell you'll often see eagles perched in spruce trees along the street!

Near the Sitka dock, heading away from town, you'll pass the tidal marsh of Starrigavan Creek with ducks, geese, kingfishers, and a summer run of pink salmon. The trail around Sitka National Historical Park follows the beach where you may see harlequin ducks and other waterfowl. In Sitka, several boat operators offer tours to the seabird rookeries on islands in Sitka Sound where you may see murres, phalaropes, auklets, oystercatchers, puffins, and many others on their nests. July is the peak month.

The Raptor Rehabilitation Center at Sitka offers your best chance to see eagles and possibly hawks and owls up close and to learn about them. There is a charge for guided presentations and donations are appreciated if you go on your own. Guided tours include films of the rehabilitation and release of birds into the wild as well as demonstrations of the medical treatment given injured and ailing birds. Bring your camera or camcorder!

Auke Bay near Juneau is a good place to watch eagles, kingfishers, and herons, especially near the ferry dock. At Juneau Airport, starting from the end of Radcliffe Road is a road/path along the dike around the floatplane pond, bordering Mendenhall State Game Refuge. In summer Arctic terns nest along the dike and may dive at you to protect their nests. Canada geese are here all year. In spring you may see a dozen species of ducks and occasionally, swans. Once I stood on the path within 30 yards of four young trumpeter swans feeding in the pond! Besides the birds, this walk has great views of Mendenhall Glacier and the expanse of wetlands.

Glacier Bay is almost as well known for birds as for whales and glaciers. The tour boats from Glacier Bay Lodge go close to bird rookeries on the Marble Islands where you can see thousands of seabirds that come ashore only to nest. Even on shore around Bartlett Cove, there's a wide variety of waterfowl and forest birds. Park rangers lead daily nature walks to help you see and recognize more. I've seen many birds in June, but more species in July.

Haines is famous for eagles, but has a growing population of nesting swans in summer. They will only stay as long as they aren't approached closely. For birding suggestions in the area, ask Chilkat State Park personnel.

A fisherman shows the salmon he caught near Klawock. It doesn't take many like that to fill the freezer.

Fishing

The water you are sailing through supports one of the world's richest fisheries. Depending on the season you may see boats trolling, seining or gillnetting for any of the five kinds of salmon, tending crab or shrimp pots or fishing for halibut or cod. When you are close to boats fishing, the ferry's officers often explain how the fishing gear works. Near the salmon fleet there will often be a large boat with a cargo boom and lights, the tender, which picks up fish from the fishing boats and hauls the load back to the cannery or cold storage plant so the boats can go on fishing. Some boats are equipped for more than one type of fishing so they can work more days a year. Most fishing "openings," or open seasons are regulated by the Alaska Department of Fish and Game. They decide how many fish must be allowed to spawn and set the times, often in hours, that fishing is allowed in an area. When the opening is only for 24 or 36 hours, the boats and crews fish all night!

In season you can sportfish for salmon, halibut, red snapper and Dolly Varden in salt water, and trout and steelhead in creeks and lakes. Prince of Wales Island, west of Ketchikan, has great fresh and saltwater fishing and hundreds of miles of logging roads. There are charter boat operators and guides in every town. Often the sporting goods store personnel can tell you where there's a good spot you can fish from shore. Don't forget the fishing license, even for salt water. Non-resident licenses are available for 4 days ($10), 14 days ($30), and a year ($50). You'll need a tide table you can get at any sporting goods store.

Fishing lodges can be reached by boat or plane (and, in some places, by car) from every town in Southeast. They offer package plans including meals, transportation, boats and guides. Most will pack your fish for you, and some will arrange for smoking it if you wish.

Kayaking

With respect for the cold water, strong tides, rain and cold, you can enjoy one of the world's finest sea kayaking areas. This is **not**, however, the place to make your first long kayak trip on your own. The rain and fog, very cold water, and changeable weather require experience or a very capable guide. Some people actually paddle from Seattle to Skagway in a summer, missing all those scenic inlets one has to pass to make such a schedule. More have discovered great shorter trips between towns, and around islands like Revillagigedo, the island Ketchikan is on, or among the islands in Sitka Sound.

A look at the Tongass National Forest map should make any kayaker dream. Where they can, most kayakers use Forest Service cabins (next section) for a spot to dry out clothing and wait out weather. If you don't have a group for such a trip, shops like **Alaska Discovery** in Juneau have guides and can offer good local info. They offer day trips as well as longer ones.

A tide table is essential. Experienced kayakers have arrived with a schedule made out showing what time they wanted to be out of camp every morning on their route so as to have the tideal current with them instead of against them. A free 5 knots is not to be ignored!

You can bring your own kayak on top of a vehicle, or carry it onto the ferry where the crew will show you where to stow it. There's a small charge for carrying boats on the ferry, so you'll need to get a ticket for it if it's not on a vehicle. Note that it's possible to launch a kayak within

100 yards of any ferry dock in Southeast. Kayaks can be rented in Juneau at Alaska Discovery, or in Gustavus for paddling in Glacier Bay. Folding boats and inflatables are usually not as efficient to paddle, but are much easier to transport, especially in floatplanes.

Prince of Wales Island, west of Ketchikan, with over 1000 miles of shoreline, has miles of sheltered water on its west side reachable easily from Hydaburg, Craig, or the road system farther north. There are several deep inlets even on the east side of the island near the ferry dock at Hollis, but some of these have exposed headlands between. Carrying the kayak by ferry to Hollis on the island saves time and leaves you much less vulnerable to the weather than attempting to paddle across Clarence Strait and its chop from Ketchikan.

Angoon is on Admiralty Island, at the mouth of Mitchell Bay, and at the west end of the Cross-Admiralty Canoe Route. Maps of this route are available from the Forest Service. Some portages have been planked and there are several Forest Service cabins that can be reserved for $20 a night (more details at the end of this section). The *LeConte* takes you and your boat to Angoon and back without having to charter aircraft or larger boats. On the east side of Admiralty Island, reachable in good weather from Juneau, is Oliver Inlet, with a hand-cart on rails for the portage across to Seymour Canal.

Another interesting canoe trip possible, thanks to the *LeConte*, goes from Hoonah to Tenakee, with only a short portage (shorter at high tide) between Port Frederick and Tenakee Inlet. The rails on this portage, making boat hauling easier, have been improved. For this trip you will want a tide table and some good judgment. Note that both of these canoe trips are on islands that have brown bears, and the portage is a bear trail.

Good kayaking is possible from Pelican, but it's more awkward to get there and back, as ferry service is limited to one trip each month all year, more in summer. Charter aircraft do serve the area regularly. In 1992 the *LeConte* will go twice a month in summer. Lisianski Inlet is sheltered, and from here you can paddle to the coast and islands of West Chichagof or even down to Sitka. En route is the Forest Service cabin at White Sulphur Springs, a hot spring, and favorite spot of those who've reached it.

Kake is a good starting point for a tour of the small offshore islands and coastlines of Kupreanof and Kuiu Islands. The bay between these islands has coves and islands enough to occupy boaters happily for a week in sheltered water with Forest Service cabins on both shores to stay in. During waterfowl migration as well as summer, this would be a beautiful trip.

And of course there's Glacier Bay where the day tour boat will drop you off at designated places and pick you up there later or leave you to paddle for several days back down the bay to Bartlett Cove.

Ferry Tale

A traveler, looking at the Tongass National Forest map, concluded "We did get a good deal from the Russians. It looks like about a dollar an island".

The Haines ferry dock at low tide. The beach has a great variety of pebbles and offers a good put-in point for kayaks.

Beachcombing

Perhaps some can resist walking down a beach to see what's there, but I think they miss a lot. Most beaches you can get to here are rocky and so far back from open ocean that they aren't known for glass float balls. However the variety of rocks you can find, including jasper, make it fun. Prince of Wales Island, with over 1000 miles of shoreline, is popular with locals. Besides interesting beach pebbles, it has inland deposits of marble (from which the columns on Alaska's capitol came), rose quartz, and other minerals. Some are on claims or other private property; don't forget to check. Ask for suggestions. The expanding road system often reaches new spots. Of course watch road banks for interesting rocks.

The beach at Hoonah, north of the cannery, has fascinating rocks carried out of Glacier Bay by the ice that once filled it. Even the beach near the Haines ferry terminal has metamorphic rocks from both sides of the fault that makes Lutak Inlet. Juneau's mining start was due to its minerals. Many locals still pan gold in streams on weekends. Wrangell's ferry terminal is built on a black slate that's easy to carve, even with a screwdriver into bas-relief scenes and figures. When oiled, the texture is like the argillite used by Haida Indians in their small totems.

At Hyder, pebbles along the road shoulder have spectacularly colored metallic ores. Be conservative with the weight of your collection if you're leaving the town by plane!

If you find eagle feathers, be warned that it's illegal to possess them. Restricting this was the only way the government could keep people from killing eagles to sell their feathers.

The tidal animals and plants to watch, as well as a few polishable rocks for your tumbler at home, make a beach walk memorable.

Shipboard Naturalist

Under an agreement between the U.S. Forest Service and the Alaska Marine Highway, there is a Forest Service naturalist aboard each of the larger ferries all summer, on trips north of Prince Rupert. You are traveling the length of the Tongass National Forest, the largest national forest in the United States. The naturalist provides a nature program aboard ship and sometimes ashore, answers your questions (or finds someone who can), and has a variety of handouts, maps, films, and a lending library. For children the naturalist has reading and coloring materials, a wildlife checklist, and sometimes a special programs. All services are free. The programs vary with the weather, the facilities aboard the ships, your interests, and the different backgrounds of the naturalists. Programs are posted at the naturalist station in the forward lounge, and announced on the ship's speakers. During the off-season the ship's purser often has a supply of Tongass National Forest maps showing the ferry route north of Prince Rupert.

Side Trips

Each town has charter planes and boats that can take you on scenic rides, and to out-of-the-way places such as Glacier Bay, Tracy Arm, the Juneau Icefields, the LeConte Glacier, and the Stikine River. They are listed under the ports where they originate.

U.S. Forest Service Cabins

If the Alaska you want to see has no roads or cars and makes few sounds but waves, wind in the trees, and waterfalls, you may find a stay in a Forest Service cabin a rare and exciting experience. For a bit of the wilderness all to yourself for a few days, this is it, with a dry roof overhead! Some are near hot springs.

Most land (aside from the towns) between the Canadian border at the Portland Canal and Skagway is in the Tongass National Forest, 17 million acres. Scattered throughout the forest are 145 cabins that can be rented (by reservation) for $20 per night, for as long as a week, longer in winter. The cabins sleep between four and eight people. Some are on the coast, and others are near freshwater lakes (these have a skiff and oars provided by the Territorial Sportsmen). Very few cabins are reached by trails, more by boat, and the majority by floatplane, your main expense in using them.

Firewood, or an axe and maul is provided. You must bring your own food, cooking utensils, stove oil if needed, sleeping bags, foam pads, life jackets, tide table, insect repellent, good rain gear and first aid kit. A small backpacking stove will be useful if the cabin has a woodstove and green wood. By fall the woodpile consists of the knotted unsplittable pieces everyone else left. The Forest Service will send you an equipment list and a description of the cabin and its facilities if you ask.

For your comfort and safety on the charter flight you'll probably use to reach the cabin, and to avoid looking like a total cheechako, it's best not to expand on the list too much. Our pilot's comment, "You people are awfully optimistic about the carrying capacity of a Beaver," as we crammed five passengers, besides the pilot, a German Shepherd, two folding boats, and a mountain of personal gear into the flying workhorse. However, I would add to the list two mousetraps. Baiting them with peanut butter, I caught twelve mice the first two nights at one cabin.

If the cabin is in brown bear country (mainland or on Admiralty, Baranof, or Chichagof Islands), you may want to take a heavy rifle or 12 gauge shotgun (if you know how to use it). Some guides now carry the more portable pepper spray gun. To avoid bear trouble for yourselves and those who come after you, don't teach the bears that humans are a source of food. Burn completely, or carry out with you all garbage and containers. If the bears are to survive and we are to use the wilderness, we must all do this.

You will be on your own, with no road or phone for help, once the pilot leaves you until the day he picks you up. If the weather gets bad, he might be a few days late. Plan your gear carefully, and **be careful** so no one gets hurt. Know how to avoid and how to treat hypothermia. Wear lifejackets in the boat. Be extra careful with axes, fire, and while hiking. If no one stays at the cabin when you leave on day trips, it's wise to leave a note telling where you went and when you'll be back.

Some cabins are booked-up regularly, while others are rarely used. A few very popular cabins are reserved by lottery drawing from the reservation requests for certain dates. All cabins are shown and num-bered on the Tongass National Forest map. The number indicates the office to which you should apply for reservations. Reservations are accepted no more than six months in advance. A table on the map lists the hunting and fishing available in each cabin's area. An Alaskan license is required, even for saltwater fishing. The table also shows how to get to the various cabins by trail, boat, or floatplane. Charter operators in each town can take you to a cabin and pick you up.

The Forest Service may be able to tell you who is using the cabin before or after you. If you can coordinate the flights so one party returns on the plane that brings the other in, you can all save money. This must be arranged ahead of time. Usually, an hour's charter will cover both trips, though some cabins are farther. For reservations, apply to:

Sitka Ranger District Box 1866, Sitka, AK 99835	Chichagof and Baranof Islands (907) 747-6671
U.S. Forest Service Information Center 101 Egan Drive Juneau, AK 99801	All other northern areas, including Admiralty Island and Yakutat (907) 586-8751
Petersburg Ranger District Box 1328 Petersburg, AK 99833	central area (907) 772-3871
Wrangell Ranger District Box 51 Wrangell, AK 99929	central area (907) 874-2323
Forest Supervisor, Ketchikan Area Federal Building, Ketchikan, AK 99901	southern area (907) 225-2148

These offices can send you a map of the forest, which is very helpful in planning your trip. It shows the entire Alaskan part of the ferry route. For a map and general information on the Tongass National Forest, you can also write: Visitor Information Service, Box 1628, Juneau, AK 99802.

You may want to read *Discover Southeast By Backpack and Paddle*, by Margaret Piggott; *Alaska*, by Norma Spring; *Milepost*, detailed annual; *Alaska's Southeast* by Sarah Eppenbach; *Birds of Alaska* by Bob Armstrong; and *Camping Alaska and Canada's Yukon* by Mike and Marilyn Miller.

Ferry Tale

Most Alaskans are used to the classic questions about what stamps and money we use, and how high above sea level we are. (The answer, looking over the side, "about 50 feet"). One traveler asked me "Do you get down to the United States very often?"

Cruise Ships

This book emphasizes the ferry system because we are writing for the traveler who wants to "see more, spend less". But during the summer many cruise ships travel through Southeastern Alaska. Compared to the ferries, they offer more comfort, more service, finer food, more shipboard entertainment, more luxuries such as swimming pools and spas, and longer daytime stops at a few of ports. If you want a considerable amount of personal service you may prefer a cruise ship with its huge staff of stewards providing for your comfort.

Side trips may be part of the tour, or available as options. A day cruising in Glacier Bay or Tracy Arm is usually included. As ship traffic in Glacier Bay is controlled, several ships go instead to Tracy or Endicott Arms, glaciated fiords south of Juneau.

The smaller ships listed in the second part of our list pass through the Narrows on cruises between Ketchikan and Skagway. Skipping expansive lounges and hundreds of passengers and staff, they enter small bays and passages surrounded by up-close scenery and wildlife. They may anchor in these spots overnight, and some will set you ashore with small boats for guided nature walks. Naturalists rather than professional entertainers may be aboard. You can fish from several of the ships or their boats. Most of these start within Southeast Alaska instead of Vancouver.

Routes and stops vary with the ships. Most offer rail, air or bus connections for tours including Anchorage and Fairbanks. Your travel agent can make arrangements for you. Most sail from Vancouver, B.C., but several start from Los Angeles, San Francisco, or Seattle. A few ships offer longer cruises all the way to Anchorage, Seward, or Whittier. Most companies offer one-way or round trip cruises, so you can have 3–14 day trips.

Cruise ships in Southeast Alaska 1992 Season

Costa Cruises, World Trade Center, 80 SW 8th St., Miami, FL 33130. (800) 447-6877. *Daphne.*

Cunard, 555 Fifth Ave., New York, NY 10017. (800) 5-CUNARD. *Sagafjord.*

Holland-America Line/Westours, Inc., 300 Elliott Ave. West, Seattle, WA 98119. (800) 426-0327. *Nieuw Amsterdam, Noordam, Rotterdam, Westerdam.*

Princess Cruises, 10100 Santa Monica Blvd., Ste. 1800, Los Angeles, CA 90067. (800) 421-0522. *Seky Princess, Regal Princess, Island Princess, Pacific Princess, Fair Princess, Dawn Princess.*

Regency Cruises, 260 Madison Ave., New York, NY 10016. (800) 388-5500. *Regent Sea, Regent Star.*

Royal Caribbean Cruise Line, 1050 Caribbean Way, Miami, FL 33132. (800) 327-6700. *Sun Viking.*

Royal Cruise Line, 1 Maritime Plaza, San Francisco, CA 94111. (800) 227-4534. *Royal Odyssey.*

Seven Seas Cruises, 333 Market St., Ste 2600, San Francisco, CA 94105. (800) 285-1835. *Song of Flower* (172 passengers).

World Explorer Cruises, 555 Montgomery St., San Francisco, CA 94111. (800) 854-3835. *Universe.*

The following firms offer tours with smaller ships to out of the way areas, sometimes staying onshore in hotels.

Alaska Sightseeing/Cruise West, 4th and Battery Bldg., Suite 700, Seattle, WA 98121. (800) 426-7702. *Sheltered Seas, Spirit of Glacier Bay, Spirit of Alaska, Spirit of Discovery.*

Clipper Cruise Lines, 7711 Bonhomme Ave., St. Louis, MO 63105. (800) 325-0010. Cruises in Southeast Alaska, Prince William Sound, even to Kodiak Island and Katmai. *Society Explorer.*

Glacier Bay Cruises & Tours, 520 Pike St., Ste. 1610, Seattle, WA 98101. (800) 622-2042. Cruises 1–7 days, most starting from Juneau. 1 day cruise to Glacier Bay. *Executive Exploreer, Spirit of Adventure, Wilderness Explorer.*

Special Expeditions, 720 5th Ave., New York, NY 10019. (800)762-0003. 11 day cruises. *Sea Bird, Sea Lion.*

The *Star Princess* backs away from Skagway's dock with the help of a tug.

The *Noordam* cruises through Canadian waters near Bella Bella.

A tour boat from Juneau pushes cautiously through floating icebergs in Tracy Arm.

Cruise ship *Song of Flower* at anchor in Sitka harbor while its boat takes passengers to shore under the eye of a young eagle on the dock piling.

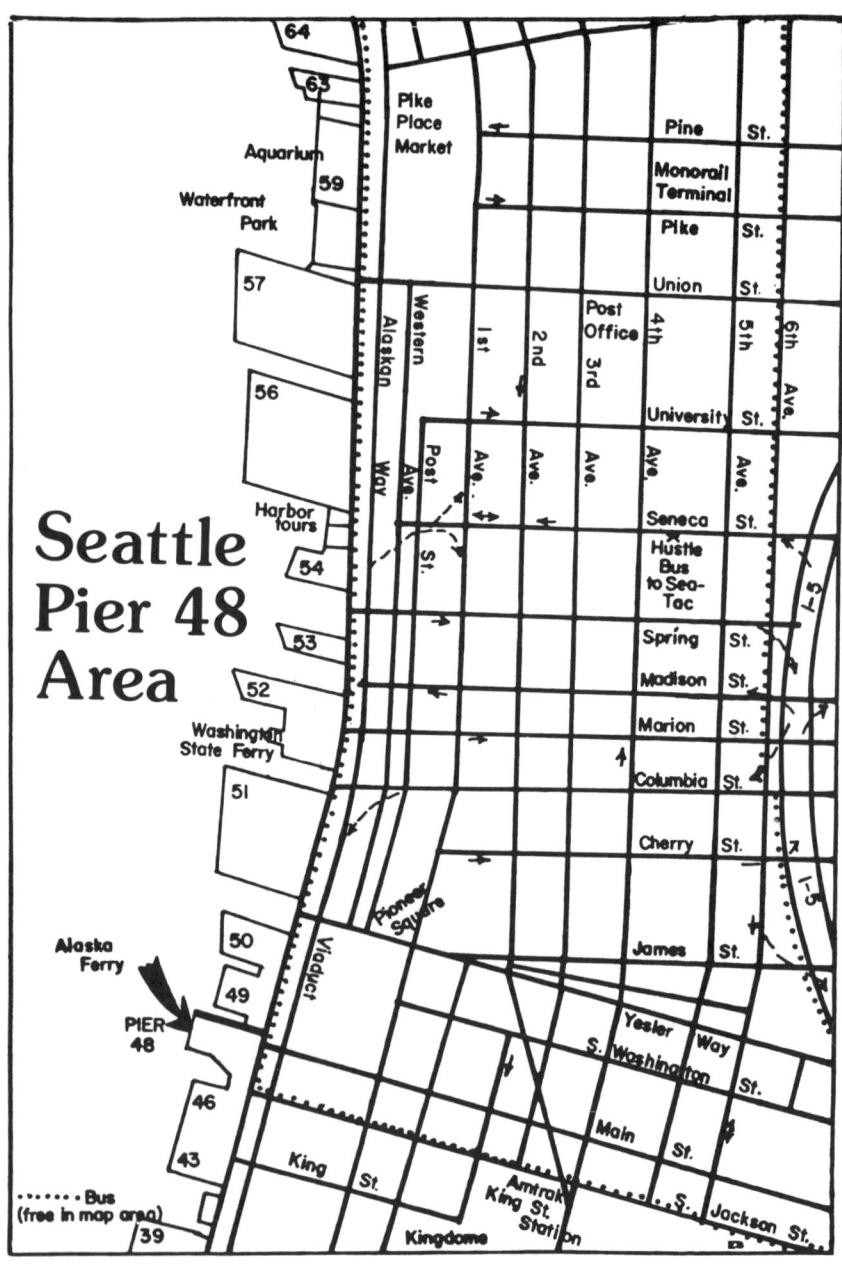

Seattle
Pier 48
Area

SEATTLE

SEATTLE is a fascinating city with a good public transit system and lots to see. You may want to allow time for its sights on your Alaskan trip. Several guidebooks are available at Sea-Tac Airport and waterfront shops, including the Washington State ferry terminal at Pier 52.

Pier 48, formerly the Alaska ferry terminal, is on the same waterfront where the Klondike gold-seekers once boarded ships for the Yukon. Nearby is Pioneer Square, part of Klondike National Historic Park (along with Downtown Skagway, and the Chilkoot and White Passes). Some original buildings remain, and many of these are being restored. Art galleries, boutiques, restaurants, and bookstores occupy many old buildings. You may want to stroll around the historic square, and share the excitement that the men of '98 felt as they packed to sail for the North.

Getting to Pier 48

FROM I-5, simply follow blue signs for ferries, directing you to Washington ferry terminals. The Madison Street interchange leads to the waterfront at Pier 52.

FROM SEA-TAC AIRPORT, the **Airporter**, airport limousine, takes you every 20 minutes to the Westin, Holiday Inn, Crowne Plaza, and restored. Art galleries, boutiques, restaurants and bookstores occupy Four Seasons Olympic hotels. From the latter you can walk about 10 blocks or take a taxi to Pier 48.

Shuttle Express, 286-4800, runs to and from Sea-Tac Airport to any destination between Tacoma and Everett. Van service, requires any airline ticket.

METRO TRANSIT (city bus) #174 runs regularly and cheaply between Sea-Tac and downtown.

RAIL—**Amtrak** station, 6 blocks, S. Jackson St. and 3rd Ave. S., on municipal bus route with line to Pier 48. Does not go to Vancouver.

BUS—**Greyhound**, 8th Avenue and Stewart, north and east of the area shown the this map. Greyhound goes to Vancouver and an affiliate continues to Prince Rupert.

TAXI—You can take any cab at a stand, not necessarily the first. Some serve certain areas of the city only. Since they have been deregulated, **Yellow**, 622-6500, and **Far West**, 622-1717, are the only ones which charge rates similar to the regulated fares. The others may charge as they choose. It's worth asking before getting in the cab.

To See and Do

Within walking distance of Pier 48 are:

- The Washington State ferry terminal for ferries to Bainbridge Island and Bremerton, Pier 53.

- Some of the 200 parks in Seattle and King County displaying public art purchased by the city.

- The Waterfront Trolley running 1.6 miles from Pier 48 to Pier 70 which has three 1927 Australian streetcars very much like the ones which plied this area in early days. They run every 20 to 30 minutes from 8 a.m. to 11 p.m. in summer and 8 a.m. to 6 p.m. in winter. Some have singing drivers. All are wheelchair accessible. They are fun!

- Many waterfront gift shops, restaurants, crafts shops (including several on Pier 70).

- The Seattle Aquarium, Pier 59. Excellent, featuring Puget Sound and nearby marine life. Open 9 a.m. daily to 9 p.m. in summer.

- Omnidome, 3D photodrama, Pier 59.

- Pike Place Market—across from the aquarium, with many shops on several levels. Open 7 days a week in summer.

- Waterfront parks next to the aquarium, fishing and shrimping.

- Several art galleries and bookstores.

- Seattle Harbor Tours, next to Pier 54.

- Cruises to Victoria on *Victoria Clipper I, II, and III,* high speed catamarans that take walk-on passengers daily from Pier 69. (206) 448-5000.

- Kingdome Sports Arena, S. King St. and Occidental Ave. S. Tours 11 a.m., 1 p.m., 3 p.m.

- Chinatown. S. Main St. at 6th and 7th Avenues. Tours available.

- The Coast Guard museum, Pier 36.

- Klondike Gold Rush National Park, Seattle unit, 117 South Main Street. Free films and slide programs 9 a.m. to 5 p.m. daily, extended summer hours.

- Underground tours in Pioneer Square, guided tours of the old Seattle neighborhood built over by the present city.

The waterfront from S. Washington Street to Pier 67 is within the free zone for the bus system. The monorail, Pike and 4th, is a fast way to the Seattle Center, 1962 World's Fair site.

Woodland Park Zoo, an easy bus ride from downtown, is one of the nation's most attractive zoos, featuring natural habitat and breeding many animals.

Annual Events

Seattle Seafair. July 10-August 2, 1992. City-wide marine festival: regattas, hydroplane races, parades, sports events, exhibits, etc. Torchlight parade, July 31, 1992. Hydroplane races, August 2. Admission fee to best viewpoint, though can be seen from wider area.

Bumbershoot, Seattle Center. Outdoor/indoor festival of arts and music. Labor Day weekend.

Folklife Festival, Seattle Center. Outdoor music and crafts. Memorial Day Weekend. Free.

4th of July fireworks are spectacular here, over Elliot Bay.

Pacific Northwest Arts and Crafts Fair, Bellevue Square (four miles east in Bellevue). Art exhibits, handicrafts. Late July. Free.

Arts and crafts fairs are held in the Seattle area almost continuously throughout the summer. The Visitors' Bureau has dates and locations.

Highland Games, traditional Scottish games and dances. Enumclaw Fairgrounds, southeast of Seattle. Late July.

ACCOMMODATIONS: Downtown lodgings range from deluxe to the YMCA, YWCA and youth hostel. On the highways north, east and south of Seattle, and especially along Pacific Avenue near Sea-Tac Airport are moderate hotels, many from the national chains.

INFORMATION AVAILABLE: Seattle/King County Convention & Visitors' Bureau, 520 Pike Street, Ste. 1300, Seattle, WA 98101. (206) 461-5800. 8:30 a.m.-5:00 p.m., Monday-Friday.

For Washington State information, call 1-800-544-1800.

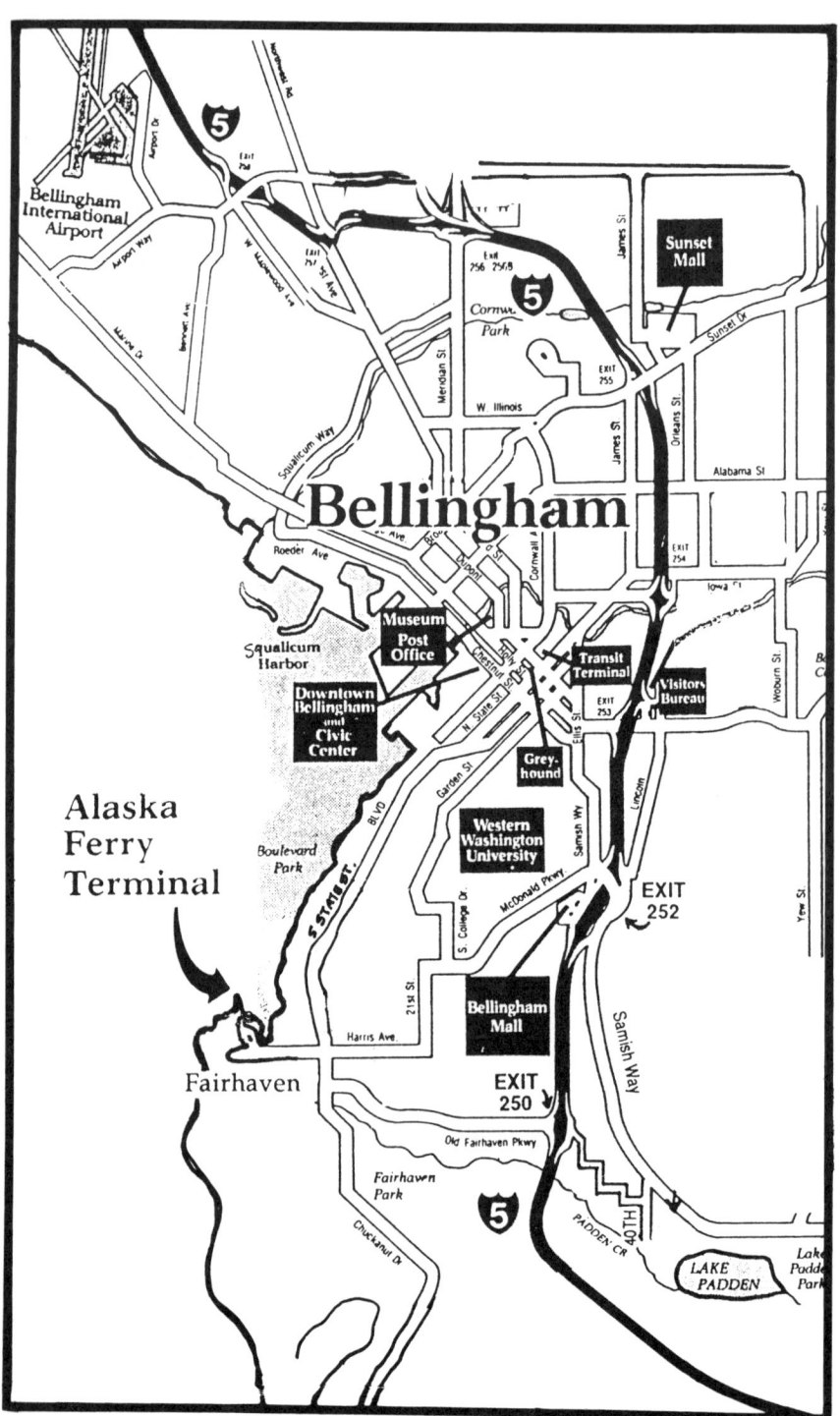

(Port of Bellingham)

Ferry and cruise terminal at Bellingham. (Port of Bellingham)

BELLINGHAM
(Area Code 206, Zip Codes 98225, 226,227)

BELLINGHAM, Washington (pop. 52,000) is the southern terminal of the Alaska ferry. It's the county seat of rural Whatcom County extending from the sea to the slopes of Mount Baker and to the Canadian boundary on the north. Seattle is 1.5 hours south (90 miles), Vancouver 1 hour north on Interstate 5.

The Port of Bellingham has built a new ferry terminal adjacent to the historic Fairhaven district on the south side of downtown. The terminal has a travel information center with very helpful people, restaurant, and rental car counters.

Bellingham is a regional shopping center with many parks, several lakes, a state university, and an international airport. Historic Fairhaven area offers restaurants, galleries, and sightseeing in restored brick buildings 1/2 mile from the terminal. It also has a supermarket, laundromat, propane, diesel, and ice. Bellingham's transit system provides 25¢ rides throughout Bellingham. Pet boarding is available. A lot for long term car storage is across the street from the terminal.

Nearby mountains, fishing, skiing, 7 golf courses, many festivals at all seasons, museums, and beautiful countryside make this an area to ex-

71

plore. Lynden, a few miles north, is a fascinating town featuring traditional Dutch shops and festivities. Just north of the international border, the Abbotsford Airshow in August is the biggest airshow in western Canada.

GETTING TO THE FERRY: **from I-5**, take Exit 250, follow signs 2 miles and 2 signal lights. **From Sea-Tac Airport**, the **Bellingham/Sea-Tac Airporter** goes 4-6 times a day each way. On Fridays only it stops twice each way at the Alaska ferry terminal. (800) BELLAIR. From Washington only, (800) 235-5247 or (206) 733-3600. Note that **Alaska Airlines, United Express**, and **Horizon** fly into Bellingham. Bellingham has daily seasonal passenger ferry service to and from the San Juan Islands and Victoria, and bus service to Vancouver and Seattle.

BUS: **Greyhound Bus Lines**, (206) 733-5251. **Whatcom Transportation Authority** (city bus), (206) 676-RIDE.

TAXI: **Superior Cabs**, (206) 734-3478.

CAR RENTAL: **Budget**, (206) 671-3800. **Hertz**, (206) 733-8336. **Denny's**, (206) 734-7262.

WHERE TO STAY: Bellingham has over 20 hotels and bed and breakfasts, almost all under $60. It also has a YWCA. The Visitors' Bureau has latest info. We strongly recommend reservations here, especially over weekends. Besides the hotels in Bellingham shown on this chart, there are many others throughout Whatcom County.

Campgrounds

There are many campgrounds and RV parks in Whatcom County, including some state parks (which fill up fast in summer). In or near Bellingham are:

Larabee State Park, 245 Chuckanut Dr., Bellingham, WA. (206) 2093. 90 sites, 26 with hookups. Shower, dump station. 7 miles from ferry with views of San Juan Islands, beaches, boat launch and hiking trails.

Crest Haven, 2500 Samish, Bellingham, WA 98226. (206) 734-9223. 4 miles from ferry. 6 sites with hookups. Tent camping, shower, laundry, dump station. Quiet adult park on bus line near Lake Padden Recreation Area. Golf.

Ferndale Campground, 6335 Portal Way, Ferndale, WA 98248. (206) 384-2622. 15 miles north of ferry. 157 sites, 57 with hookups. Dump station, shower, laundry, picnicing, playground, river access.

Lake Samish Terrace, 910 N. Lake Samish Dr., Bellingham, WA. 98226. (206) 671-2741. 10-15 miles from ferry. 10 sites with hookups, tent camp-

Port of Bellingham with Northern Cascade Mountains in background (photo: Tore Ofteness).

ing. dump station, shower, laundry. Lake Samish Recreation Area.

BAGGAGE STORAGE: in minimum size lockers in the terminal, available when the terminal is open.

INFORMATION AVAILABLE: **Bellingham Whatcom County Visitors & Convention Bureau**, 904 Potter St.-ip, Bellingham, WA 98226. (206) 671-3990. Fax (202) 647-7873. From I-5, take Exit 253 to find them. Very helpful people with lots of good, current info!

Happenings

Ski to Sea, Memorial Day weekend. Five stage county-wide relay race from Mt. Baker to Bellingham Bay. Parade and festivities. Free.

Deming Loggerodeo, mid-June. Traditional logging contests and barbecue, in Deming.

Northwest Washington Fair, mid-August. Agricultural fair with farm animals, crafts, music, and carnival in Lynden.

BELLINGHAM ACCOMMODATIONS

For more information contact the
Bellingham/Whatcom County
Visitor and Convention Bureau
904 Potter St. I-5 Exit 253 Bellingham, WA 98226
Phone (206) 671-3990 1-800-487-2032
FAX (206) 647-7873

	Phone	Rates	# of Rooms	Meeting Room Capacity	Restaurant/Lounge Entertainment	Pool, Jacuzzi, Hot Tub, Sauna	TV	Phone	Kitchens	Pets	Handicapped	Transportation	Credit Cards
Aloha Motel 315 N. Samish Way, Bellingham 98226	733-4900	BC	28		near		•	•			•		•
Anderson Creek Lodge 5602 Mission Road, Bellingham, 98225	966-2126	C-	6	40	BFST	PSH	•	•			•		•
A Secret Garden B&B 1807 Lakeway Drive, Bellingham 98226	671-5327	BC	2		BFST		•	•					
*Bab's Reservation Service P.O. Box 5025, Bellingham, 98227	733-8642	AB			BFST								
*Big Trees B&B 4840 Fremont Street, Bellingham, 98226	647-2850	C	2		BFST		•			•	•		
Bell Motel 208 N. Samish Way, Bellingham, 98225	733-2520	BC	27		near		•	•	•				•
Best Western Heritage Inn Meridian Plaza, Bellingham, 98226	647-1912	BC	92	60	near	PJ	•	•	•	•	•		•
*Best Western Lakeway Inn 714 Lakeway Drive, Bellingham, 98226	671-1011	C	132	900	RLE	PSJ	•	•		•	•		•
*The Castle B&B 1103 15th Street, Bellingham, 98225	676-0974	AC	2		BFST		•			•			
*Circle F B&B 2399 Mt. Baker Hwy., Bellingham, 98226	733-2509	AB	5		BFST		•	•		•			
*Coachman Inn 120 N. Samish Way, Bellingham, 98225	671-9000	BC	60		near	PSJ	•	•	•	•	•	•	•
*DeCann House B&B 2610 Eldridge Ave., Bellingham, 98225	734-9172	AB	2		BFST		•	•			•		
*Evergreen Motel 1015 Samish Way, Bellingham, 98225	734-7671	AB	11				•		•				•
*Hampton Inn 3985 Bennett Drive, Bellingham, 98225	676-7700	C	133		near	PH	•	•		•	•		•
Key Motel 212 N. Samish Way, Bellingham, 98225	733-4060	B	40	10	near	PSH	•	•	•				•
Lions Inn Motel 2419 Elm Street, Bellingham, 98225	733-3118	B	33		BFST	P	•	•	•	•	•	•	•
*Mac's Motel 1215 E. Maple, Bellingham, 98225	734-7570	A	36		near		•	•	•				•
Motel 6 3701 Byron Street, Bellingham, 98225	671-4494	AB	60		near	P	•	•			•		
*North Garden Inn B&B 1014 N. Garden, Bellingham, 98225	671-7828	BC			BFST								•
*Park Motel 101 N. Samish Way, Bellingham, 98225	733-8280	BC	56	55	near	SJ	•	•		•	•		•
*Ramada Inn 215 N. Samish Way, Bellingham, 98225	734-8830	BC	65		near	P	•	•					•
*Schnauzer Crossing 4421 Lakeway Drive, Bellingham, 98226	733-0055	C	2			J		•					•
Samish Arms Inn 1015 Otis, Bellingham, 98225	671-0393	AB	31		near		•	•	•		•		•
*Seagoat House 2115 Lummi Shore Drive, Bellingham, 98225	676-0974	C				Beach					•	•	
*Shangri-la Motel 611 Holly Street, Bellingham, 98225	733-7050	ABC	20				•	•	•	•	•		•
*Sudden Valley Resort 2145 Lake Whatcom Blvd, Bellingham, 98226	734-6430	C	50	80	RLE	PS	•		•		•		
*Sunrise Bay B&B 2141 N. Shore Drive, Bellingham, 98226	647-0376	C	2		BFST	P	•	•		•	•		
*Travelers Inn 3570 Meridian, Bellingham, 98225	671-4600	AB	126		near	PH	•	•			•		•
Travel Lodge Railroad & Holly, Bellingham, 98225	734-1900	AB	49	24			•	•			•		•
*Val-U Inn 805 Lakeway Drive, Bellingham, 98226	671-9600	BC	80		BFST	H	•	•		•	•		•

*Indicates VCB Member   Rates: A=$30-45; B=$45-60; C=over $60

Boat Bluff Lighthouse on the British Columbia coast marks a tight turn for the ferry.

PORT HARDY

This town of 5,000 on the north end of Vancouver Island is the southern end of the British Columbia ferry route to Prince Rupert. Fishing, scenic trails and native Indian art are some of its attractions. It is 320 miles north of Victoria, about an 8 hour drive on a 2-lane road. Here, for the convenience of readers who may spend the night when connecting in either direction with the B.C. ferry, is a short list of relevant facilities.

Reservations for rooms or campsites are advised. A shipload of passengers headed in either direction fills the town. As an alternative, Port McNeill, 30 miles south of Port Hardy, has 2 hotels with a total of 98 rooms and a campground with 26 sites.

INFORMATION AVAILABLE: **Port Hardy & District Chamber of Commerce**, Box 249, Port Hardy, B.C. V0N 2P0. (604) 949-7622. Located at 7250 Market Street.

Hotels
(Prices are in Canadian $. * indicates 1991 rates last reported.)

Airport Inn—Box 2039 Airport Rd., Port Hardy, B.C. V0N 2P0. (604) 949-9434. Fax (604) 949-6533. 45 rooms, coffee shop. Single $54.95, Double $59.95, Twin $64.95. Add'l. $6. Kitchen $6.

Waterfalls from lakes above line Grenville Channel—enough so you can each name one!

Best Western Port Hardy Inn—9040 Granville St., Box 1798, Port Hardy, B.C. V0N 2P0. (604) 949-8525. Full service hotel, indoor pool. 84 rooms, wheelchair accessible, pets allowed. Single $68 Double $72, Twin $76. Add'l $10. *

Glen Lyon Inn—6435 Hardy Bay Road, Box 103, Port Hardy, B.C. V0N 2P0. (604) 949-7115. 29 rooms, restaurant, boat launch and moorage adjacent. Wheelchair accessible. Single $42–52, Double $42–58, Twin $46–66. Add'l $10.

Thunderbird Inn—Box 88, Port Hardy, B.C. V0N 2P0. (604) 949-7767. Fax (604) 949-7740. 50 rooms, dining room, live entertainment, pets allowed. Single $61–66, Double $72–78, Twin $72–82. Add'l $12.

North Shore Inn—7370 Market St., Box 1888, Port Hardy, B.C. V0N 2P0. (604) 949-8500. Full service hotel, 30 rooms, ocean view with balconies. Restaurant, lounge. Single $48, Double $54, Twin $56. Add'l $5. *

Pioneer Inn—Box 699, Port Hardy, B.C., V0N 2P0 (604) 949-7271. Adjacent to Quatse River campsite in park-like setting. Kitchenettes, laundry room. Open hearth cuisine. Single $54, Double $60. Add'l. $6. Kitchen $8.

Seagate Hotel—8600 Granville St., Box 28, Port Hardy, B.C. V0N 2P0. (604) 949-6348. (800) 663-3676. 84 rooms, kitchenettes $10, restaurant. Live entertainment. Single $30-59, Double $40-64, Twin $45-69. Add'l $10.

Campgrounds

Quarterdeck Marina & RV Park—6555 Hardy Bay Rd., Box 910 Port Hardy, B.C. V0N 2P0. (604) 949-6551. Fax (604) 949-7777. Next to fishermen's wharf. Moorage, marine fuels, propane, ice, charts, boat and tackle rentals, laundromat, store, full hookups, 20 sites. $22.43.

Quatse River Campground—Box 1409, Port Hardy, B.C. V0N 2P0. (604) 949-2395. 1 mile from Port Hardy, off Hwy. 19 on Old Island Hwy. Laundromat, showers, dump station. 61 sites, 39 with electrical and water hookups. Shaded sites, fishing. $12/vehicle. Elec. $3.

Sunny Sanctuary Campground—Box 552, Port Hardy, B.C. V0N 2P0. (604) 949-8111. On Hwy. 19 near ferry. Adjacent to river and wildlife sanctuary. Full hookups, store, dump station, hot showers, laundromat, tent areas. Fire pits, RV and boat storage. Weekly & monthly rates. 70 sites, tents, $7. RVs, $12. 30 amp electricity, $2 add'l. Sewer, $1.

Wildwoods Campsite—Box 801, Port Hardy, B.C. V0N 2P0. (604) 949-6753. On road to ferry, nearest to terminal. Forested, with fireplaces, firewood, tables, beach access. Moorage. Pets allowed. 66 sites. Hot showers. $10-15. *

Car Parking & Storage

Daze Parking—Box 1, Coal Harbor, Port Hardy, B.C. V0N 2P0. (604) 949-7792. Fenced lot. *

Sunny Sanctuary Campground, listed under campgrounds. *

Wildwood Campsite, listed under campgrounds. *

* Rates not recently reported.

Canadian Maple Leaf flies from stern of the *Queen of the North*.

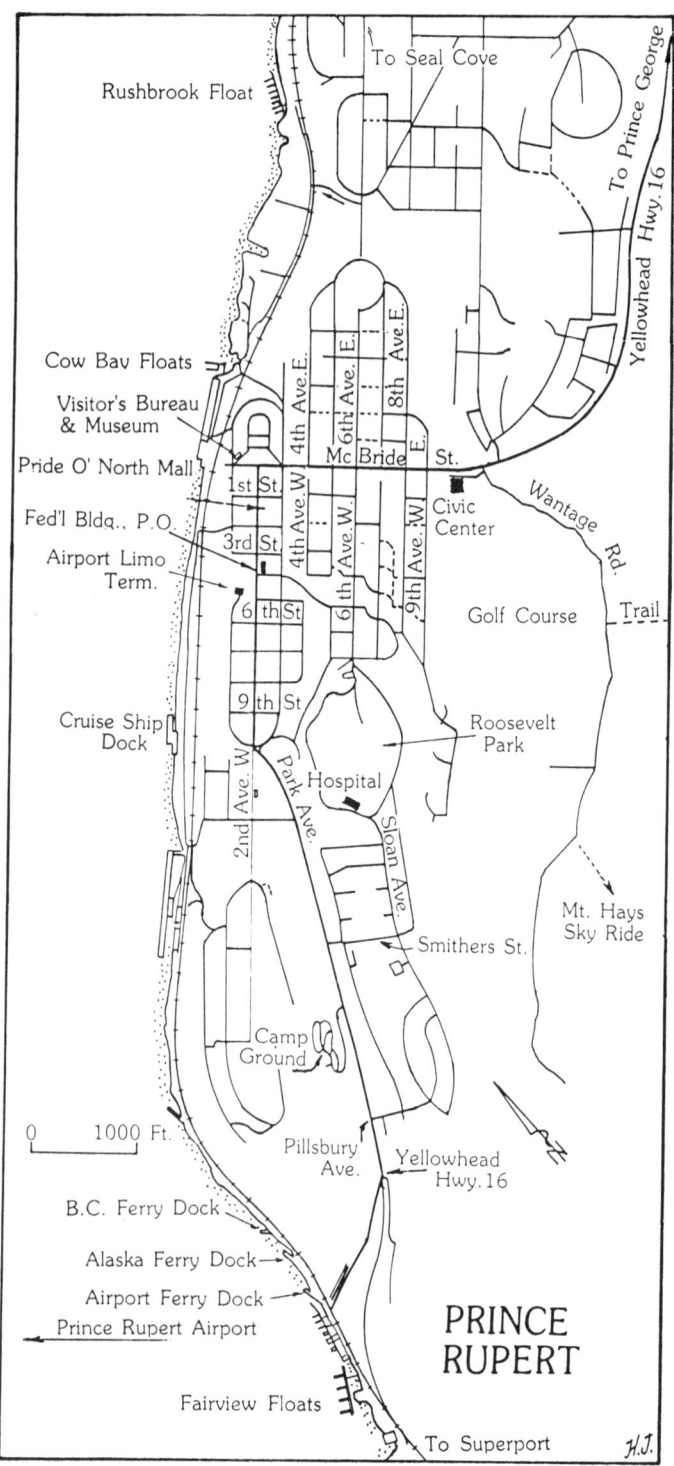

Rushbrook Float

To Seal Cove

To Prince George

Yellowhead Hwy. 16

Cow Bay Floats

Visitor's Bureau & Museum

Pride O' North Mall

4th Ave. E.

6th Ave. E.

8th Ave. E.

McBride St.

1st St.

Civic Center

Fed'l Bldg., P.O.

4th Ave. W.

6th Ave. W.

9th Ave. W.

Wantage Rd.

3rd St.

Airport Limo Term.

6 th St

Golf Course

Trail

9 th St

Cruise Ship Dock

2nd Ave. W.

Park Ave.

Hospital

Roosevelt Park

Sloan Ave.

Mt. Hays Sky Ride

Smithers St.

Camp Ground

0   1000 Ft.

Pillsbury Ave.

Yellowhead Hwy. 16

B.C. Ferry Dock

Alaska Ferry Dock

Airport Ferry Dock

Prince Rupert Airport

PRINCE RUPERT

Fairview Floats

To Superport

H.J.

78

Totems stand in front of Prince Rupert's Performing Arts Centre—two of more than 25 in town.

PRINCE RUPERT
(phone area code 604)

PRINCE RUPERT (pop. 17,500) is Canada's northernmost ice-free port, the third largest naturally deep harbor in the world. It is a lumbering and fishing center (mainly for halibut and salmon), and a transportation hub. Here the Yellowhead Highway and the Canadian Railroad from the interior meet passenger ships and freighters.from all over the world. It is the main trading center for the Canadian coast north of Vancouver. The British Columbia Ferry from Port Hardy and the Alaska Ferry arrive here several times a week in summer. The B.C. Ferry has added ferry service to the Queen Charlotte Islands several times a week. It is worth taking time to explore Prince Rupert and enjoy the views over its harbor.

Bald eagles dive beside the fishing boats and deer walk on the railroad tracks. Atlin Fish Company has a cold storage room filled with frozen halibut (each over 100 pounds!) stacked like firewood. Lots to see here besides the fog.

To See and Do

See 25 totems standing throughout the town

Enjoy the view of the harbor from Roosevelt Park.

Visit the Museum of Northern British Columbia (Art Gallery and Infocentre in the same building). The Museum offers archeology and guided harbor tours in season. Open 9 a.m.–9 p.m., Mon.–Sat., 9 a.m.–5 p.m. Sun., mid-May through mid-September. Off season, 10 a.m.–5 p.m., closed Sunday. Donations. Two miles from ferry, McBride and First Avenue. 624-3207.

Visit Kwinitsa Station Railway Museum across from Via Rail on the waterfront.

Visit the North Pacific Cannery Museum in Port Edward. Living museum in historic cannery building. Demonstration of net-mending and ropemaking some days.

Ride Mt. Hays Gondola. Three miles from ferry. Information: 624-2236, or 624-5637.

Explore the waterfront of this busy port.

Take a city walking tour (maps and tapes available at Infocentre).

Fish from boat, shore, or in the Skeena River-with B.C. license. Check fish and game or sporting goods stores to find out where and when the closures are.

Take some of many tours available through the Infocentre, including grain terminal, walking tours of town, archeology tour of harbor by boat.

Visit Chatham Village Longhouse, across from the Museum of Northern B.C., adjacent to Pacific Mariners Memorial Park.

Visit the Firehall Museum in the present firehall 2 doors up 1st Avenue from the Longhouse.

Watch reversible Butze Rapids from the highway. Best time is on an ebbing tide, 1/2 hour after high tide. (Add an hour to the tide table for Daylight Savings Time.)

Ride harbor tours, with trips to Venn Passage and Metlakatla.

Hike the trails on Mt. Hays. Guided nature trail tours available.

Enjoy the beautiful parks and gardens throughout the city.

Pick wild berries in summer (get suggestions from Infocentre).

Take a B.C. ferry side trip to the Queen Charlotte Islands with or without your car. Call the Infocentre or B.C. Ferries for schedules and information.

Play golf on Prince Rupert's golf course or watch one of the summer tournaments. In this climate players often wear rubber boots. The course has an unusual hazard—ravens sometimes steal the balls!

World War II historians or veterans of war in the Aleutians will find bunkers on shore, some visible from the ferry and some covered with undergrowth. Thousands of U.S. troops came by train to Prince Rupert and went from here to the Aleutians by ship. Several buildings near Seal Cove housed some of them. Roosevelt Park and a plaque near the hospital across from the park commemorate the action.

EARLY MORNING COFFEE SHOPS for those early arrivals! Prince Rupert Hotel, 2nd Avenue West & 6th Street. **Raffles Inn,** 1080 3rd Avenue West. **The Coast Highliner Inn,** 815 1st Avenue West, 6 a.m. **Crest Motor Hotel,** 222 1st Avenue West, 5:30 a.m. **Moby Dick Motor Inn,** 935 2nd Avenue West, 24 hours and **McDonald's,** 99 11th Avenue East, open at 7 a.m. daily. There's also a Mohawk Station and 24-hour convenience store at 201 2nd Avenue West.

INFORMATION AVAILABLE at **Prince Rupert Infocentre,** First and McBride, 9 a.m.–9 p.m. Mon.–Sat., 9 a.m.-5 p.m. Sun., mid-May to mid-September. Off season 10 a.m.–5 p.m., closed Sunday. Very helpful people. 624-5637. P.O. Box 669ip, Prince Rupert, B.C. V8J 3S1 Canada. The infocentre is in the Museum Building at the lower (west) end of McBride.

If you haven't yet acquired a copy of the current Tourism British Columbia Accommodation Guide, this is a good place to get one. It lists hotels and useful info for every B.C. town and village. As a small fee is charged for listing, you will find some hotels not listed. Free.

Transportation

FERRY: **Alaska Marine Highway,** May, 3-6 ships/week; June, July, August, September, 7 ships/week. Winter, 2-3 ships/week. All larger ships have cabins. Drivers should look over terminal area in daylight. Alaska Ferry Office, Box 457, Prince Rupert, B.C. V8J 3R4 Canada. 624-1744.

B.C. Ferries run from Port Hardy at the north end of Vancouver Island. Box 697, Prince Rupert, B.C. (604) 624-9627, 28, 29. Reservations:

British Columbia Ferry Corporation, 1112 Fort St., Victoria, B.C. V8V 4V2. (604) 386-3431.

In summer 1992 the B.C. ferries are running all daylight cruises between Port Hardy and Prince Rupert, with all departures at 7:30 a.m. and all arrivals about 10:30 p.m., with a stop at Bella Bella on some runs.

Schedule:	Lv Port Hardy	Lv Prince Rupert
June	odd days	even days
July	odd days	even days
August	even days	odd days
September	odd days	even days

To the Queen Charlotte Islands at Skidegate from June through September, the *Queen of Prince Rupert* goes 4–5 sailings weekly from each port. Fall through spring, 3 sailings weekly each direction. Sailing time 8 hours (Hecate Strait can be rough). Adult passenger $16, car and driver $77.

BUS: **Greyhound Bus Lines** (Canadian Coachways), 106–6th St., Prince Rupert, V8J 3L7, 624-5090, connects at Prince George to Vancouver. **Farwest Bus Lines,** 624-6400, and **Haida Coach Lines,** 624-6236, local only, bus tours.

TAXI: **Skeena Taxi,** 624-2185.

CAR RENTAL: **Budget,** 624-5144, and **Tilden,** 624-5318, 624-9470, are located in Rupert Square Shopping Mall, near the Canadian Airlines terminal, 500-2nd Ave. West, Prince Rupert, B.C. V8J 3T6.

RAIL: **Via Rail,** Waterfront, at foot of 2nd St., Prince Rupert, 627-7589. Train service to Prince George several times weekly. Reservations office in Winnipeg is open Mon. 10:30-7:30, Tues. closed, Wed., Fri., Sun. open 7:30-4:30, Thurs. and Sat. 7:30-4:30. For reservations call toll free in British Columbia (800) 561-8630 in Canada, (800) 561-3949 from the U.S., or see a travel agent. Amtrak unfortunately runs only as far north as Seattle. The fares between Prince Rupert and Prince George were being revised at presstime. The train leaves Prince Rupert at 10:30 a.m. M, Th, S. It arrives in Prince Rupert on M, W,S at 1 p.m. Sometimes, by prior arrangement, the train will stop for passengers at the ferry dock en route to Prince George.

AIR: Canadian **Airlines International (CAI),** to and from Vancouver, Rupert Square, 624-9181. 500 2nd Ave. West, Prince Rupert, V8J 3T6. Three flights daily in summer. **Air B.C.** offers regular flights between Prince Rupert and Vancouver. For schedule and fares, call 624-4554. Note: airport ferry to CAI and Air B.C. flights leaves dock near Alaska and B.C. ferries, but passengers must check in at airline office downtown and ride out to the ferry. Do allow time for this! Airport ferry fare: Adult $9 one-way, seniors and children $4. Same day return, add $1.

North Coast Airlines & Charters, Seal Cove. 627-1351. Serves Queen Charlotte Islands and other coastal communities.

Trans Provincial Airlines, Seal Cove. 627-1341. Also serves Queen Charlotte Islands and coastal communities. Scheduled flights three times a week to Ketchikan in summer.

Vancouver Island Helicopters, Seal Cove, 624-2792. No passenger service to Queen Charlotte Islands.

TOURS: Bus tours and service to interior points available from bus lines listed above. A full list of tours is available at the Infocentre.

Car and Baggage Storage

Moby Dick Motor Inn, 935 2nd Avenue West, Prince Rupert, B.C. V8J 1H8, 624-6961, $5. per day. **Philpott Evitt & Company Ltd.** (Indoor), 101-500 2nd Avenue West, Prince Rupert, B.C. V8J 3T6, 624-2101, $4 per foot per month.

BAGGAGE STORAGE at B.C. Ferry office (check for hours). Most hotels allow storage on day of departure for patrons.

Suggestion

For reasons possibly known to themselves, the U.S. and Canadian mails frequently take three weeks to get airmail between the U.S. and Prince Rupert. We advise using the telephone or fax freely to make reservations or get information here.

Hotels

Prices in Canadian dollars. Room tax is 6% to $49, 8% above that. Reservations advised in summer. 1992 rates not reported. Most have lower off season rates.

Aleeda Motel—900 3rd Avenue West, Prince Rupert, B.C., V8J 1M8. 627-1367. Quiet, Clean, 31 rooms (some with kitchens), phone, TV. Single $46, Double $55, Twin $62. Add'l, $5/person, kitchen $5.

Commercial Hotel—901 1st Avenue West, Prince Rupert, V8J 1B4. 624-6142. 24 rooms (some with bath), restaurant, TV. Rates low but not reported. Usually not space for visitors.

Coast Highliner Inn—815 1st Avenue West, Prince Rupert, B.C., V8J 1B3. 624-9060. Fax 627-7759. Reservations: 1-800-663-8158. Restaurant, lounge, banquet facilities, wheelchair accessible, non-smoking rooms, balconies with all rooms. Single $80, Double $85, Twin $90. Triple $95. Quad $100.

Crest Motor Hotel—(1 mile from dock) 222 1st Avenue West, Prince Rupert. Mail: Box 277, Prince Rupert, V8J 3P6. 624-6771. Fax 627-ROOM. 100 rooms, restaurant, coffee shop, cocktail lounge, TV, wheel-chair accessible, pets allowed. Fishing charters. Single $90, Double $95, Twin $105. Add'l $10. Day Room $30. Cot/crib $15. Seniors 10%.

Moby Dick Inn—935 2nd Avenue West, Prince Rupert, B.C. V8J 1H8. 624-6961. Fax 627-3760. Sauna and whirlpool. 24 hour restaurant. Coin-op laundry. Car rental package available. Near B.C. and Alaska ferries. Single $51–54, Double & Twin $56–60. Add'l $8.

Neptune Motor Inn—1051 Chamberlin (Yellowhead Centre on Hwy. 16). Mail: P.O. Box 966, Prince Rupert, B.C. V8J 4B7. 627-1377. Restaurant, cable TV, pets allowed. Kitchenettes. 45 units. Car and trailer storage. Single $40, Double $45, Twin $50. Add'l $5. Kitchen $6.

Ocean View Hotel—950 1st Avenue West, Prince Rupert, V8J 1A9. 624-6259. Restored older hotel. 55 rooms (some with bath, TV). Shared bath, single $28, double $30. Private bath, single $35, double $39. Pub downstairs with ocean view.

Parkside Resort Motel—2 miles, 101–11th Avenue East, Prince Rupert, V8J 2W2. 624-9131. Fax 627-8547. 35 rooms (18 with kitchen), phone, complimentary coffee, Satellite TV, pets allowed. Single $52, Double $58, Twin $64. Kitchen $6. Suite $12 add'l, weekly rates, senior and family rates. Camper and trailer parking. 7 campsites with hookups, $10.00. Car storage $3/day.

Pioneer Rooms—167 3rd Avenue East, Prince Rupert, B.C. 624-2334. Boarding house in historic building "with colourful past". Popular with backpackers. $15–35.

Prince Rupert Hotel—2nd Avenue West & 6th Street. Mail: Box 700, Prince Rupert, V8J 3S1. 624-6711, or 1-800-663-7760 (in B.C.). Fax 624-3288. 95 rooms, harbor view, dining room, lounge, cabaret, wheelchair accessible, satellite TV. Single $59, Double $69, Twin $77 Add'l $10.

Raffles Inn—1080 3rd Avenue West, Prince Rupert, V8J 1N1. 624-9161, or 1-800-663-3207 in B.C.. Fax 627-7500. 52 rooms, restaurant, lounge, TV. Single $52, Double $62, Twin $69. Add'l, $4/person. $5 cot. Seniors, 10%.

Rupert Motor Inn—1 mile, corner 1st Avenue West & 6th Street. Mail: Box 700, Prince Rupert, B.C. V8J 3S1. 624-9107. Fax 627-8232. 51 rooms, restaurant, phone, satellite TV, sauna. Single $62, Double $72, Twin $71. Add'l $8/person.

Slumber Lodge—1.5 miles, 909 3rd Avenue West, Prince Rupert, V8J 1M9. 627-1711, or 1-800-663-2831 in B.C. 73 rooms, restaurant, lounge, cable TV, sauna. With continental braakfast, Single $50, Double $60, Twin $65, Triple $65. Children under 12 free. Add'l $4. Senior rate about 15%.

Totem Lodge Motel—1 mile, 1335 Park Avenue, Prince Rupert, V8J 1K3. 624-6761. 31 units, phone, TV, car storage. Coin-op laundry. Single $50, Double $58, Twin $64. Add'l $6. Kitchen $5. Rollaway bed $5. Pets, $4. Car storage $3.

No Youth Hostel. Note some inexpensive hotels in Prince Rupert.

Bed & Breakfasts

Eagle Bluff B & B, in renovated heritage building near the waterfront and yacht club. 100 Cow BAy Rd, Prince Rupert. 627-4955. Choice of breakfasts. Shared bath, single $40, double $50. Private bath, single $44, double $55. Suite for 6, more with cots, $65.

Rose's B & B. across the street from the Oceanview Hotel. 943–1st Avenue West, Prince Rupert, V8J 1B4. 624-5539. Single $40, Double $50.

Campground

Park Ave. Campground—1/2 mile from ferry, 1750 Park Ave., Box 612-IPT, Prince Rupert, B.C. V8J 3R5. 624-5861. Visitor information. 87 sites, some pull-throughs, tent camping available. Overflow parking. Showers, toilets, full hook-ups, dump station. $11 unserviced site, tenting $9, $15 full serviced. Reservations recommended. Vehicle storage in winter only.

There are other campgrounds along the highway and river east of Prince Rupert, but no others in town.

Facilities

LAUNDROMAT—**McBride Street Laundromat**, 326 McBride Street. 627-7755. Open till 9 p.m. **King Koin**, 743-2nd Ave. W. **Maytag**, 226 7th St.

ICE—any gas station. **Park Avenue Corner Store** across from campground. **Safeway.**

PROPANE—**Canadian Propane Ltd.**, 170 George Hills (near Cow Bay). **Park Avenue Corner Store**, 1665 Park Ave. **Mt. Hays Service**, 537 Hays Cove Circle, 627-7005.

DUMP STATIONS—**Campground** and **Park Avenue Corner Store**, 1665 Park Ave., across from campground.

HOSPITAL—**Prince Rupert Regional**, 1305 Summit Avenue. 624-2171.

PETS—**Veterinary Services**, 975 Chamberlin, 627-1161. Boarding $4-6.25/day. **SPCA**, 2200 Seal Cove Circle. 624-2859. $4-6.50/day. Male cats must be neutered. Will take ferrets.

Boats

CHARTERS: For current information on boat charters, ask at **Infocentre**. 624-5637 or **Prince Rupert Charter Operators**, 627-7777.

PUBLIC FLOATS, FUEL. **Fairview Public Floats** just south of ferry dock. Fishing boat traffic is heavy here during summer. **Cow Bay Floats**, north of Atlin Fish Co., fuel. **Rushbrook Public Floats**, north of main part of town and fish canneries. Can be reached on land by going north on 3rd Avenue past Court House, taking second left. Launching ramp. Fuel at Cow Bay.

Happenings—1992

Year-round	Bingos at Rupert Bingo Centre. Bowling, at Totem Lanes Bowling Centre,. Art exhibits changed monthly at the Prince Rupert Museum Art Gallery. Performances at Performing Arts Centre
May 7–9	B.C. Annual Jazz Dance Competition
May	National Tourism Week
May 18	International Museum Day
June 11–14	Seafest. Parade, Children's events. Land and water events. Native Cultural Days.
June 13, 14	Ladies' Open Golf Tournament. Call 627-2000 for info on all golf events.
June 18	All That Jazz recital, Performing Arts Centre, 7:30 p.m. 627-8888
June 19–21	Men's Open Golf Tournament
June 27, 28	Seniors Open Golf Tournament
July 1	Canada Day Activities.
July, early	Fishing Derby, date not confirmed.
July 19	International Scramble—Golf
September 12, 13	Duffers Mixed Tournament—Golf

A full list of things to see and do is available at the Infocentre. Throughout the year and particularly in summer, there are musical, dance, and drama performances, many not announced at presstime.

Canadian Customs and Regulations

Vehicles can be left in Canada for up to 45 days without a permit, under supervision in a lot, not on street. Report leaving car to Customs,

Room 105, Federal Building, or at Alaska ferry terminal. When driving in Canada, especially the Yukon, carry proof of adequate liability insurance, at least $200,000. Seat belts must be used and children under 6 or under 40 lbs. must be in infant or child seats. Blood alcohol levels over .08% are illegal in Canada and penalties are severe.

Carry money sufficient to pass through Canada by your planned route and method of travel, allowing for emergencies, to avoid being refused entry to Canada.

Personal identification is required for everyone, including infants.

Firearms. Handguns are not permitted into Canada. Rifles and shotguns for personal use are allowed. If they will be in B.C. for a week or longer, you need a $1 permit, available from the RCMP or Fish & Wildlife. Some sports stores may sell the permits.

Pets (cats and dogs), over 3 years of age, must have proof of rabies vaccination within past 36 months. Health certificate advised, within 30 days of trip.

Pilots. Canadian Customs now have 24-hour service, free of charge, at Digby Island Airport, Prince Rupert. For others, including boats and floatplanes, customs inspections free at Seal Cove between 7 a.m. and 10 p.m. in summer. After hours, by reservation made during above hours, the charge is $50. Winter hours are 7 a.m.-4:30 p.m.

Boats. Pleasure craft have free clearance 7 a.m.-10 p.m. daily. Overtime charges apply at other hours.

Seal Cove—loading a DeHavilland Beaver on floats with groceries for a logging camp.

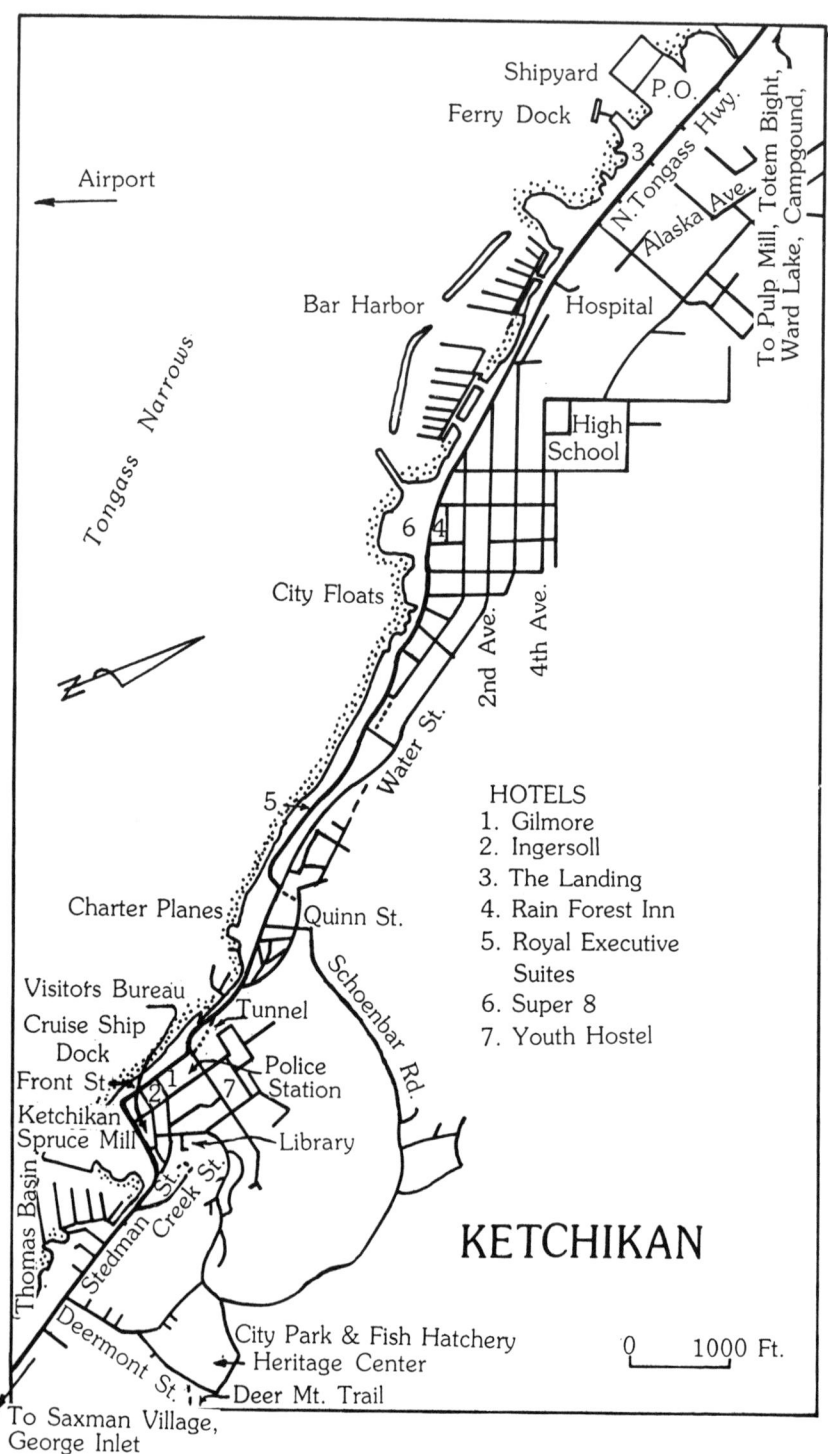

Airport

Shipyard
Ferry Dock
P.O.
N. Tongass Hwy.
Alaska Ave.
To Pulp Mill, Totem Bight, Ward Lake, Campgound,

Tongass Narrows

Bar Harbor
Hospital

High School

City Floats

6 4

2nd Ave.
4th Ave.

Water St.

5

HOTELS
1. Gilmore
2. Ingersoll
3. The Landing
4. Rain Forest Inn
5. Royal Executive
   Suites
6. Super 8
7. Youth Hostel

Charter Planes
Quinn St.

Schoenbar Rd.

Visitors Bureau
Cruise Ship Dock
Tunnel
Front St.
Ketchikan Spruce Mill
2 1
7
Police Station
Library

Thomas Basin
Stedman St.
Creek St.

KETCHIKAN

City Park & Fish Hatchery
Heritage Center
Deer Mt. Trail

Deermont St.

To Saxman Village,
George Inlet

0   1000 Ft.

Camping near Ward Lake north of Ketchikan.

KETCHIKAN
(Area code 907, Zip code 99901)

KETCHIKAN (pop. 14,000) is the fourth largest city in Alaska and the commercial center for most of Southeastern Alaska. Early Indians settled here. Later, salmon canneries and sawmills were built, and gold was discovered in the area. In 1954 the Ketchikan Pulp Company mill was constructed at Ward Cove, just north of town. From Ketchikan, planes and boats work in all directions, supplying logging camps, fishing resorts, and settlements on other islands.

The town, like most in Southeastern Alaska, is linear, never more than 10 blocks wide, but several miles long. Tongass, the main street, is built on pilings that take it out over the water in several places. Some of the cross "streets" are really wooden steps climbing the steep hillside.

The largest collection of totems anywhere in the world is found here in three locations: at Totem Bight, 7.5 miles north of the ferry dock. Saxman State Park, 4.5 miles south of the ferry dock, and the Totem Heritage Center, 601 Deermont Street, 4 miles south of the dock.

The ferry terminal is 2.5 miles north of downtown Ketchikan.

To See and Do

Take a walking tour of Ketchikan. Maps available at ferry terminal and Visitors Bureau on downtown dock. Covers all the sights within walking distance of downtown. The city bus stop on Tongass Ave., in front of the ferry terminal parking lot, has buses every half hour to downtown.

Take a taxi tour, including totem parks if you wish. **Alaska Cab** charters cabs for $42/hr. for 1–6 people.

Gray Line offers sightseeing tours from hotels and from the ferry parking lot during longer ferry stops.

Visit totem parks. Saxman Village, 4.6 miles from ferry, Mile 2.3 S. Tongass Highway. Totem Bight, totems and ceremonial house, 7.6 miles, Mile 9.9 N. Tongass Highway.

Totem Heritage Center, 4 miles, 601 Deermont St., 8 a.m.–5 p.m. Mon-Sat and9–5 p.m. Sun, during tour season. May 16 through September. Tues–Fri 1–5 p.m. October through May. $2 admission.

See Deer Mountain fish hatchery with observation platforms and signs and videos explaining the life cycle of salmon.

See the Ketchikan Historical Museum, 2.4 miles, Dock St., adjacent to the library. Pioneer and Indian artifacts, minerals, shells. $1 admission.

Tour Dolly's House, 2.4 miles, Creek St. This residence of Ketchikan's last "madame" has been opened as a museum, with other Creek Street houses in this professional district. Summer hours, 9 a.m.–5 p.m. $2.50.

Visit boat harbors and the waterfront. Nearest to ferry dock is Bar Harbor, about 1 mile, with most types of fishing and pleasure boats. Much of this can be seen during a regular ferry stop if you have at least an hour on shore-walk briskly, and keep track of the time. This is a good chance to see all types of fishing gear close-up, talk to fishermen, and see jellyfish and sea anemones under floats.

Tour fishing harbor and fish processing plant (includes free samples). **Outdoor Alaska**, Box 7814, Ketchikan. (907) 225-6044. Pulp mill, **Ketchikan Pulp Company**, Box 6600, Ketchikan. (907) 225-2151.

Ward Lake Recreation Area, 5.8 miles from ferry, turn off at Mile 6.8 N. Tongass Highway. Nature and hiking trails, picnic area, and campgrounds. A good place to explore and learn about a temperate rain forest.

See U.S. Forest Service Visitor Center on ground floor, Federal Building. Shows films, has historical and cultural displays and a variety of free handouts, maps, and information. (907) 225-3101. Open 8-5, Mon-Fri until late May. Open 8–5, Mon–Sat through first week in September.

Hike trails to top of Deer Mountain (from Deermont) for spectacular view over town, waterways and islands. Perseverance and Talbot lakes, and White River. Maps available from Forest Service in Federal Building, or from information centers.

Ride the *Aurora* on her local runs to Metlakatla and Hollis. Hollis has no facilities, but offers road access to Craig, Klawock, Hydaburg, and Thorne Bay. Check the ferry schedule.

Ride the *Aurora* on her cruise up the Portland Canal to Hyder and back on Fridays, or ride one way and fly the other with a local air taxi. Ask the ferry terminal if one is offering a package rate. Portland Canal is a long fiord marking the US and Canadian boundary which early explorers hoped would be a Northwest Passage. Rock walls over 1000 feet high line it on both sides, broken by the occasional waterfall. At its end are the villages of Stewart, B.C. and Hyder, AK with glimpses of icefields and hanging glaciers above.

See Misty Fiords via tour boat from Ketchikan. Ketchikan Visitors' Bureau has information at their building on the city dock. All air charter companies will make flightseeing excursions.

Fish or kayak in Misty Fiords using Forest Service cabins or camping out. Kayak rentals $20/day, or bring your own. Transportation via air and *M/V Misty Fjords* on Sun., Wed., Fri. **Outdoor Alaska**, Box 7814, Ketchikan, AK 99901. 225-6044.

Fish from shore or boat. Mountain Point, 8.5 miles from ferry, is a favorite fishing spot for pink salmon, from mid-June on. There is a boat launching ramp and parking area. Residents can tell you the current hot spots. Fishing is *the* local sport here. Charter a boat, rent one, or bring your own. Do respect the tides, currents, weather, and cold water. Traffic, especially in Tongass Narrows, is heavy with ships, tugs and barges, boats, and floatplanes. The Visitors Bureau has a current list of charter operators. Fishing license info is listed for Ketchikan under Facilities.

Enjoy miles of sheltered water for boating or kayaking. Apply the cautions above, but enjoy easy access to such areas as Behm Canal, the passage around Revillagigedo Island, the island Ketchikan is on.

Pick berries in season-July, August, September for blueberries, red huckleberries, salmon berries. The big clearcut above the north end of town is a huge berry patch. It's less than half a mile straight up the hill from the ferry terminal.

Transportation

FERRY: Runs daily in summer; fewer sailings in winter. Dock and terminal are at Mile 2.3 N. Tongass Highway (north of town). Airport ferry dock 1/2 mile farther north, serves the ferry to Ketchikan Airport (across the Narrows on Gravina Island).

BUS: North end of the line is at the ferry parking lot. Buses run from here to the center of town, and south, every half hour 6:45 a.m.-6:45 p.m. Mon.-Sat. $1. Senior and child fares.

TAXI: **Alaska Cab**, 225-2133. **Yellow Taxi**, 225-5555. **Sourdough-Ingersoll**, 225-5544. **Classic Chauffeur Limousine**, 225-9159.

CAR RENTAL: At airport, **Alaska Car Rental**, 225-5123. **Avis**, 225-4515.

TOURS: around Ketchikan and to totem parks, Ward Lake, etc. Most operate mid-May to late September. **Alaska Sightseeing**, summer number, 225-2740. **Alaska Travel Adventures**, 789-0052 (Juneau office), cruises of Ketchikan area. **Cape Fox Tours**, 225-5163. **Classic Chauffeur Limousine**, 225-9159. **Classic Tours**, 225-3091 (in 1955 Chevy with retired high school teacher). **Gray Line of Alaska**, 225-5930. **Ketchikan Local Tours**, 225-1989. **North Wind Expeditions**, 225-4751, rainforest and tidepools. **Orca Tours**, 225-0411. **Seahorse Trolley's Tours**, 225-5713, by horse-drawn trolley. **Specialty Tours**, 247-8625.

KAYAK TOURS: **Outdoor Alaska**, 225-6044. **Southeast Exposure**, 225-8829. These companies offer half day tours of Ketchikan's waterfront and Tongass Narrows as well as multi-day trips to the backcountry.

AIR: **Alaska Airlines** has daily jet flights between Ketchikan Airport and Seattle, Anchorage, Juneau, Sitka, Wrangell, and Petersburg. **Markair** serves Seattle, Sitka, Juneau, and Anchorage daily.

The airport is served twice hourly by 5-minute ferry from its dock 1/2 mile north of ferry terminal, $2.50. Be sure to allow time for the airport ferry in making connections. It departs from Ketchikan at 15 and 45 minutes past each hour. The uphill walk from ferry to airport terminal is two blocks. The airport shuttle, for a higher charge, stops at hotels and delivers you to the terminal door. 225-5429.

AIR CHARTERS: **Ketchikan Air Service**, 1600 Ketchikan Int'l. Airport, Ketchikan, AK 99901. 225-6608.

Taquan Air Service, 501 Water St., Ketchikan 99901. 225-9668. Offers flightseeing tours by floatplane, some with stops at native villages, overnight package tours to lodges.

These charter services are based along the waterfront, and their take-offs and landings provide much of the action in the harbor. Some also have bases on the airport. All can fly you into fishing resorts, Forest Service cabins, and virtually any place in Southeastern Alaska.

INFORMATION AVAILABLE at **Ketchikan Visitors Bureau** on the downtown dock. Very helpful people. 131 Front St., Ketchikan, AK 99901. Phone: 225-6166. Fax: 225-4250. **Chamber of Commerce**, Box 5957,

Ketchikan, AK 99901. Phone: 225-3184. Also check with Fish and Game and Forest Service offices downtown. The Forest Service has an information center in the lobby of the Federal Building.

BAGGAGE STORAGE available at hotels, for patrons, on day of departure (check with individual hotels).

Worker waters a hanging flower basket on Ketchikan's dock.

Hotels
(plus 9% room and sales tax. * 1992 rates not reported)

Alaska's Rain Forest Inn—1/2 mile from from ferry. 2311 Hemlock, Ketchikan 99901. 225-9500. Eight rooms, some available on per bunk, dormitory basis. Coffee free. Restaurants nearby. Clean. Open all year. $19.27 in dorm. $41.28 private room, single or double. $6 Add'l adult.

Best Western Landing: across the street from ferry dock, 3434 Tongass, Ketchikan 99901. 225-5166. 48 rooms newly remodeled, restaurant, lounge, TV. Freezer space for your fish. Courtesy van. Single and Double $82–98.

Clover Pass Resort—13 miles from ferry, Mile 15, North Tongass. Box 7322, Ketchikan 99901. 247-2234. Lodge, cabins, restaurant, lounge, marina, boat rentals and supplies, fishing information and charters. Boat moorage. Package tours for three to eight days include cabin, boat, motor, fuel, bait, rod and reel, breakfast, lunch, dinner, fish packing boxes, transportation to and from Ketchikan. $970-2240 for 3-8 days. Deluxe package includes chartered boat with guide. Trailers and campers $20 for 2 people. Add'l, $2/person. Season runs from April 2 to October 1.

Gilmore Hotel—2.2 miles from ferry (downtown), 326 Front St., Ketchikan 99901. 225-9423. 40 rooms, color TV, direct dial phones, Annabelle's Keg and Chowder House in building. Courtesy van. Call on arrival. Double room, $60, higher rate for waterfront view. Small pets allowed, $50 deposit.

Ingersoll Hotel—2.3 miles from ferry (downtown corner of Front and Mission), 303 Mission St., Ketchikan 99901. 225-2124 or 800-478-2124 within Alaska. Fax 225-8530. 60 rooms. Double $95, continental breakfast included. Corporate, government, senior, and group rates.

New York Hotel—3 miles from ferry, next to Creek Street. built in 1925, restored hotel with 8 rooms furnished in period style plus cable TV, phone, queen beds, full baths. Continental breakfast, local phone calls included. Single/Double $79. 225-0246.

Super 8 Motel—1/2 mile from ferry, 2151 Sea Level Drive, P. O. Box 8818, Ketchikan 99901. 225-9088 or 800-800-8000. 82 rooms. Pets with $25 deposit. Free airport shuttle. Double $88.88.

Royal Executive Suites—1471 Tongass, Box 8331, Ketchikan 99901. 225-1900. Fax 225-1795. 14 rooms, sauna and jacuzzis, waterfront views. Rooms $85 single/double. $105 with jacuzzi. Suite with jacuzzi, $145.

Salmon Falls Resort—15 miles from ferry on N. Tongass Highway. Box 5700, Ketchikan 99901. 225-2752 or (800) 247-9059. Fax 225-2710. Restaurant, lounge. Conference room. Fishing package rate includes room, meals, airport transfes, guided fishing, fishing gear and bait, and fish processing, $659 incl. tax. Room only, single $115, Double $139, incl. tax.

Westmark Cape Fox Lodge: 800 Venetia Way, Ketchikan, AK 99901. 225-8001 or 800-544-0970. Fax 225-8286. New hotel on hill above city with funicular down to Creek Street. 70 rooms, 2 suites, restaurant, conference rooms. Wheelchair accessible. Courtesy van from airport and ferry terminal. Double $144–150.

Youth Hostel—First Methodist Church, 400 Main, P. O. Box 8515, Ketchikan, AK 99901. 225-3319. Bring sleeping bag to use male and female dormitories. Register 6 p.m.–11 p.m. $5, with AYH pass, $8 for nonmembers. Open Memorial Day to Labor Day.

Bed & Breakfasts

Bed & breakfasts are increasing rapidly throughout Alaska, and our readers enjoy them. Prices usually range from $45 to $80 depending on season and facilities. Each town's visitors bureau has a list of the homes in that town, individual or organized under an association. Some homes are open all year, while others operate seasonbally. To save space and the book weight you carry, I list associations and the local visitors bureau rather than individual homes. I use the same policy for fishing charters in larger towns where there are many, constantly changing.

Alaska Bed & Breakfast Association—P. O. Box 21890, Juneau, AK 99802. 586-2959. Fax 463-6788. Lists homes in most S.E. Alaska towns, including Ketchikan.

Ketchikan Bed & Breakfast—P.O. Box 3213, Ketchikan 99901. Phone 225-8550. The association books travelers into private homes, can arrange tours, fishing charters. $50 for 1 person. $10 for each add'l. Up to 20 rooms available. Confirms reservations with 1 night's deposit.

Ketchikan Visitors Bureau, 225-6166, has a current list of individual bed & breakfasts, some in town, some surrounded by forest, and some on the waterfront. Fishing charters, skiff rentals, and airport/ferry transfers may be offered.

Guard Island Light, now automated, marks the north end of Tongass Narrows.

FLY-IN RESORTS: Near Ketchikan, offer a variety of rustic to modern facilities, and excellent fishing. Included are **Yes Bay Lodge, Humpback Lake Chalet, Misty Fiords Resort, Unuk River Post, The Floating Fishing Lodge**, and **Waterfall Resort**, 225-9461, 800-544-5125. On Prince of Wales Island (and described in that section), some reached by ferry and bus as well as plane are **Boardwalk Wilderness Lodge**, 800-372-9382, **Coffman Cove Wilderness Lodge, Fireweed Lodge**, 755-2930, **Gold Coast Lodge**, 225-8375, 800-333-5992, **Karta Inn, Haida Way Lodge**, 826-3268, **Silver King Lodge, Sportsman's Cove, Lodge**, 800-962-7889, **Whale Pass Resort, Log Cabin Resort & RV Park**, 755-2205, 800-544-2205, **McFarland's Floatel**, 828-3335. Information available from air charter services and Ketchikan Visitors' Bureau, 225-6166.

Campgrounds
(14 day limit)

Signal Creek—5.2 miles from the ferry, Mile .7 on Ward Lake Road, on the shore of Ward Lake. 24 units. Firewood, toilets, water, tables. $6. Open Memorial Day–Sept. 30.

3 C's Campground—5.4 miles from ferry, Mile 1 on Ward Lake Road. Water, firewood, grates, tables, toilets. 4 units. $6. Open mid-May through mid-Sept.

Last Chance Campground—7.2 miles from ferry, on Ward Lake Road. Opened as needed for overflow from other campgrounds. Firewood, water, tables, grates, toilets. 25 units. $6. Open mid-June through mid-Sept. These U. S. Forest Service campgrounds have no hookups.

Settlers Cove—16 miles from ferry, Mile 18.2 North Tongass Highway. State campground. Adjacent parking, with overnight parking allowed. Picnic area, beach, fishing, swimming, firewood, tables, grates, toilets, water. No hookups. Super view. Good berry picking in August. 12 units, $6.

Clover Pass—private campground, RV hookups, laundry, dump station, 12 miles from ferry, $20/night for 2 people. Add'l $2. P.O. Box 7322, Ketchikan, AK 99901. (907) 247-2234.

Facilities

LAUNDROMATS: **The "Mat"**, 989 Stedman, 225-0628. **Highliner Laundromat**, 2703 Tongass, 225-5308.

SWIMMING POOL: Ketchikan High School. Scheduled open hours. Sauna. 225-2010.

HOSPITAL: **Ketchikan General** 3100 Tongass, 225-5171.

DIESEL: **Gas At Last,** 655 Stedman. **White Pass Alaska,** S. Tongass Hwy.

PROPANE: **White Pass Alaska,** S. Tongass Hwy. **Petrolane**, N. Tongass Hwy.

DUMP STATION: **Public Works Warehouse,** 3291 Tongass Ave., 2 blocks north of ferry terminal. 24 hours/day, 7 days/week, all year. Free.

ICE: All supermarkets.

PETS: Vet **Dr. Vern R. Starks**, mile 3, North Tongass. Mail: Rt. 1, Box 863, Ketchikan 99901. 225-6051. Pet boarding and dog grooming: **Gail Oaksmith** 225-6393, and **Debbie Turner,** 225-6786. Boarding: **Claudia Brooks** (at vet clinic).

FISHING GEAR REPAIR: **Butch's Rod & Reel Repair**, 225-5155, 225-4656.

FISHING LICENSES: Required even for salt water fishing, are available at **The Outfitter**, 3232 Tongass Ave., at **Plaza Sports** in the Plaza Port West Mall, and at **Tongass Trading Company** on the downtown dock. Non-resident licenses, 1-day $10, 3-day $15, 14-day $30, and year $50.

Boat Rentals

Clover Pass Resort—Rentals, supplies, launching. 247-2234. **Knudson Cove Marina**,—Rentals, supplies, launching. 247-8500.

KAYAK RENTALS—**Outdoor Alaska**, 225-6044. **Southeast Exposure**, 225-8829.

Charters

Outdoor Alaska, P.O. Box 7814, Ketchikan 99901. 225-6044. Sightseeing to Misty Fiords, canoe and kayak transportation trips. Licensed for 32 people. Cruise/fly $175. Cruise both ways, $135.

Ketchikan Sportfishing, P.O. Box 7896, Ketchikan 99901. 225-3293, 225-9505. Day & overnight charters. Book for 40 boats, 22 to 54 feet.

Ketchikan Visitors Bureau, 225-6166, in office on the downtown dock, has a current list of individual charter boats with local owner/guides.

Happenings

Fish Pirate's Daughter, Ketchikan's very well-done summer musical melodrama about its wilder days, July 3 through September. 7 and 8 p.m. most nights, 338 Main St. 225-4792. Adults, $6.

Ketchikan King Salmon Derby, Memorial Day weekend and following two weekends, May 22–26, 30, 31, and June 6, 7, 13, and 14, 1992. Prizes and fish are big.

Killer Whale Halibut Derby, mid-May through Labor Day.

4th of July celebration, July 3-5, 1992, is Ketchikan's big holiday, with parade followed by a logging show with contests at the ballpark. Fireworks over the channel at night and many other events.

Blueberry festival on August 8, 1992 with crafts show, basement and lower floor of state office building.

Christmas Festival of Lights, November 30–Dec. 2, 1992. Community lights up, Santa arrives by helicopter, and there's a formal ball.

Festival of the North, last three weekends of February. Variety of performing & visual arts events including drama, ballet, literary readings, piano & jazz programs, and art walk.

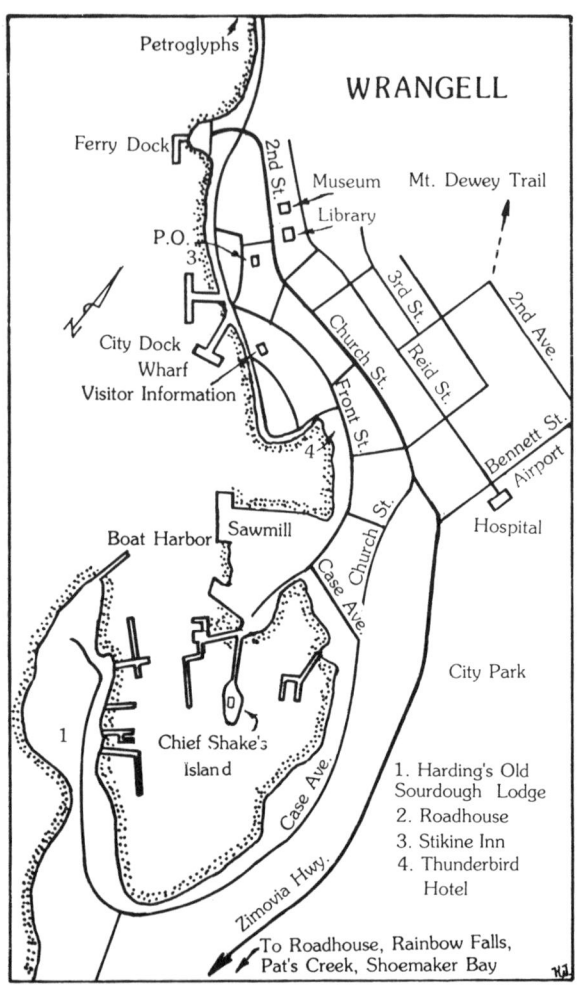

WRANGELL

Petroglyphs

Ferry Dock

2nd St.

Museum   Mt. Dewey Trail

Library

P.O.
3.

3rd St.

Reid St.

2nd Ave.

Church St.

City Dock
Wharf
Visitor Information

Front St.

4

Bennett St.
Airport

Boat Harbor — Sawmill

Church St.

Hospital

Case Ave.

City Park

1

Chief Shake's
Island

Case Ave.

1. Harding's Old
   Sourdough Lodge
2. Roadhouse
3. Stikine Inn
4. Thunderbird
   Hotel

Zimovia Hwy.

To Roadhouse, Rainbow Falls,
Pat's Creek, Shoemaker Bay

Wrangell children sell garnets pried from Garnet Ledge to ferry passengers, making pocket money for school clothes, bicycles, even trips to Disneyland!

WRANGELL
(Area code 907, Zip code 99929)

AT THE MOUTH of the Stikine River, Wrangell (pop. 3,100) is the only town in southeastern Alaska to have flown 3 flags. The Russians built Fort St. Dionysius here in 1834 to guard the mouth of the Stikine against Hudson's Bay Company trappers hunting sea otters. Later the British leased most of the area, calling their post Fort Stikine. Under the American flag, Wrangell, named for Russian Baron Von Wrangell, became the jump-off point for gold miners headed up the Stikine to the Klondike and Cassiars. Today Wrangell is an important lumber exporting port and processes shrimp.

Its attractions include excellent fishing, a totem park, a good museum, petroglyphs, and a variety of minerals, including the garnets sold by local children at the ferry dock.

To See and Do

Visit Chief Shakes Island, one mile (a brisk 15 minute walk each way from ferry), in boat harbor just south of the lumber mill. You will find a good collection of totems and a ceremonial house. Normally locked, it is open regular hours in summer, when tour ships are in, or on request in IRA Council office, 874-3505. Donations appreciated to help maintain the building.

Tour the museum, two blocks up 2nd St. (the main street leading away from the ferry dock). Artifacts from Wrangell's early days, fishing, and mounted game specimens. Open 1-4p.m. Mon-Sat., open for cruise ships and ferries in summer. Winter hours: Wednesday 2-4 or by appointment. Wrangell Museum, P.O. Box 1050, Wrangell, AK 99929. 874-3770. Admission $1, children under 16 free.

See the Wrangell Art Gallery adjacent, open same times as museum.

Take the Wrangell walking tour of sights, totems, etc. Map available at hotels and information centers.

See the new Totem Park on Front St. across from City Market. The totems were recently carved in Wrangell.

See petroglyphs carved by prehistoric Indians. The nearest is on the library lawn, next door to the museum. At least 20 more are carved in black argillite rock on the point about 1/2 mile north of the dock. From a sign on the road, walk down a boarded path to the beach. A few yards to your right you will see scattered black rocks with designs and faces carved on them. It is possible to make rubbings from them with paper and charcoal. Locals recommend laying rice paper on the petroglyphs and rubbing the paper with a wad of the bracken fern that grows along the boardwalk. These are prehistoric artifacts—please treat them with respect. Some may be 2,000 years old. Rice paper is available at Norris's Gift Shop. Use a cool iron on paper later to take out wrinkles and set dye.

Hike to Rainbow Falls. The trail begins at Mile 4.7 Zimovia High-way. It is maintained.

Fish in the harbor, or up Stikine River. Hunting also in Stikine Valley. Licenses and info at Angerman's Sport Shop, and Ottesen's Hardware.

Hike up Mt. Dewey for great view over harbor, 1 mile. Trail starts at 2nd Ave. and Mission St. Trail is only maintained and marked at start.

Charter a boat or fly up Stikine River for rockhounding (including garnets), river touring, and animal and bird watching (this is a major migratory flyway).

Charter a plane to fly up over the LeConte Glacier and the mouth of the Stikine River.

Watch black bears catch salmon at Anan Creek 30 miles south of Wrangell. Get there by boat or floatplane. Viewing platform. Day trip or use USFS cabin a mile away with reservation. July, August peak months.

Meet local children (to whom the Garnet Ledge claim has been turned over) at the ship, and see or buy the garnets they have gathered. Their salesmanship is often hilarious.

Buy local garnets through the Boy Scouts at Wrangell Museum. Permits to collect your own are available for a nominal fee at the museum. Garnet Ledge is 7.5 miles from Wrangell by boat or plane.

Note the small flattened pieces of dark-grey slate around the ferry terminal building. These are similar to the argillite used in Haida carvings and can be carved. Experienced carvers easily make bas-relief scenes and figures even with a screwdriver.

The Wrangell stop is usually only 1/2 hour southbound, 1 hour northbound, but it can be longer depending on the tide in Wrangell Narrows. The Zimovia Highway (called 2nd St. there) starts at the ferry dock.

INFORMATION AVAILABLE at the museum, 2nd St., **Wrangell Visitors Bureau**, Box 1078, Wrangell, AK 99929. 874-3770. **Wrangell Chamber of Commerce** office is in an A-frame next to the City Hall offices on Outer Drive, about two blocks from the city dock. Box 49, Wrangell, AK 99929. 874-3901. **U.S. Forest Service**, Box 51, Wrangell, AK 99929. 874-2323. USFS cabins and trails.

Transportation

FERRY: Runs daily in summer, fewer sailings in winter.

AIR: **Alaska Airlines** daily, year-round.

AIR CHARTER SERVICES: **Wrangell Air Service**, 874-2369. **Diamond Aviation**, 874-2319.

AVIATION FUEL: **Wrangell Air Service** has 80/87 and 100 octane. **Diamond Aviation** has 100 octane and jet fuel. Aviation fuel at Wrangell costs about $.30 per gallon less than at Ketchikan or Juneau. Wrangell has customs service.

BUS: There is no scheduled bus service.

BUS TOURS: Bus tours are available from the owners of the **The Roadhouse**, 874-2336. They also run shorter narrated tours when ships wait for tides. Salmon bakes on request. **C.E. Bradley's Inc.,** 874-3611. Offers 1.5 hour tour. Ten people minimum.

BOAT TOURS: **Jerry Elliott**, 65' boat, 3-to 9-day trips, 4 person minimum. 874-3030. **Doug Smith**, fishing, sightseeing. 874-3447. **Dan Rob-**

erts, fishing, sightseeing, LeConte Glacier tours, 874-3637. **Bob Gillen,** Stikine River, 874-3191. **TH Charters,** 874-3613. Fax 874-2285. Boat tours up Stikine River, jet boat day trips to Anan Creek.

BICYCLE RENTALS: **James Jones.** 874-2248.

TAXI: **Star Cab,** 874-3622, 874-3511.

CAR RENTAL: **Rent-A-Dent,** Thunderbird Hotel, 874-3322. Late model cars in excellent condition.

BAGGAGE STORAGE at hotels, for patrons, on day of departure.

Hotels
(6% tax additional plus $3 per room)
Hardings Old Sourdough Lodge—1 mile, Shustak Point south of town. Box 1062, Wrangell, AK 99929. 874-3613. Courtesy transportation from ferry or airport. 20 rooms, laundry, TV, sauna/steam bath. Fishing and hunting trips. $65/person, double occupancy, including meals. Bed and breakfast only, Single $63, Double $71. Rooms only, $55 1–2 people. Fishing tour package rate. Open all year.

The Roadhouse—4 miles from ferry, Zimovia Highway, across from the new boat harbor at Shoemaker Bay, Box 1199, Wrangell, AK 99929. 874-2335. Motel, courtesy car, restaurant, lounge. Salmon bakes, sightseeing tours, raft trips, fishing, and hunting charters. Car rentals. Pets allowed. Single $50, Double $58.

Stikine Inn—1 block on Front St., Box 990, Wrangell, AK 99929. 874-3388. Fax 874-3923. 34 rooms with telephone, restaurant, lounge, dance band, liquor store, gift shop. Open all year. Single $70, Double $75. Children under 12 free.

Thunderbird Hotel—6 blocks, 223 Front St., Box 110, Wrangell. 874-3322. Courtesy coffee, laundromat, TV. Restaurant next door. Open all year. Single $50, Double $59, Twin $64. Winter, weekly, monthly rates.

Clarke Bed & Breakfast—Box 1020, Wrangell. 874-3863 or 874-2125. 732 Case Ave., near Chief Shakes Island. Ferry transfers. Year around. Cooking facilities for more than one-nighters. $40-50.

Campgrounds
(free)

City Park—Mile 1.7 Zimovia Highway. Restrooms, flush toilets, sinks.

Shoemaker Bay—Mile 4.5 Zimovia Highway. Self-contained recreational vehicles may park here. No hook-ups. Near new boat harbor. Tennis court, dump station, tent campsites.

Facilities

ICE—supermarket.

LAUNDROMAT—**Thunderbird Hotel**—5 blocks from ferry, on Front St. 12 washers, dryers.

DUMP STATION—Near Front St. and Case Ave.

HOSPITAL—**Wrangell General** on Bennett St. north of Zimovia Hwy.

Boats

No rentals known. Charters can be arranged to Garnet Ledge, Stikine River, Anan Creek, and for fishing. See list under boat tours and check latest list at **Wrangell Visitors Bureau**, 874-3770 or at the **Wrangell Visitors Information Center** on Outer Drive, 874-3901.

Transient moorage available at boat harbors downtown and at Shoemaker Bay, south of town. Fuel, **Union** and **Chevron**, at waterfront.

Happenings

Tent City Winter Festival— celebrating gold rush in 1890's. First weekend in February. Fun, food, games.

Salmon Derby—Last 2 weeks of May. Dick Angerman, mgr. 874-3279.

Fourth of July festival—Logger's contests, Queen contest drawing for big prizes, food and games, boats, parade at 11 a.m. Midnight fireworks Wrangell put on the finest fireworks I've seen in 1987. Our skipper held the departing ship out in the bay so we could watch.

Annual Doll Show—in March. Sponsored by the Wrangell Historical Society, 874-3770.

Fishing gear exhibit in Wrangell Museum includes handmade seat to keep fisherman above water in bottom of boat.

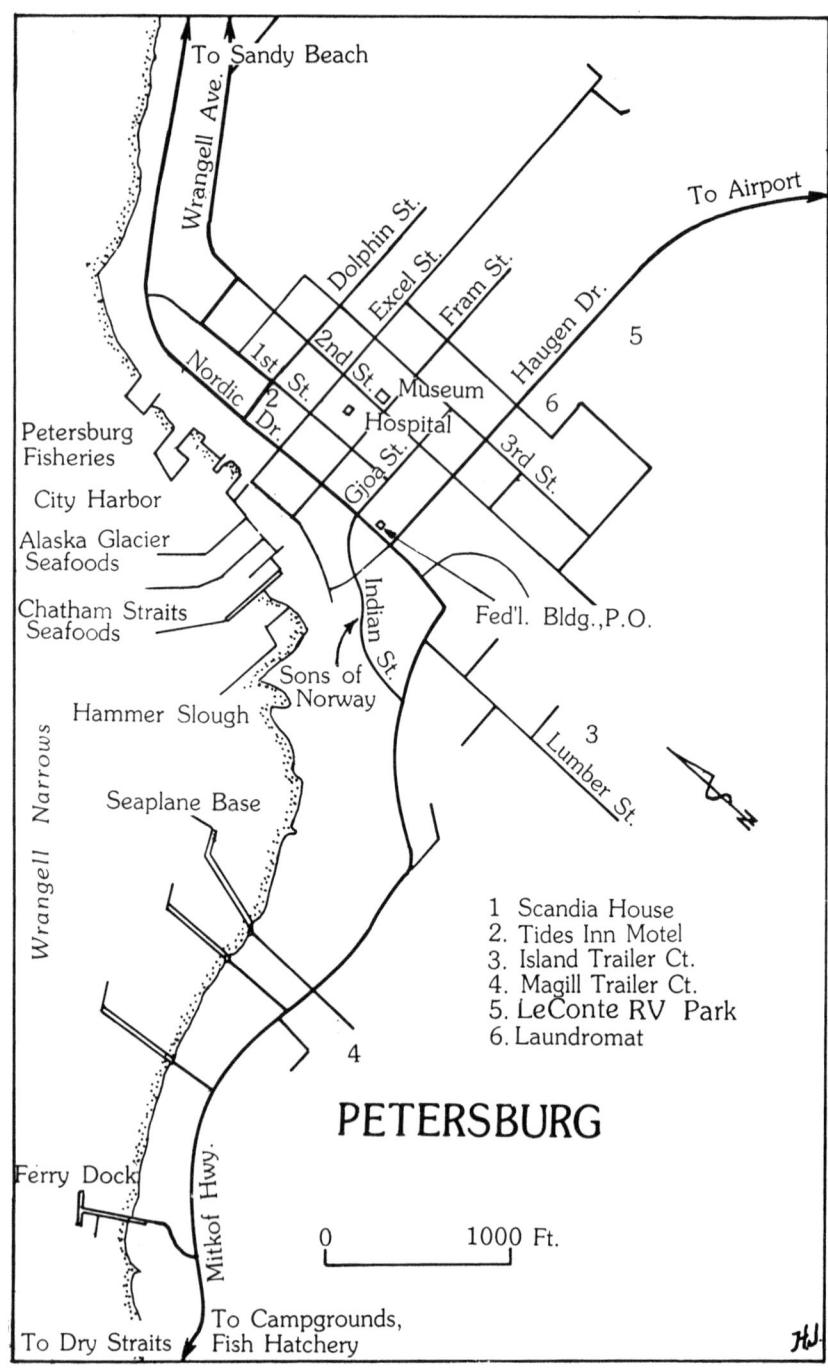

To Sandy Beach

To Airport

Wrangell Ave.

Dolphin St.

Excel St.

Fram St.

Haugen Dr.

5

1st St.

2nd St.

6

Nordic Dr.

2

Museum

Hospital

Gioa St.

3rd St.

Petersburg Fisheries

City Harbor

Alaska Glacier Seafoods

Chatham Straits Seafoods

Fed'l. Bldg.,P.O.

Indian St.

Sons of Norway

Hammer Slough

3

Lumber St.

Wrangell Narrows

Seaplane Base

1. Scandia House
2. Tides Inn Motel
3. Island Trailer Ct.
4. Magill Trailer Ct.
5. LeConte RV Park
6. Laundromat

4

PETERSBURG

Ferry Dock

Mitkof Hwy.

0   1000 Ft.

To Campgrounds, Fish Hatchery

To Dry Straits

104

Norwegian rosemaling designs decorate entrance of Petersburg home.

PETERSBURG

(Area Code 907, Zip Code 99833)

Petersburg (pop.3,400) was named by its founder, Peter Buschmann who, with his wife and eight children, moved here in 1897. The similarity of the geography to his native Norway, the mountain peaks, the fiords, availability of good lumber for building, abundant ice from nearby LeConte Glacier, a good natural harbor and its position in the center of the world's richest fishing grounds made this an idea site for his new home. Today it is the main fish processing port in Southeastern Alaska, with four canneries, a cold storage plant, and a fish meal plant that reduces scrap. In season they handle five kinds of salmon, crab, shrimp, halibut, and herring.

Many people in Petersburg are of Norwegian descent, and the town is proud of its ancestry. Its Norwegian character is evident in its houses, gardens, and boats. In May, on the weekend nearest May 17, Petersburg celebrates a "Little Norway" festival, with Viking boats and Norwegian dancing, lots of terrific food, costumes, street booths, games, and competions.

To See and Do

Visit the Museum, 1 mile, 2nd and Fram streets, open daily 11–4 in summer through September. Wed. Thurs. and Sun. 1–4 in winter and by appointment. It has a section on fish and fishing, including the world-record king salmon (126.5 pounds), Cape Decision Lighthouse lens, Norwegian costumes, and other historical items.

Walk self-guided tours along waterfront and Hammer Slough in town. Great photography possible. Take a 5 mile loop walk via Sandy Beach. Get a brochure at Chamber of Commerce's new Visitor Center at First and Fram Streets.

Walk on floats in fishing boat harbor, children with an adult, for safety.

Tour the shrimp cannery, forestry farm and fish hatchery with the **Tongass Traveler**. **Tides Motel** and **Chamber of Commerce** have info. Special tours on request.

Watch salmon at Falls Creek Fish Ladder, 10 miles, at Mile 10.8 Mitkof Highway. Allows spawning salmon to pass falls into good spawning waters above.

Tour Crystal Lake Fish Hatchery, 16.5 miles, Mile 17.5 Mitkof Highway. This modern hatchery raises both salmon and trout. Employees will explain the operation. Fish are sent from here to much of Southeastern Alaska. Open 8 a.m.– 4 p.m., weekdays.

Take a self-guided tour of Falls Creek clearcuts. A brochure is available at the Forest Service office in Federal Building, Main Street and Haugen Drive. You can see different stages of regrowth, experimental thinning, and fertilizing plots. Also a good view of Wrangell Narrows. Berrypicking in season.

Hike out to Hill, Crane, and Sand Lakes on Three Lakes Loop Road Trail, mostly a boardwalk, built by the Youth Conservation Corps. There's good berry picking in several areas, and the lakes have trout fishing and a skiff on each.

Fish in Scow Bay, Blind Slough, Frederick Sound, and streams. If you fish in the Narrows, beware of tidal currents and the suction and force of ship wakes. Do not get in the way of ships, tugs, and ferries.

Watch wildlife. In the Narrows, along the Mitkof Highway, and on the logging roads you may see bald eagles (this is a nesting area), otters, porpoises, bear, deer, and porcupines. Eagles often fish beside the ferry dock and perch in trees near the waterfront in town.

Note that some of the best birdwatching on the ferry route is from the ferry decks while it's docked here. You can watch gulls, ducks of many kinds, loons, and great blue herons if you step out on deck. Southbound, watch for cormorants perched on the channel markers just after the ship leaves the dock.

Enjoy Blind Slough Recreation Area. 16.5 miles from ferry, Mile 17.5 Mitkof Highway. Swimming, picnic area, daytime use only.

From the wildlife viewing blind at Blind Slough, watch wintering swans, migrating waterfowl in spring and fall, a variety of birds and an occasional bear in summer.

Hike to Raven's Roost on mountain behind town, about 4 miles each way. Camping possible on upper part. Overnight shelter available by reservation, $15, from U.S. Forest Service in Federal Building. Trail starts from road to airport.

See the LeConte Glacier by charter plane, boat, or kayak.

Mountaineering for experienced, well-equipped climbing teams. This is the jump-off point for Devil's Thumb and other major peaks on the mainland.

INFORMATION AVAILABLE at **Chamber of Commerce and Visitor Center**, corner of First and Fram Streets, Box 649, Petersburg, AK 99833. 772-3646. **U.S. Forest Service** information desk is in same office. **Harbormaster's Building**, 221 Harbor Way.

Transportation

FERRY: Runs daily in summer, fewer sailings in winter. Dock is at the south edge of town, .9 miles from the Federal Building.

BUS: None

TAXI: **City Cab**, 772-3003. **Chris West Cab**, 772-WEST.

CAR RENTAL: **Avis Car Rental**, Box 1048, Petersburg, AK 99833 at Tides Inn. 772-4716. **All Star Rental**, 772-4281, Scandia House. (Some people rent a car to get to out of town campgrounds.)

TOURS: Boat and floatplane tours to LeConte Glacier (sail among icebergs in the fiord). **Chamber of Commerce Office**, 772-3646.

Viking Travel Agency, Box 787, Petersburg, AK 99833. 772-3818, 800-327-2571, has a list of boats for tours, including fishing en route to the glacier. Day to day availability varies with seasonal fishing openings. Bus tours of Petersburg and fish ladder and fish hatchery by arrangement.

AIR: **Alaska Airlines** has daily jet service, year-round.

AIR CHARTERS: Charter service and flight to Kake: **Temsco Helicopter**, Box 829, Petersburg, AK 99833. 772-4780. **Pacific Wing Charters**, Box 1560,

Petersburg, AK 99833. 722-9258. **Nordic Air,** Box 1292, Petersburg, AK 99833. 772-3535. **Kupreanof Flying Service,** Box 867, Petersburg, AK 99833. 772-3396

BAGGAGE STORAGE by arrangement with hotels.

Hotels
(9% city sales tax extra)

Beachcomber Inn and Motel—3.1 miles from ferry, built on the water out of a restored cannery, overlooking Wrangell Narrows. Box 570, Petersburg, AK 99833. 772-3888. Restaurant (dinner only), lounge, entertainment. Private dock for boats, planes and fishing. Salmon and halibut fishing in season at lodge. Courtesy van to/from town for dinner or room guests. Single $60, Double $65.

Green Rocks Lodge—12 miles from ferry, 10.5 Mi. Mitkof Hwy. Box 110, Petersburg, AK 99833. 772-3245. Cabins and dock very near Green Rocks, the tightest turn in Wrangell Narrows. Fishing package for up to 4 people includes cabin with kitchen, breakfast, skiff and outboard with radio, fishing gear, raingear, fish processing and airport/ferry transfers, $200/day. Very good value. Guided fishing available.

Narrows Inn—across street from ferry. Box 1048, Petersburg, AK 99833. 772-3434. 25 refurbished rooms, TV, phones. Kitchens available. Pets allowed. Single $55, Double $65.

Scandia House —1 mile from ferry, downtown, Nordic Drive between Fram and Gjoa. Box 689, Petersburg, AK 99833. 772-4281. Scandinavian decor. American and European style rooms, kitchenettes. Courtesy car from airport and ferry. Complimentary rolls and coffee. European rooms, shared bath, Single $50, Double $55, American rooms, private bath, Single $65, Double $70. Kitchenettes $78. Add'l $5. Fishing tour packages. Boat, car, bike rentals, tours.

Tides Inn Motel—1.3 miles from ferry, 1st St. corner of Dolphin St., Box 1048, Petersburg, AK 99833. 772-4288. 46 rooms, queen-size beds, con-ference room, courtesy refreshments, phone, color TV with movie channel. Wheelchair accessible. Single $65, Double $80. Kitchenette, no extra charge. Can issue fishing and hunting licenses 24 hours/day.

Bed & Breakfasts—Chamber of Commerce, 772-3646, has lists, including lodges and bed & breakfasts outside of Petersburg along Wrangell Narrows. **Alaska Bed & Breakfast Association,** 586-2959, has listings in Petersburg.

Jewell's By The Sea—1/2 mile from dock, on waterfront. Box 1662, Petersburg. 772-3620. Owner has art gallery and shop featuring local artists on ground floor. Open year around. Single $50, Double $60.

Frigidland, Icicle Seafoods tender, hauls fresh-caught salmon on ice back to the fish processing plant in Petersburg. It also carries supplies for fishing boatsworking night and day during an "opening".

Campgrounds

Ohmer Creek Campground—21 miles from ferry, Mile 22 Mitkof Highway. Bring water or boil creek water. Barrier-free trail. Free.

Sumner Strait Campground—26 miles from ferry, Mile 26.8 Mitkof Hwy. Unimproved site on state land. Road to it is washed out 1/4 mile away; you can walk in. Boat launching. Bring water. Free.

Tent City—3 miles from ferry, out Haugen Dr. past airport. 31 tent pads, 62 people maximum. Purpose is to house cannery workers. Not family oriented. Restrooms, sinks, firepits, wood, picnic tables. No vehicles permitted. Daily $3, weekly $17.50/person. Weekly deposit $25. Pay at Parks & Recreation, 12 S. Nordic St., 772-3392, or manager on site.

Twin Creeks—6 miles from ferry, 7.5 Mi Mitkof Hwy. Box 90, Petersburg, AK 99833. 772-3282 and 3244. 20 spaces with bathhouse, laundromat, dump station, convenience store. $10/night.

LeConte RV Park—1.2 miles from ferry, Haugen at 4th St., P.O. Box 1548, Petersburg 99833. 772-4680. Full hookups for 13 vehicles up to 35' long. Laundry with shower. $15/day.

Boats

RENTALS: **Scandia House**, 772-4281. **Aaristos**, 772-4281.

CHARTERS: Check with Chamber of Commerce Office for charter boat listing.

HARBOR: Moorage available. See Harbormaster. Restrooms, Grids to handle boats up to 200 tons. Water and electricity. Public showers and hot water. **Harbormaster's Office**, Box 1047, Petersburg 99833. 772-4688. Channel 16 VHF and CB Channel 9.

Petersburg Shipwrights, boat pull out and grid. 772-3596.

Facilities

LAUNDROMATS: **Glacier Laundry & Dry Cleaning**, on Nordic Drive., near the corner of Excel Street. **LeConte RV Park**, Haugen at 4th.

PROPANE: **Skylark Welding**, Box 654, Petersburg, 99833. 772-3145.

DIESEL: **Union Oil** on Union Oil dock. 772-4219.

AVIATION FUEL: **Temsco Helicopters**, 772-3728.

DUMP STATION: **Alaska Chevron Gas Station**, one block north of ferry terminal. 772-3740. **LeConte RV Park**, Haugen at 4th.

ICE: **The Trading Union, Inc.** general store. **Hammer & Wikan, Inc.**, general store. All liquor stores.

HOSPITAL: 13 Beds with limited medical capabilities. Two doctors, six emergency medical technicians, city operated ambulance. Two dentists, 772-4291, or 9246.

HOT TUB AND SAUNA: at **The Spa** in Scandia House, Nordic Drive. Also tanning beds.

SWIMMING POOL: **Roundtree Swimming Pool**, behind Petersburg High School on 2nd Street. Charge for swim, lower for shower and locker only. Call for open times, 772-3392.

VET: **Jane Egger**, Box 328, Petersburg, AK 99833. 772-3191.

Happenings

Little Norway festival on May 15–17, 1992, celebrating Norwegian Independence Day (May 17), Petersburg's *big* festival. You need a reservation for rooms or a sleeping bag.

Annual Chamber Salmon Derby, Memorial Day weekend. Cash and prizes for largest salmon. May 22–25, 1992.

Fourth of July enthusiastically celebrated by visitors and residents.

Logging and fishing competitions, street games, fireworks display. July 3–4, 1992.

Silver Salmon & Halibut Derby—September 5–7, 1992.

All activities above sponsored by the Petersburg Chamber of Commerce, 772-3646.

Private floatplanes on ramp next to Petersburg ferry dock give their owners access to spectacular back country lakes and bays.

Ferry Tale

A traveler standing in the *Malaspina* solarium looked ahead and announced to his girl "There's another glacier coming up." Without rising, she asked "Is it just your basic glacier?"

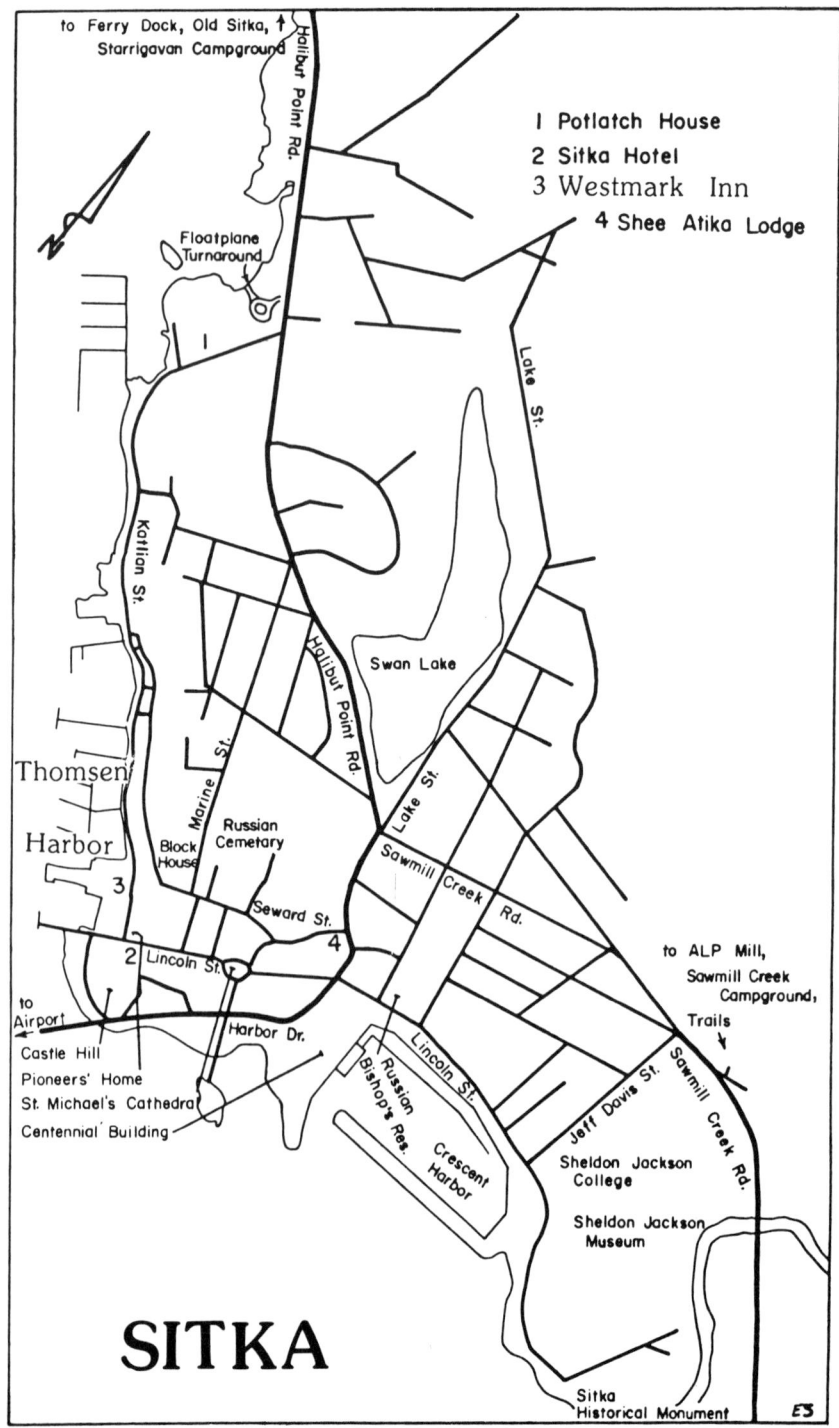

1 Potlatch House
2 Sitka Hotel
3 Westmark Inn
4 Shee Atika Lodge

to Ferry Dock, Old Sitka,
Starrigavan Campground

Halibut Point Rd.

Floatplane
Turnaround

Katlian St.

Lake St.

Halibut Point Rd.

Swan Lake

Thomsen

Harbor

Marine St.

Russian
Cemetary

Block
House

Lake St.

Sawmill Creek Rd.

Seward St.

Lincoln St.

to
Airport

Harbor Dr.

Castle Hill
Pioneers' Home
St. Michael's Cathedral
Centennial Building

Russian
Bishop's Res.

Lincoln St.

Crescent
Harbor

to ALP Mill,
Sawmill Creek
Campground,
Trails

Jeff Davis St.

Sawmill Creek Rd.

Sheldon Jackson
College

Sheldon Jackson
Museum

SITKA

Sitka
Historical Monument

E3

Lighters, small boats carried on cruise ships, ferry passengers ashore in Sitka near the Russian Bishop's House and fishing boats.

SITKA
(Area Code 907, Zip Code 99835)

Sitka (pop 8,500) was the site of the first Russian Settlement in Southeast Alaska, established by Baranof in 1799. Originally located just north of where the ferry terminal now stands, it was wiped out by Tlingit Indians. A new fort and town were built at the present townsite. For several years Sitka was the European cultural center of the Pacific. It had the first shipyard and built the first steam-driven vessel in the Pacific. American, Spanish, and British ships came here to trade with the Russians for otter pelts. When the United States bought Alaska from the Russians in 1876, the change-over took place in Sitka. Her Russian heritage, her historic sites and buildings, the Sheldon Jackson Museum (with its excellent Indian collection), and the Sitka National Historical Park make a stopover here very rewarding. The Alaska Pulp Company's pulp mill, just south of town, provides much of the economic support for this area.

To See And Do
(Ferry dock is 7.1 miles north of town)

Tour Sitka National Historical Park, about 9 miles from the ferry. See its program on Sitka's history and Tlingit culture. Visit workshops teaching Tlingit arts. This is the site of the Tlingit fort and "Battle of Sitka."

Walk forest and beach paths with totems. Park is open 8–11 in summer. Picnic area.

See the museum at Sheldon Jackson College, 8.5 miles from ferry. It has large collection of artifacts from all the Alaska native cultures. Summer hours: 9–5, daily. Winter hours: 1–4, Tues.–Sat. Donation, $2.

Visit the Centennial Building's wildlife exhibit and the Isabel Miller Museum of Sitka history. Open 8–5 Mon.–Sat., 8–1 Sun., June 1–October 1. Winter, 12–4, Mon–Fri., 10–4 Sat.

Tour the Russian Bishop's House, still being restored. Open 8–5 daily, May through September.

See the New Archangel Dancers in a program of Russian folkdances at the Centennial Building (downtown). Check there for times of programs. $4 admission. Excellent performance.

Tour St. Michael's Cathedral, 7.1 miles from Ferry, at center of town. This is a Russian Orthodox cathedral, replica of the original which burned in 1966. The icons, doors, and other items were saved from the original. Open 11–3, Monday–Saturday. On cruise ship days 9–3, Sunday 12–3 in summer. By special appointment the rest of the year. Check with Father Eugene, 747-3340. Donations $1.

Walk or take a bus tour to Sitka's historical sites. These include: Castle Hill, Russian cemetery, blockhouse, Russian cannons, Russian Bishop's Residence, Pioneer's Home, Sitka Nat'l. Cemetery (veterans).

On the bus tour you will see the site of Sitka National Historical Park, Sheldon Jackson Museum, St. Michael's Cathedral, Old Sitka, Castle Hill, and the Russian Bishop's House. Some days admission to the New Archangel Dancers is included. Stops vary with time of day.

Watch pink salmon and a few kings and cohos migrate up Starrigavin Creek along road 1/2 mile north of ferry terminal, late July through September. Eagles usually in trees. Good walk for the children or pets.

Hike local trails, including Mt. Verstovia (past Russian charcoal pits, and through 130-year-old clearcut) and Harbor Mt. trail (for an easily accessible look at alpine tundra, and a good view of the Sitka area). Remember this is brown bear country!

Visit Old Sitka, 1/2 mile north of the ferry dock. This is the site of the first Russian settlement (1799), destroyed by the Tlingits (1802).

Boat tour Sitka Sound. Special tours to bird refuge islands.

Fly over Mt. Edgecumbe, Southeastern Alaska's only volcano (dormant except on April Fools' Day). You can reach the top by trail from the beach on Kruzof Island if you go by boat or plane.

Fish from boat or shore. Inquire locally about hot spots.

Bald eagles recovering from injuries perch in front of the Raptor Rehabilitation Center.

Visit Southeast Alaska's first Raptor Rehabilitation Center in Sitka. Taking in sick and injured eagles, hawks, and owls, staff treats and releases about 50% of the birds. Birds that can't be restored to survive in the wild are often sent to zoos or breeding centers, some in the Lower 48. The center offers your best chance to see and photograph eagles close-up. It's off Sawmill Creek Rd., on Indian Creek, about 1.5 miles from town. 747-8662. Guided tours including demonstration of treatment and feeding are given in the morning during summer when cruise ships are in, $11. Open 3–5 daily in summer for self-guided visits. Gift shop has great posters, photographs, T-shirts. Winter hours, 8–5, M–F.

INFORMATION AVAILABLE from the **Sitka Convention & Visitors Bureau,** Box 1226, Sitka, AK 99835. 747-5940. Located in the Centennial Building (it has a Tlingit log canoe in front) in the Isabel Miller Museum. Open 8–4, daily.

The **U.S. Forest Service** office is in a new building on Katlian Street next to the Potlatch House, three blocks from the center of town. Forest Supervisor, Chatham Area, Box 1980, Sitka, AK 99835. 747-6671. They have information on USFS cabins reached by plane or boat from Sitka and a booklet, *Sitka Trails*, with maps and information about the trails leading out from town up the nearby mountains.

Sitka National Historical Park. Box 738, Sitka, AK 99835. 747-6281, also has information. **Alaska State Division of Parks,** HPR Box 142, Sitka, AK 99835. 747-6279.

Transportation

FERRY: Alaska Marine Highway. Eight ships per week (both north-bound and southbound) in summer; fewer in winter. Dock is 7.1 miles north of town.

BUS: **Sitka Tours,** 747-8443. Buses meet ferry for ride downtown. They leave very shortly after ship docks. $2.50 one way.

TAXI: **Arrowhead Taxi,** 747-8888. **Baranof Taxi,** 747-3366. **Sitka Taxi,** 747-5001. **T & H Taxi,** 747-6621. Inquire about rates. Car rental may be cheaper if you need more than two rides.

CAR RENTALS: **AAA Auto Rental,** 747-8228. **Avis,** 966-2404. **All Star,** 966-2552.

TOURS: **Sitka Tours,** 747-8443. The tour lasts 3 hours and costs $21 per adult, children 1/2 price. Morning and afternoon tours daily in summer with pick-ups at all four hotels. Ferry stopover tour is two hours, $8 adults, $4 child, when the ferry arrives at a reasonable (even 5 a.m.!) hour and will be in port long enough. Excellent guides.

Alaska Adventures Unlimited, Box 6244, Sitka, AK 99835. 747-5576. One-stop agency for fishing, photo, nature tours, guided trips of all kinds, boat and canoe rentals.

BOAT TOURS: **Silver Bay Nature Cruise,** *M/V St. Maria* and *M/V St. Aquilina* leave Crescent Harbor. **Allen Marine Tours,** Box 1049, Sitka 99835, 747-8100. $25/adult, $10/child. Two-hour tour. Reservations advised. Also offer half day wildlife and sea otter tour up to Salisbury Sound, with wildlife guaranteed. $80 adult, $60 child 12 and under.

Alaska Sea Tours, 747-5576. Tours from Sitka to bird, seal and sea lion rookeries. Motor yacht/large inflatable boats. 3 1/2 hour tour.

Several fishing charter boats also offer nature tours, some with very knbowledgeable guides and even hydrophnes for listening to whales. Check with Visitors Bureau for list.

AIR: **Alaska Airlines** has daily service to Seattle, Anchorage, Juneau, Ketchikan, Petersburg. Get airline reservations early in summer as some flights fill with passengers on cruise-fly package tours with cruise ships. **Markair** flies to Juneau and Ketchikan daily. A shuttle bus does serve the airport to and from downtown hotels at airline flight times.

AIR CHARTERS: **Bell Air**, Box 371, Sitka, AK 99835, 747-8636. **Mountain Aviation**, at Sitka Airport. Box 875, Sitka, AK 99835. 747-6000.

BAGGAGE STORAGE in hotels, for patrons only, on day of departure.

Sun sets behind Mt. Edgecumbe as a fishing boat towing its skiff heads for Sitka.

Hotels
(rates plus 4% hotel tax and 4% sales tax)
Senior citizens with Medicare cards are exempt from tax.

Potlatch House (motel)—5.5 miles from ferry. 713 Katlian St., Sitka 99835, (907) 747-8611. 30 unit, dinner restaurant, lounge. Direct dial phones, no charge for local calls. Cable TV. View of harbor, Mt. Edgecumbe. Recently remodeled. Single $67, Add'l $8. No pets. Courtesy pick-up service. Car/room package available with cars starting at $19.95 and hotel room at regular rates.

Sitka Hotel—7.1 miles from ferry dock. 118 Lincoln St., Sitka 99835. 747-3288. 60 rooms, downtown. Restaurant. Single w/o bath $45. Double w/o bath $50. Single w/bath $50, Double $55. No pets. Larger rooms additional. Credit cards accepted.

Super 8 Motel—7.1 miles from ferry. 404 Sawmill Creek Blvd., Sitka 99835. 747-8804. 35 rooms. Complimentary morning coffee. Car/room package available. Single $64.88, Double $68.88/1 bed, $70.88/2 beds.

Westmark Shee Atika--7.3 miles from ferry. 330 Seward St., Sitka 99835. 747-6241. 93 rooms, dining room, bar. Double $118. No pets. (800) 544-0970 for U.S. including Alaska and Hawaii.

Youth Hostel—United Methodist Church, Edgecumbe and Kimsham Streets. Mail: Box 2645, Sitka 99835. 747-8356. Open June 1-August 31. Check in 6–10. Out by 8:00 a.m. $5 with AYH card, $8 without. Sleeping bags required. No kitchen.

Bed & Breakfast

Sitka Visitors Bureau, Box 1226, Sitka 99835, 747-3940, has current lis, some on nearby islands reached by boat. **Sitka Total Vacation Island Cabins**, Box 2487, Sitka, AK 99835. 747-6562. Fax 283-8090. Fishing packages including boat for salmon and halibut. **Alaska Bed & Breakfast**, 586-2959. Fax 463-6788.

Special Restaurant: **The Channel Club**, Halibut Pt. Rd, 747-9916 may have the best salad bar in Alaska, with at least 20 kinds, cold and hot. Well known for steaks.

Campgrounds

Starrigavan Campground—.7 miles north of ferry dock. 30 spaces among trees near creek. Fills fast when ferry arrives. Picnic tables, firepits, toilets, water. Spaces not drive-through. 14 day limit. (USFS)

Sawmill Creek—13 miles from ferry, off Sawmill Creek Road, near the pulp mill take spur road 1.4 miles. 9 sites. Picnic tables, firepits, toilets. No water. Large spaces but none drive-through. Free. 14 day limit. (USFS)

Sealing Cove—8 miles from ferry on Japonski Island, next to Sealing Cove Boat Harbor. 26 RV sites, no reservations. Water and electrical hookups. Limit 15 nights. $10. 747-3439. (City & Borough of Sitka)

Sportsman's Campground—1 block toward Sitka from ferry dock. 8 sites, water and electrical hookups. Reservations, 747-8791 (Sitka Sportsman's Association). $10.40.

Boats

Information on fishing charters and charters to offshore bird rookeries with skippers licensed by the Coast Guard is available at the Centennial Building and from Sitka Tours. Boat fuel at three fuel docks in Sitka Channel near Thomsen Harbor. Boats can be moored overnight at certain stalls on floats in Thomsen Harbor, Crescent Harbor behind Centennial Building. Contact the Harbormaster, VHF Channel 16 or 747-3294.

KAYAK RENTALS: **Bidarka Boats**, P.O. Box 2158, Sitka AK 99835. (907) 747-8996.

Facilities

LAUNDROMAT: **Duds & Suds**, 908 Halibut Point Rd. 747-5050. Showers. Open 8 a,m,–8 p.m. **Homestead Laundromat**, 619 Katlian St. at Thomsen Harbor. 747-6995. Showers. Open 8 a.m.–8 p.m.7 days/week

PROPANE: **Service Transfer**, 321 Lincoln St. 747-3276. **Texaco Station**, 613 Katlian Ave. 747-8460.

DIESEL: **Sitka Fuels** on Katlian St., **Chevron** station on Lake St.

ICE at canneries on Katlian St. and at supermarkets.

DUMP STATIONS: **City Maintenance Shops**, 1410 Halibut Point Rd. 747-3887. **Wastewater Treatment Plant**, Japonski Island. Big grey building on airport side of Sealing Cove, 966-2256.

OUTBOARD MOTOR REPAIR: across from ferry terminal at **Southeast Marine**. Also repairs motorcyles.

HOSPITAL: **Sitka Community Hospital**, Halibut Pt. Rd. 747-3241.

PETS: Vet is **Dr. Burgess Bauder**. Office is behind the city garage on Halibut Point Rd., open 3 p.m.–5 p.m., Monday–Friday. 747-3056. No boarding facilities in town.

Happenings

Sitka Music Festival (chamber music) in Centennial Building, with performances June 5–26, 1992. Some of the world's finest musicians perform.

Salmon Derby, Memorial Day weekend, May 23–26, 1992 and May 3–31, 1992.

All-Alaska Logging Championships, June 27–28, 1992.

Alaska Day Festival, Oct. 14–18, 1992, celebrating the Russian transfer of Alaska to the United States. Transfer is reenacted with period costumes, muskets and flags. Week-long celebration.

See the **Sitka Convention & Visitors Bureau** for a complete list of activities, some not scheduled at presstime. Visitor Information Center in the Isabel Miller Museum in the Centennial Building. 747-5940.

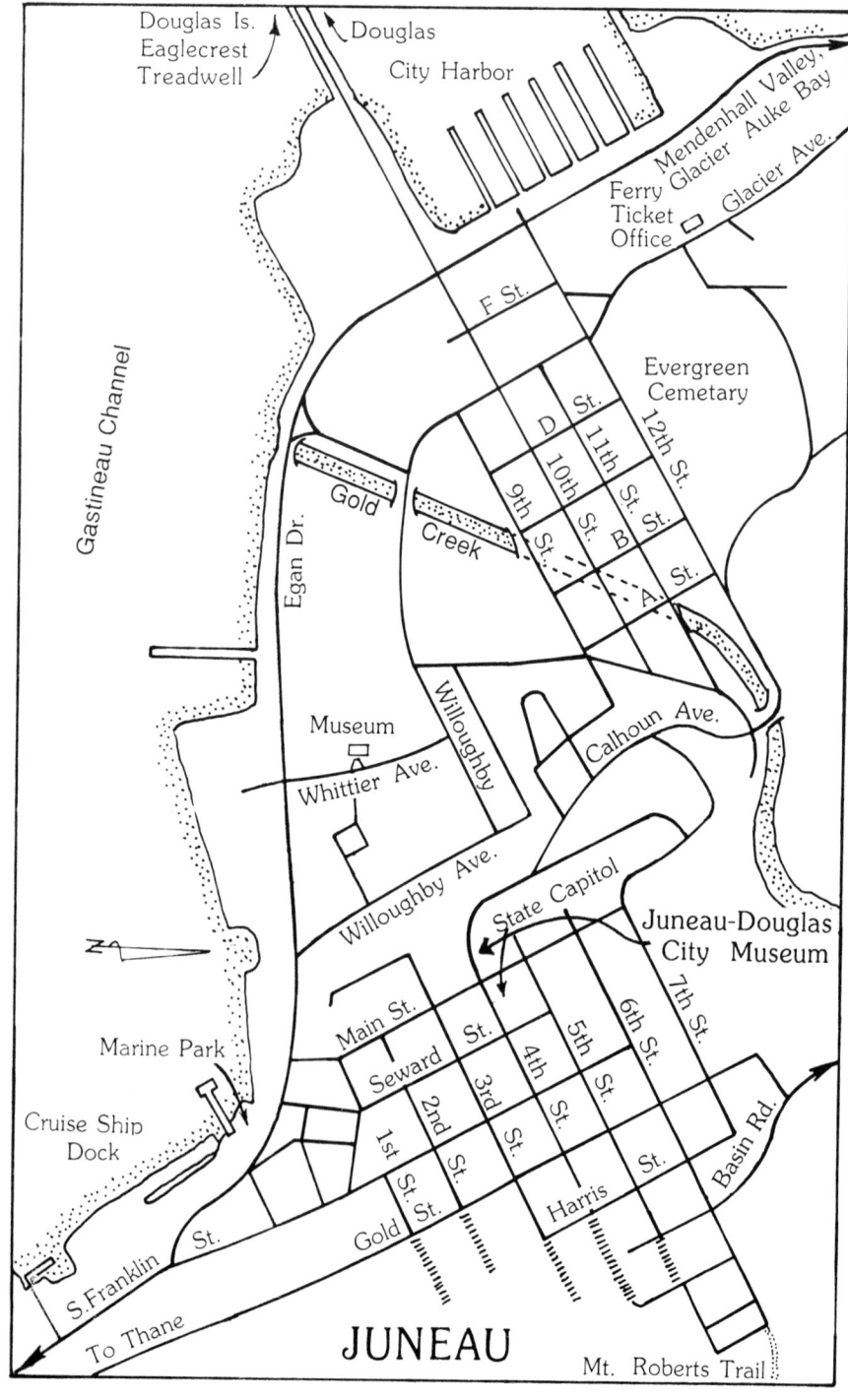

JUNEAU

Raftload of sightseers floats in front of the Mendenhall Glacier before starting down Mendenhall River rapids.

JUNEAU
(Area Code 907, Zip 99801,2,3,11)

Juneau (pop. of city and borough 29,946) is Alaska's state capital. It is nestled on the slopes between Gastineau Channel and Mounts Juneau and Roberts, which rise over 3,000 feet above the town. In 1880, prospectors Joe Juneau and Dick Harris were hired by geologist George Pilz to contact Auke Chief Kowee and confirm the presence of gold. They found gold in what is now Gold Creek, and a mining camp sprang up, named Juneau in 1881.

Besides placer gold from the creeks, gold was mined in two deep shaft systems: the Alaska Juneau Mine, and the Treadwell Mine on Douglas Island (extending under Gastineau Channel). Over $66 million in gold was removed before gold mining was declared a "nonessential wartime activity" during World War II, and the Alaska-Juneau Mine was closed. The Treadwell was closed some years earlier when the shafts under the channel caved in and flooded with sea water.

Mining is again important to Juneau. Greens Creek on northern Admiralty Island produces silver and lead from a large deposit. Crews live in Juneau and commute to the mine by bus and boat from a dock near the Auke Bay ferry terminal. Meanwhile a Canadian company is preparing to reopen the Alaska Juneau mine and another north of Berners Bay.

As Juneau grew past Sitka in size and activity, the district capital in 1906, the territorial capital in 1912, and later the state capital, were established here. Distances in Alaska are so great that most state departments have additional offices in other towns as well.

Juneau has so little flat ground in the downtown area that building has extended northwest into the Mendenhall Valley, where most residents now live. The airport and the Mendenhall Glacier also occupy the valley.

Since the glaciers dump sediment carried by the Mendenhall River and Lemon Creek into the channel, ships cannot pass north of Juneau, and must go back down the channel and around Douglas Island. In order to avoid many miles of extra sailing, the ferries use a terminal at Auke Bay, 14 miles north of town. Distances are given from the **downtown docks** unless otherwise noted.

There is minibus and taxi service in summer, taxi service in winter from Auke Bay terminal plus limited van service to town and to the airport when the larger ferries dock. The hourly city bus runs between DeHart's store, 2 miles toward town from the dock, and town 6:50 a.m.– 11:36 p.m. Mon.–Sat. with fewer runs on Sundays.

In daylight you have a fine view of the Mendenhall Glacier as you enter and leave Auke Bay. Unfortunately, many landings are scheduled at night, so if you want to see Juneau, you should stop over. For most summer arrivals there's a tour bus to the glacier or into town during longer daylight stops. Sharing a taxi for a trip to the glacier or town is another option, but do keep track of time if you're continuing on the ship. The drive from downtown to Auke Bay is a half hour one-way. Often the taxi must come from town to pick you up.

To See and Do

Take a walking tour of downtown Juneau. Maps are available at the waterfront Marine Park information center (kiosk), most hotels, at the airport, and the Juneau Visitor Information Center in the log cabin at 3rd and Seward Streets. The tour passes historic sites and buildings of interest on Juneau's hills and waterfront.

Notice bald eagles on beaches, pilings, and trees around town and on the road north. There are several nests near the Auke Bay dock. Once I saw an eagle swim ashore to the parking lot with his fish. Another day a land otter used the culvert pipe as an underpass to gecross under the road and popped out on the beach and down to the water beside the ship.

Visit the Alaska State Museum, on Whittier St. Open 9 a.m.–6 p.m. Mon–Fri., 10 a.m.–6 p.m. weekends in summer. Native culture, wildlife, historic exhibits, changing art exhibits. $2 charge. Closed Sunday and Monday in winter. Winter hours, 10–4, Tues. through Sat.

See St Nicholas Orthodox Church, 326 5th St., built in 1894. Frame building with a dome, icons, artifacts. Guided tours in summer. Donation requested, $1 per person.

Enjoy the view over Juneau and Gastineau Channel from Juneau's new library atop the parking garage next to the cruise ship dock.

See the Mendenhall Glacier, 13 miles from downtown, 5 miles from Auke Bay ferry dock. Reach by car, bus tour, or municipal bus (daily, $1, you must walk the last 1.5 mile). You will find a U.S. Forest Service Visitor Center with programs, naturalists to answer your questions, nature walks, trails, and a good view of the glacier face. The Visitor Center is open weekends all year. From mid-May to September 30 it's open 9 a.m.–6:00 p.m., seven days a week. Sockeye (red) salmon spawn in the stream in July and August, Arctic terns nest in the gravel, and you may even see mountain goats above by telescope.

Auke Lake, 12 miles from downtown. Also the location of Chapel By-The-Lake, and the University of Alaska campus. Get there on bus tour, or on municipal bus (except Sundays). The chapel has a famous view of the Mendenhall Glacier across Auke Lake.

Auke Bay Marine Lab, by car or municipal bus. Research lab has self-guided tour and exhibits, 9 a.m.-4 p.m., weekdays.

Auke Bay ferry terminal, 14 miles from downtown. In daylight, watch eagles, herons, a kingfisher who likes to dive off the dock, porpoises, seals, and an occasional whale. Eagles are often perched on the piling below the grocery store at Auke Bay small boat harbor.

Fish by boat or from shore. For rental and fishing charter information ask at Visitor Information Center, 3rd and Seward. Beach fishing on Douglas Island, and north of Juneau. For a recorded fishing report, call Alaska Fish and Game, 465-4116, April through November.

Fly over the Juneau Icefield. On a clear day this is an unforgettable experience. The icefield, which feeds the Mendenhall Glacier, covers 1500 square miles, supplying 39 glaciers. Many spectacular peaks. Local plane charters run about $80-90 per person. **Temsco Helicopters**, 789-9501, adjacent to the airport 9 miles from town, will fly you to Mendenhall Glacier and land. $125. ($199 gets you a flight of an hour and a half with two stops on the glacier.)

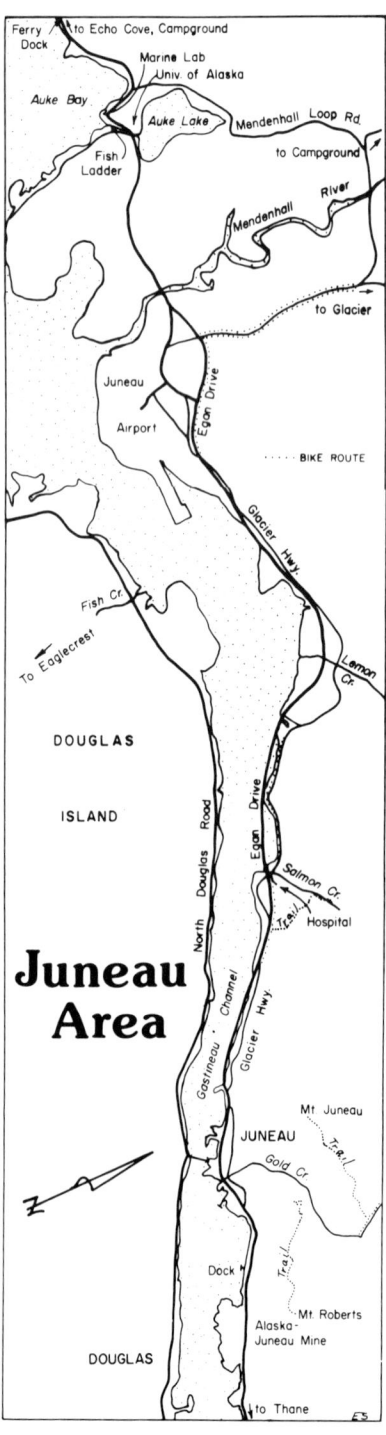

ERA Helicopters offers a 45 minute flight over the Icefield plus 15 minutes on the glacier for $145 per person.

State Office Building, 4th and Main. Free Concerts on old theater pipe organ, Friday noons, in spectacular 8th floor lobby with totem and view over channel.

Juneau Douglas City Museum, at 4th and Main St. Exhibits and audio-visual programs, emphasizing local mining history, early social life, ships and planes of pioneer days. Special glacier exhibit. Summer hours—9–5 weekdays, 11–5 weekends, mid-May–mid-Sept. Winter hours—12–4:30 Thurs.–Sat. of by appointment. Admission $1. 586-3572.

Alaska Department of Fish and Game, 3/4 mile Egan Drive, behind KINY Radio, has wildlife notebook series with information on all major land and water wildlife in Alaska.

State Capitol Building, 4th between Seward and Main. Free tours daily in summer.

Federal Building, Glacier Avenue and 9th, houses the offices of most federal agencies. Bureau of Indian Affairs, 3rd floor, exhibit of native artifacts.

Cooperative Extension Office, now across from Mendenhall Mall in the Valley, has free or inexpensive leaflets on everything from rhubarb and sourdough recipes to how to tan hides with battery acid and salt!

Gold Creek Salmon Bake, at the end of Basin Rd. beside Perserverance Creek. Courtesy bus picks visitors up at Baranof Hotel at 6 p.m. Music, entertainment. Operates nightly outdoors (under a roof), 5:30– 9, mid-May to mid-September. All you can eat and your first beer, $20. 586-1424.

Thane Ore House Salmon Bake, 4 miles south on Thane Road. Tickets available at the Baranof Hotel. Salmon, halibut, BBQ ribs. Mining operation, gold panning, mining exhibit. Indoor and outdoor seating. Handicapped accessible. Lunch and dinner daily, noon-9:30 p.m, mid-May-mid-Oct.. 586-3442. Courtesy transportation from down-town if you call them. All you can eat $15, with follies show, $19.95.

Hike trails in Southeastern Alaska's most extensive system. Guidebook *Juneau Trails*, $3, is available from the Forest Service, and at bookstores. *90 Short Walks around Juneau* by Mary Lou King is a book featuring many delightful places to spend a few hours. The trail up Mt. Roberts (fine view of town) begins at the end of 6th St. The trail up Mt. Juneau (requires respect for weather and snow on trail) starts beyond Salmon Bake Turnoff, at end of Basin Road. The trail to Pt. Bishop from end of Thane Road is 8 miles of flat hiking, through forest and along shore. Good camping and fishing at Dupont, 3 miles from start of trail.

Guided all day hike with Juneau Parks and Recreation, Wednesdays and Saturdays. Cross-country ski tours in winter. Distances and exertion vary. Free. Call 586-5226 for info.

Tour the **Gastineau Salmon Hatchery**, 2697 Channel Drive (frontage road adjacent to Egan Drive), 463-4810, to see salmon climbing a fish ladder, eggs taken for hatching, and saltwater aquariums with many local fish and sea plants. Gift shop offers smoked and canned salmon and salmon leather crafts. Open 8–6 weekdays, 12–5 Sat., 10–6 Sun. Adults $2.50, children under 12 $1.

Visit **Alaska Brewing & Bottling Co.**, Alaska's only brewery, 5429A Shaune Drive. 780-5866. Taste Chinook Alaskan Amber Beer, daily, 11–5, in summer. Shorter hours in winter. Thursday is the best time to go as that's the day they bottle the brew! T-shirts, caps, etc. with label for sale. In the Lemon Creek area, from Glacier Highway turn north on Anka St., then right on Shaune Dr.

Drive your car or a rented one "out the road," a phrase Juneau-ites use to describe any place north of Auke Bay, for a picnic and beautiful view. Fire pits and picnic shelters (open with roofs for rain) at Auke Bay Recreation Area and Lena Cove. Fire pits and shelter at Eagle Beach. Pit toilets at all areas. Good picnicking and views from North Douglas Road. Some tourists drive these roads simply because they've never been where all the roads have ends!

Visit the lovely Shrine of St. Terese, 23 miles out Glacier Hwy. on a scenic rocky point. Excellent shore fishing from rocks below.

Ride the ferries on one day or overnight excursions if you're using Juneau as a base. In summer the *Taku*, *Malaspina*, and *Columbia* stay in Skagway one afternoon a week. You would have time to explore either Haines or Skagway on a one-day trip. Check ferry schedule or our comments on the current season earlier in this book.

The *LeConte's* trips to Pelican, Hoonah, Tenakee, Angoon, and Sitka are popular. On her run leaving Juneau, Friday afternoon and returning early Sunday, you can go all the way to Sitka and have several hours Saturday in town or get off at any of the other ports and catch her on the return trip. At Tenakee for example, you would have nearly 24 hours. Remember that seniors can ride the smaller ferries free all year, space available.

Join an adventure tour with **Alaska Travel Adventures**, 9085 Glacier Hwy., Juneau 99801. 789-0052. Three-hour float trips on the Mendenhall River, May 15-Sept. 26, Adults $75, Children $48. Gold panning and gold

Above timberline on the Mt. Roberts trail, view of Juneau harbor, Gastineau Channel and north Douglas Island out to airport and Auke Bay.

mining tour, 1 and 1/2 hours, Adults $24, Children $16. Will pick you up at hotels. Nature tour to bird rookeries near Sitka. and canoe trip in Ketchikan. Grayline desk in Baranof Hotel also books these tours.

Kayak Juneau's sheltered waters or take off from here for longer trips. For kayak equipment, instruction, guiding, rentals, **Alaska Discovery**, 369 S. Franklin, 586-1911.

For small-group personalized tours of the rain forest without the rigors of a wilderness trip, early morning birdwalks, tours of art galleries to meet the artists, special tours arranged according to your interests, including van transportation, call **Alaska Up Close**, 789-9544, P.O. Box 32666, Juneau, AK 99803. For similar tours conducted in German, call **German Connection Fototour**, 780-4911. P.O. Box 32925, Juneau, AK 99803.

Hike with **Alaska Rainforest Tours**, 463-3466. 369 S. Franklin Street, Juneau, AK 99801. Day hikes, backpacking (including the Chilkoot Trail), and nature tours according to your interests. Rain gear provided.

Enjoy a Juneau Icefield flight and a salmon bake at fly-in **Taku Glacier Lodge**, 586-8330. Leaves from seadrome in front of Merchants' Wharf for 3.5 hour trip, mid-May-late Sept. $130. One hour icefield flight only, $85.

At Sandy Beach on Douglas Island, a vent tunnel and pilings remain since the Treadwell mine under Gastineau Channel caved in.

See Tracy Arm, a winding glaciated fiord about 60 miles south of Juneau. With granite walls several thousand feet high on both sides, waterfalls, and icebergs, it's like a flooded Yosemite without the people. The floating ice gets thicker as you reach the upper end where the North and South Sawyer Glaciers reach the water, calving off icebergs while you watch. Seals often lie on the icebergs with pups. You may also see mountain goats, black bears, humpback and orca whales, and many bald eagles and sea birds on this trip. Companies offering tours to Tracy Arm are listed under Boats and Boat Tours later in this Juneau chapter. Some offer you a floatplane flight one-way and the boat ride the other. All serve meals on the boat. The tour takes 7-12 hours. Suggestions: go as early in the summer as possible for longer daylight hours. Take a parka and cap for standing out on deck. This can be an alternative to longer, more expensive trips to Glacier Bay.

Watch brown bears and cubs catching salmon at Pack Creek on Admiralty Island. For a one day trip, charter a plane to take you over and pick you up later. With kayak or boat, you can get there and back in several

Overhanging face of the Mendenhall Glacier calves off into Mendenhall Lake, feeding the Mendenhall River. This ice fell as snow on the Juneau Icefield 250 years ago.

days. The viewing area is at least 100 yards from most bears. Call the U.S. Forest Service, 586-8790, and see them for a permit for the time you want to be there, as they now limit the number of people at one time. Some guide services have permits to lead groups there—the Forest Service can tell you which.

For further info on events and activities, check with the **Davis Log Cabin Visitor Information Center**, 134 3rd St., corner of 3rd and Seward. 586-2201 or the information kiosk in Marine Park in summer. Dial 586-JUNO for a 24 hour recorded message of current scheduled events.

"Lady Lou Revue", Gold Rush musical, Elks Hall, near Baranof Hotel, 109 N. Franklin Street. Almost daily mid-May to mid-Sept. Shows 8 p.m. plus some extra performances.

Tour "House of Wickersham", former home with memorabilia of Judge Wickersham and Alaska's early days. 7th Street, up hill from State Capitol. 465-4563, 586-9001. Open noon–5 daily except Sat., in August, 1992.

Tours of Governor's Mansion only available on certain days, by prior arrangement. 465-3500.

INFORMATION AVAILABLE at **Visitor Information Center** in Davis Log Cabin, 134 3rd St., Juneau AK 99801, 586-2201. To learn about current happenings in Juneau, dial 586-JUNO for a recorded message.

For hiking, kayking, and mountaineering trips and information, stop at the **Foggy Mountain Shop**, 134 N. Franklin. **U. S. Forest Service** information desk in Centennial Hall, 101 Egan Dr., 586-8751, has films, slide shows, maps, brochures, and makes Forest Service cabin reservations. Open 9–6 daily Memorial Day to mid-September, 8–5 Mon.–Fri. rest of the year. Information on Glacier Bay National Park also at the information desk in Centennial Hall in summer. The **Juneau Convention & Visitors Bureau** operates an information kiosk in Marine Park, adjacent to the cruise ship dock and desks in cruise ship terminal, and in the airport terminal, summers (airport counter is self-service in winter).

Transportation

FERRY: **Alaska Marine Highway,** daily in summer from Auke Bay terminal, 14 miles north. Ferry office for information, reservations, tickets, 1.5 miles, 1590 Glacier Ave. For time of arrival it's best to call the terminal 789-7453. Terminal opens an hour or two prior to arrival, otherwise the message is recorded. Vehicle check-in time is at least 2 hours prior to departure. Reservations, 465-3941; daily recorded ferry arrivals 465-3940.

CITY BUS: Runs daily, less frequently on Sunday. Route goes from downtown cruise ship terminal through town to airport and DeHart's store at Auke Bay, 1.9 miles from Auke Bay ferry terminal. Some buses go to Douglas. Hourly, 6:50 a.m.–11:45 p.m., depending on route. Check schedule as some hours are omitted at night. Ask for the express bus schedule (M-F) as well—it's separate. The express bus stops at the airport. There is no city bus service to the Auke Bay terminal.

Bus and Van service to airport and ferry: **MGT** meets ferries year round. Will transport ferry passengers to downtown for $5 or to airport for $3. When ships are in port for several hours at a reasonable time of day, **MGT** offers a tour of the Mendenhall Glacier and town with return to the ferry terminal for $7. **MGT** buses offer city/glacier 2 1/2 hour tours from the downtown cruise ship terminal and kiosk for $9. 789-5460.

Note that buses, and sometimes taxis, are parked in Juneau *behind* the ferry terminal building. You may not be able to see them from the parking lot until you walk around the building. All leave soon after ferry arrival, so you need to go up there as soon as the ship arrives or you will miss them. For pick up downtown to ride out to the ferry, ask at hotel desks or call the bus company.

The **Eagle Express Line,** a van service, offers custom sightseeing tours. 789-7111.

Gray Line runs a bus from Juneau Airport to downtown, $6. 586-3773, -9625.

"Alaska cotton" grows in swamps, including Brotherhood Park beside Glacier Highway in the Valley.

TAXI: **Taku Taxi**, 102 Franklin St., Juneau, 586-2121. **Capital Cab**, 586-2772. Fare from town to Auke Bay terminal $21, $1 per add'l person.

BUS TOURS: Starting in downtown Juneau, **Gray Line /Westours**, 586-3773, ticket desk in Baranof Hotel, June 1–September 30. Tours to Mendenhall Glacier and around Juneau. **Alaska Sightseeing**, 586-6300, desk in Baranof Hotel. **MGT** from the ferry dock, 789-5460.

CAR RENTAL: **Hertz**, Juneau Airport, 789-9494. **Avis**, Juneau Airport, 789-9450, **Payless Rent-a-Car**, 5245 Glacier Hwy., 780-4144. **National**, Juneau Airport, 789-9814. **Allstar**, across from Mendenhall Mall, 790-2414, 800-722-0741. **Budget**, Juneau Airport, 789-5186. **Mendenhall Auto Center**, 789-1386. **Evergreen Ford**, 789-9386. **Rent-A-Wreck**, 789-4111. **Ford Rent-a-Car**, 586-2050, at Inn at The Waterfron, 455 S. Franklin (the only agency located downtown).

AIR: **Alaska Airlines**, 789-0600, 800-426-0333, to Ketchikan, Sitka, Gustavus, Petersburg, Wrangell, Anchorage, Seattle, and other West Coast cities.

Delta Airlines, 800-221-1212, Fairbanks, Seattle, and routes in the "Lower 49."

Air North, 789-2006, Fri. and Sun. to Whitehorse and Fairbanks all year. (405) 668-2228, Whitehorse (Juneau call 789-2006)

CHARTERS: Some operators have mail contracts requiring scheduled flights to outlying towns, on which you can ride at a flat rate (you don't don't have to charter the whole plane).

Alaska Coastal Airlines, 1873 Shell Simmons Dr., Juneau, AK 99801. 789-7818.

Glacier Bay Airways, Terminal Building, Juneau Airport, 789-9009. Scheduled flights to Gustavus, Glacier Bay and Juneau Icefield tours.

LAB Flying Service, Terminal Building, Juneau Airport, Juneau, AK 99803, 789-9160. Scheduled flights to Haines, Skagway, Gustavus, Hoonah, Excursion Inlet.

Loken Aviation, 1873 Shell Simmons Dr., Juneau, AK 99801. 789-9160. Flightseeing Juneau Icefield and Glacier Bay.

Skagway Air Service, Terminal Building, Juneau Airport, 789-2006. 2 people minimum. Flies to Skagway, Haines, Hoonah, Gustavus.

Ward Air, Terminal Building, Juneau Airport, 789-9150. Strictly charter.

Wings of Alaska, Terminal Building, Juneau Airport, 789-0790. Mailing address: 1873 Shell Simmons Dr., Suite 119, Juneau 99801. Scheduled service to Angoon, Gustavus,Hoonah, Pelican, Tenakee, Petersburg, Haines, Skagway, Kake, Elfin Cove.

The following helicopter services offer flightseeing which can include landing on a glacier or the Juneau Icefield, letting you out to walk around and peer down crevasses. Bring your camera!

ERA Helicopters, P.O. Box 1468, Juneau, AK 99802. 586-2030 or 800-843-1947 outside Alaska. Fax 463-3959.

Temsco Helicopters, 1650 Mapelsden Way, Juneau, AK 99801. 789-9501.

BIKE ROUTE: A cycle path follows the Mendenhall Loop Road from near the glacier to Egan Drive and along it to the Old Glacier Hiway near Switzer Village. Another segment follows Old Glacier Hwy. beside Twin Lakes from near Lemon Creek to Salmon Creek. From there a path follows north of Egan Drive to Glacier Highway in town. Thus it is possible to cycle from DeHart's Store at Auke bay to Juneau without getting on the freeway. You'll want time and daylight the first time. Bicycle lanes also parallel some other main roads, including the Douglas Bridge and Douglas Hwy. to downtown Douglas, 4.5 miles from downtown Juneau.

BAGGAGE STORAGE at hotels, for patrons, on day of departure. Juneau Airport terminal has lockers and is open more hours than the ferry

Hole in The Wall Glacier, a branch of the Taku Glacier near Juneau, is a rare advancing glacier, pushing over the grove of trees on the right.

terminal. Auke Bay ferry terminal has lockers, but is locked when ships aren't in. **Alaskan Hotel**, bags of non-patrons, space available, (small fee).

Hotels
11% tax extra.

Alaskan Hotel—167 S. Franklin St., Juneau, AK 99801. 586-1000. For reservations 800-327-9347. Fax 463-3775. Sauna, hot tubs. Cable TV, phone. Single w/o bath, $40. Single with shower, $50. Double $10 more. Add'l, $10 adult, $5 child. Kitchenettes at no extra cost. No pets.

Baranof Hotel—127 N. Franklin St., Juneau, AK 99801. 586-2660, 800-544-0970. Fax 586-3815. Housekeeping units, restaurant, lounge, hairstyling shop, travel agency, gift shop, coffee shop. Single $110, Double $120. Add'l, $15/person. No pets. Commercial and government rates.

Bergmann Hotel—434 Third St. Juneau, AK 99801. 586-1690. Restaurant, lounge, parking. Single $55 incl. tax. Double $65, weekly rates. All rooms with shared bath. No pets.

Best Western Country Lane Inn—9300 Glacier Hwy., Juneau, AK 99801. 789-5005. Reservations 800-528-1234, in Alaska 800-478-5005. Fax 586-3815. 4 miles from Mendenhall Glacier, near airport. Courtesy transportation to airport, ferry, and downtown Juneau. 50 rooms. Complimentary continental breakfast. Free local phone calls, cable TV with HBO. Indoor pool and jacuzzi. Pets OK. Single $100, Double $106, to $130 for suites.

Breakwater Inn—1711 Glacier Avenue, Juneau, AK 99801. 586-6303. Fax 463-4820. 41 rooms have 2 double or 1 king-size bed. Dining room, lounge. Good view of waterfront, boat harbor. Mountain view, Single/ Double $75. Harbor view Single/Double $85. Add'l, $15/person. Deluxe unit add'l. Children under 12 free.

Cashen Quarters—Downtown. 315 Gold Street, Juneau, AK 99801. 586-9863. 5 units. 3/4 baths and kitchenettes. No phones or TV. Single $45, Double $60.

Driftwood Lodge—435 Willoughby Avenue, Juneau, AK 99801. 586-2280, 800-544-2239. Fax 586-1034. 62 rooms. Kitchen units. Color TV, HBO, laundry facilities. Courtesy van to ferry and airport. Pets OK. One block from Alaska State Museum. Near federal Building, convention center. Restaurant adjacent. Single $55, Double $68. Add'l, $7/person.

Grandma's Feather Bed—A Country Inn—9300 Glacier Hwy., Juneau, AK 99801. 789-5005, 789-5566. Fax 789-2818. near airport. Victorian farm-house-style. 7 rooms. Jacuzzi. Courtesy van. $100–105.

Inn at the Waterfront— 55 S. Franklin St., Juneau, AK 99801. 586-2050. Restored hotel across from cruiseship dock in historic district. Restaurant, lounge, steam bath. 21 rooms. Rates from $38 for single w/o bath to $115 for 3-room suite with 2 baths. Rental cars available.

Juneau Airport Travelodge—9200 Glacier Hwy., Juneau, AK 99801. 789-9700, 800-255-3050. Half mile from airport, 5 miles from Auke Bay terminal. 86 rooms. Restaurant, lounge, indoor pool, jacuzzi. Courtesy transportation from airport/ferry terminal. Wheelchair accessible. No pets. Single $105, Double $115. Children 17 and under free with parents.

Prospector Hotel—375 Whittier St., Juneau, AK 99801. 586-3737. Reservations: in Alaska 800-478-5866, elsewheres, 800-331-2711. Fax 586-1204. 60 rooms, restaurant, lounge, live entertainment. Single $80, Double $90, Suites $95-1115. Pets allowed with manager's okay.

Silverbow Inn—120 Second St., Juneau, AK 99801. 586-4146. 6 room restored hotel in historic building downtown. Excellent restaurant. Single $99, Double $109, includes continental breakfast. Senior citizen rates.

Super 8 Motel—Near airport, 2295 Trout St. (behind McDonald's). Juneau, AK 99801. 789-4858, 800-800-8000. 75 rooms, cable TV, direct-dial phone, elevator, coin-op laundry, conference room. Queen-size beds, paraplegic room. Courtesy transportation to airport and ferry. Pets with deposit. Rooms $59.88–$98.88.

Westmark Juneau—51 West Egan Drive, Juneau, AK 99801. 586-6900, 800-544-0970. Fax 258-0560. 104 rooms. Restaurant, lounge, dancing. Wheelchair accessible. Conference rooms. Rooms $98–144, varying with mountain or channel view. Add'l $15. Children under 12 free in room with parent. Commercial and government rates. No pets.

Hostel—Hill overlooking downtown 614 Harris St., Juneau, AK 99801. 586-9559. Dorm rooms, cooking facilities, showers, living room, dining area. Groups welcome. No pets. Register 5:00–11:00 p.m. Closed 9:00 a.m.–5:00 p.m. 3-day limit. $8 AYH members, $11 non-members.

Alaska Bed & Breakfast Associatiation, P.O. Box 21890, Juneau 99802. In Alaska, 586-2959. Fax 586-2959. Personalized reservation service, offering homes that specialize in hospitality. Serves all of Alaska and the Yukon. Rates average $50/Single, $60/Double. Reservations advised. Brochure and directory free..

For other homes, call or write the **Visitors Bureau**, 134 3rd St., Juneau 99801. 586-2201.

Campgrounds

Mendenhall Lake—5 miles from Auke Bay ferry dock, off Mendenhall Loop Road (turn right leaving ferry and follow signs for camping), 2 miles northwest of Visitor Center. USFS $5 per day, June 1–September 15. May be open free a few days before and after according to snow. Great views of glacier, hiking. Some mosquitos. Firewood scarce and possibly green. Tables, fire grates, water, restrooms, central dump station. 60 spaces, some drive-through. Some walk-in tent spaces where you get away from vehicle sounds. No reservations taken.

Auke Village Recreation Area—2 miles northwest of Auke Bay ferry terminal. (turn left as you leave terminal) USFS. $5 per day. 11 sites. Boating and beach adjacent. Fewer bugs, Flush toilets. Same info as above but no dump station.

With regret, I advise not leaving valuables in camp when you leave, and recommend marking equipment obviously and permanently with your name.

City and Borough of Juneau allows parking for self-contained RV's only, $5/night, limit 3 nights, at several sites. Permits available at Juneau Harbormaster's Office, across Egan Drive from high school. 586-5255, 586-5337. Sites: Juneau Yacht Club, Savikko Park (Douglas). No hookups. Mid-May to Sept. 30.

Auke Bay RV Park—11930 Glacier Hwy., 1.5 miles from ferry terminal toward downtown. P.O. Box 210215, Auke Bay, AK 99821. 789-9467. 25

Purse seiner, fishing boat for salmon and herring, is easily recognized by the power block hanging from overhead boom and the powerful seine skiff carried on its stern.

spaces with full hookups. $16 per night. Reservations taken.

Facilities

LAUNDROMATS: **Harbor Wash Board**, 1111 F. St., Juneau. Off Glacier Ave., behind Alaska Laundry, also has showers. There are several others in the area. **The Dungeon** is in basement of the Mendenhall Apartments, 326 4th Street, 586-2805. **Mendenhall Laundromat**, 789-4224, adjacent to supermarket off Mendenhall Loop Road in the Valley.

SWIMMING POOL: **Augustus Brown Pool** next to Juneau-Douglas High School on Glacier Avenue has open hours, weight equipment, a sauna, and showers. 586-2055, 586-5325.

DUMP STATIONS: **Mendenhall Campground, City Borough shop** in Douglas at 3rd and Front St. **Valley Chevron**, Mendenhall Mall.

PROPANE: **Petrolane Alaska Gas Service**, 3850 Mendenhall Loop Rd. (road to glacier). **Valley Chevron** in Mendenhall Shopping Center. **Aurora Basin** fuel dock. **Eagle Propane**, 5716 Glacier Hwy.

DIESEL: **Valley Chevron** in Mendenhall Shopping Center. **Gas 'N Go**, Grant's Plaza on Glacier Highway at Lemon Creek. **Airport Union**, Glacier Hwy. & Airport Rd. **Aurora Basin** fuel dock.

ICE: All supermarkets. **Breeze Inn,** convenience late night grocery, Glacier Hwy. and Trout St., across from McDonald's.

Island Princess, one of the ships used to film "Love Boat", cruises the Inside Passage in summer, stopping in Juneau and other ports.

HOSPITAL: **Bartlett Memorial Hospital**, 3.5 miles, Glacier High-way, (907) 586-2611. Ambulance, fire department, dial 911.

PETS: Veterinarians, **Juneau Pet Clinic**, 8367 Old Dairy Rd., Juneau 99801. 789-3444 **Southeast Alaska Veterinary Clinic**, 7691 Glacier Hwy., Juneau 99801. 789-7551. Boarding, **Gastineau Humane Society**, 7705 Glacier Hwy., Juneau 99801. 789-0260. Dogs, $7.50 and up/day. Cats, $6/day.

Boats

CHARTERS: **Juneau Sportfishing**, P.O. Box 20438, Juneau, AK 99802. 586-1887. Boats 28–50 ft. available for fishing, wildlife viewing, over-nights, Tracy Arm, mid-April through September. Courtesy shuttle to boat. Snacks provided. Wheelchairs accommmodated. Several are sail-boats; others can transport for diving. Half day $110, Full day $185. Overnights $275–375 depending on size of boat.

List of licensed charter operators available through **Visitor Information Center**. Boats can be hired for Tracy Arm (a spectacular fiord with glaciers), Berners Bay, Taku Inlet, or for **good** fishing. Rates from $100 for half day, $180 all day. 586-2201.

BOAT TOURS: **Alaska Sightseeing**, 586-6300. Overnight trips to Tracy Arm on Sundays. **Glacier Bay Cruises**, 463-5510. Daily trips to Tracy Arm, $99. **Rainforest Tours**, 463-3466. $140 to Tracy Arm.

Princeton Hall—15225 Point Louisa Rd., Juneau 99801. 789-7558. Classic restored former missionary cruiser gives 3 and 5 day nature-watching tours around Admiralty Island, Tracy Arm, and other Southeastern spots. Fish, go ashore to beachcomb, etc. Charters for small groups.

Alaska Discovery, 586-1911. Kayaking trips with guide, 6 hours, also overnights and multi-day trips.

FUEL AND MOORAGE at Aurora Basin, Harris Harbor, Douglas and Auke Bay. Dock space limited, especially in summer. Harbormaster, Ch 16 or 586-5255.

Happenings

Concerts in The Park, June 5–August 14, 1992. Friday evening concerts in Marine Park, downtown, by local and visiting groups. Free.

4th of July, July 3-4, 1992. Parades, fireworks over channel, races, contests.

Salmon Derby, August 3-5, 1992. Big prizes. Winners got $15,000 in recent years.

Five Finger Lighthouse, between Juneau and Petersburg, was the last lighthouse in Southeastern Alaska to be automated. Until then it was manned by a crew of Coast Guardsmen stationed there for a year with just one short break at six months. But for reading and bird and whale watching, ti was a great station!

A humpback whale sounds or dives. The white makings on its tail are distinctive and allow this whale to be identified wherever it goes—migrating between Alaska and Hawaii, possibly Mexico.

GLACIER BAY NATIONAL PARK AND PRESERVE

This spectacular 60 mile-long bay is fed by a dozen glaciers at its upper end. It has bears, seal, whales, tufted puffins, and lots of icebergs. Many seabirds come ashore only to nest here.

The park is some distance by boat or plane from Juneau—there is no ferry service. The nearest glaciers are 45 miles from park headquarters. You may get there using the following:

A chartered flight over the bay from Juneau, Haines, Skagway or Gustavus. Flights are cheapest from Haines, but the clouds, must be high enough for the plane to get over the mountains, or at least between them.

The **Alaska Airlines** air-boat tour from Juneau. This can include a night at Glacier Bay Lodge, round trip boat service to the glaciers with a Park Service naturalist, and return flight to Juneau. Additional nights at the lodge can be added, as well as an overnight near a glacier on an excursion boat with staterooms. For package prices contact the airline or tour operators below. At presstime even the airline couldn't tell us their exact dates for summer flights to Glacier Bay! However the season is about May 20-Sept. 15.

Air fare from Juneau—regular coach $130 round trip, $65 one-way. Special summer fare until September 10 with a $25 fee for cancellation,

$88 round trip, $44 one-way. There are senior rates. Does not include airport transfer at Juneau and Gustavus ($15).

Glacier Bay Airways, Box 1, Gustavus, Alaska 99826, 697-2249, in Gustavus. 789-9009, in Juneau Airport. Scheduled air service between Juneau and Gustavus. Air charter service to Juneau, Haines, other Southeastern points. Sometimes is the cheapest way to move a group of people, boats, gear. Also does flightseeing in the park from Bartlett Cove.

One option, if you get to park headquarters at Bartlett Cove, is to take camping gear and a small boat or kayak "up bay" on the con-cessionnaire's boat. For a small additional fee, you can be left off at camper drop-off points. You can be picked up some days later, or you may want to camp and paddle your way back down the bay to Bartlett Cove. You can thereby have a longer trip in this wild area for only a bit more than the overnight trip.

There is a small extra charge for kayaks taken as hand luggage on the ferry to Juneau, and they are difficult to hitch with around town. Taku Taxi in Juneau will carry them on top. Kayaks are available for rent in Gustavus, so you don't have to bring your own.

The Park Service has a helpful information sheet for back country users and conducts an orientation session for kayakers at 6 p.m. nightly at Bartlett Cove in summer. Kayaks to be dropped off the following day are loaded on the dayboat ahead of time. Arrangements must be made with the lodge.

A day in Glacier Bay with a Park Service naturalist is included in the itinerary of most of the cruise ships running in Southeast Alaska.

Some air-boat packages as well as some of the charter boat trips include an overnight anchored near one of the glaciers.

FOR INFORMATION about the park, write **Glacier Bay National Park**, Box 140, Gustavus, AK 99826, (907) 697-2230. Good people to call for bear information, and suggestions for trips at all times especially off-season, when the lodge is closed and excursion boats and some flights aren't running.

Gustavus Visitor Association has a brochure, info on local boat charters, bed & breakfasts. There are now several bed & breakfasts as well as numerous charter boats for fishing or nature tours. P.O. Box 167. Gustavus, AK 99826. (907) 697-2288.

Hotels and Lodges

Annie Mae Lodge— Box 80, Gustavus, AK 99826. Phone/fax 697-2346. Family owned 5 room lodge near Good River. Good food, wildlife watching, hiking, biking, Glacier Bay tours and fishing optional. Courtesy van. Package includes meals, bicycle, and ground transportation to airport and Bartlett Cove, Single $100, Double $175, Child under 12, $75.

Fairweather Lodge—Box 148, Gustavus, AK 99826. 697-2334. Three rooms with four beds each. Package tours include guided fishing for halibut and salmon. Room and breakfas only, adult, $120.

Glacier Bay Country Inn—Box 5, Gustavus, AK, 99826. 697-2288. Fax 697-2289. Open May–Sept. Winter, October–April: P.O. Box 2557, St. George, UT 84771. (801) 673-8480. Fax (801) 673-8481. Secluded retreat with 6 rooms, private baths. Price includes meals and transportation to and from airport, use of bikes. Glacier Bay boat/plane tours and fishing charters arranged. Offers fishing, whalewatching, and sightseeing on 42' yacht. Open year round. Adults $99/day. Child, aged 3–11, $54/day.

Glacier Bay Lodge—For info and reservations all year: Glacier Bay Lodge, Inc, 520 Pike St., Ste. 1610, Seattle, WA 98101. (206) 623-2417 in Washington. Toll-free from rest of U.S. (800) 451-5952. Fax (206) 623-7809. Dining room, lounge, gift shop, day and overnight tour boats, charter fishing, boat fuel. Package tours available from Juneau: 2 day/1 night tour $339, 3 day/2 night $408. A one-day fly/cruise trip from Juneau to Bartlett Cove, up to the glaciers and back is $269. Tours starting from Haines and Skagway cost somewhat more. Single or double room/ $126. Dormitory, $26 per person. (Plus tax.)

Gustavus Inn—P.O. Box 60ip, Gustavus, AK 99826. (907) 697-2254, Fax (907) 697-2255. Open May 15–Sept. 15. Winter: 7920ip Outlook, Prairie Village, KS 66208. Phone/fax (913) 649-5220. Family, farm style, fireplace, private baths, 14 rooms. Meals are famous, featuring home-grown produce, local seafood. Glacier Bay fishing and sightseening packages available. All inclusive tour, one night/two days, $275, all meals, lodging, transfers, and all day cruise to Glacier Bay's West Arm. We can help with flights to and from Juneau (especially useful outside airline summer season). Overnight Glacier Bay cruises and fishing charters on our four boats. Daily rate, including all meals, use of bikes, fishing poles, transfers to/from airport and Bartlett Cove, $120 per adult, $50 per child.

Salmon River Cabin Rentals—Box 13, Gustavus, AK 99826, (907) 697-2245. Housekeeping cabins, close to good fishing. Bicycle rentals. Walking distance from beach. Bus service to Glacier Bay Nat'l Park. Cabin for 1 to 4 persons. $40/day, $200/week. Free transportation to and from airport.

W.T. Fugarwe Lodge—Box 27, Gustavus, AK 99826. (907) 697-2244. 12 rooms. Fishing package rates, flightseeing, boat charters. Room and meals, $120. Open June 1-Sept. 15. Winter: P.O. Box 459, Georgetown, CO 80444.

Bed & Breakfasts

While these may change, the following are listed in 1992—**Beyond Good River**, 697-2241. **Good River Bed & Breakfast**, 697-2241. **Noah's Ark**, 697-2307. **Puffin's Bed & Breakfast**, 697-2260, fax 697-2258, May–Sept. Winter: phone/fax 789-9787. All of these can arrange tours to the glaciers, transport you to the day boat from Bartlett Cove to the glaciers, and offer guided fishing or arrange it. Several offer bicycles or rent them for exploring around Gustavus.

Campgrounds

Bartlett Cove, in park. Walking distance from lodge, on shore. Tables, pit toilets. Seals and whales often just offshore. You can sometimes buy fresh seafood from commercial fishing boats at the dock. Pets allowed in Bartlett Cove area on leash. Not allowed in back country.

Boats

EXCURSION boat cruise from Bartlett Cove on *M/V Spirit of Adventure*, $144.50 round-trip to glaciers. Child under 12 $72.25. Infant under 2 free.

MOORAGE, but no dock space, fuel at Bartlett Cove. Private boats need permit to enter park during June, July and August.

KAYAK rentals from **Glacier Bay Sea Kayaks** in Gustavus. 697-2257. may 15–Sept. 15. **Spirit Walker Expeditions**, 697-2266 (800-478-9255 in Alaska), offers guided kayak trips, 1–7 days.

Facilities

Gustavus has gift shops, an art gallery, restaurants, and a hair salon.

GROCERIES: **Beartrack Mercantile**, 1/4 Mile, Dock Rd., 697-2358. Groceries, camping supplies, batteries, film. Open Mon.–Sat. For boat orders delivered, call VHF "WRS 957".

SMOKED FISH: **The Salmon River Smokehouse**, 697-2330. On main road, west side of Salmon River. Sell smoked fish or will process your salmon, halibut, trout. Open 9–9.

FUEL: **Gustavus Dray**, 697-2299, on and across from airport. Plane, boat, car, and stove fuels, lubricants.

AIRFIELD: Runways at Gustavus Airport 7,500' and 5,000' paved. Avgas 100LL and Jet A fuel, **Gustavus Dray**, 697-2299. Radio repeater 122.5 to Juneau on field.

In this roadless region, a tug and barge move a trainload of freight—here approaching the terminal at Haines. Notice the vehicles and small boats often stacked atop cargo containers. Other barges support movable logging camps and even village schools. One "logging camp" is the only one in the nation licensed by the Coast Guard as a vessel!

A bald eagle climbs out near the ship with the fish he just caught in the narrows.

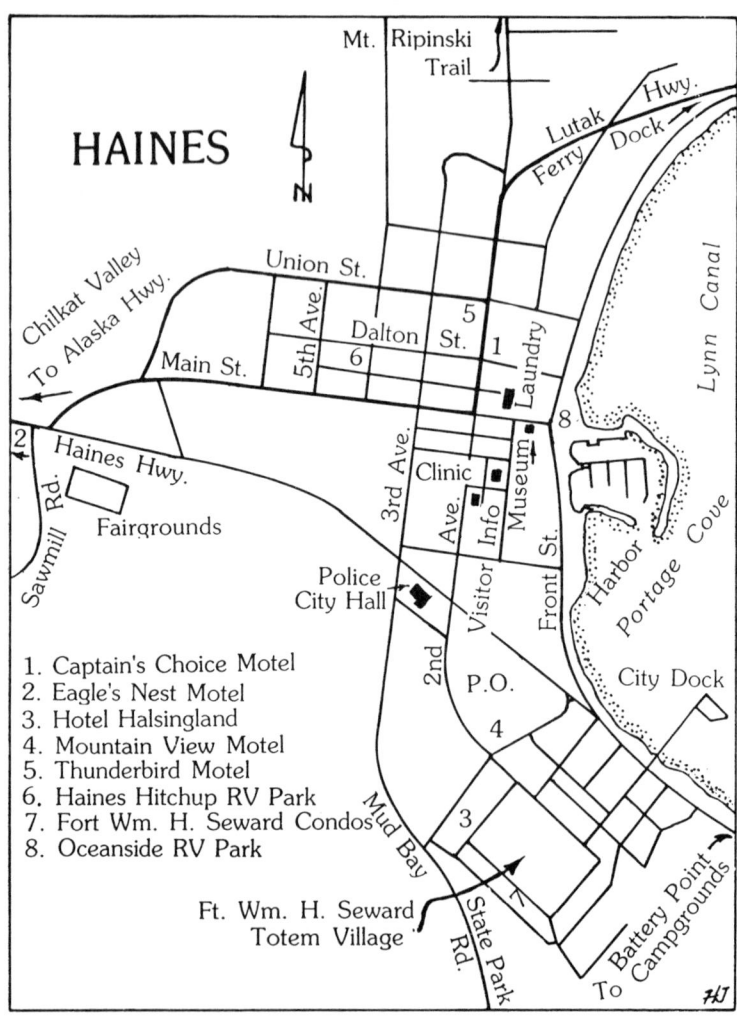

HAINES

N

Mt. Ripinski Trail

Lutak Ferry Dock Hwy.

Lynn Canal

Union St.

Chilkat Valley Hwy.

To Alaska Hwy.

Main St.

5th Ave.

Dalton St.

5

6

1

Laundry

8

Haines Hwy.

Sawmill Rd.

Fairgrounds

3rd Ave.

Clinic

Ave.

Visitor Info

Museum

Front St.

Harbor

Portage Cove

Police City Hall

2nd

P.O.

4

City Dock

1. Captain's Choice Motel
2. Eagle's Nest Motel
3. Hotel Halsingland
4. Mountain View Motel
5. Thunderbird Motel
6. Haines Hitchup RV Park
7. Fort Wm. H. Seward Condos
8. Oceanside RV Park

Mud Bay

3

Ft. Wm. H. Seward Totem Village

State Park Rd.

Battery Point Campgrounds

To

Successful fishing party with halibut and salmon after a morning charter out of Haines.

HAINES
(Area Code 907, Zip Code 99827)

CHILKAT INDIANS lived in this area and traded with inland natives long before John Muir and S. Hall Young arrived in 1879 and selected it as a mission site. The mission was established in 1881, followed by salmon canneries, mining, and an army post in 1903. During the Klondike Rush this was the southern end of the Dalton Trail, a toll road over which stock could be driven to supply meat to the northern settlements. The Haines Highway, connecting the Inside Passage with the Alaska Highway, generally follows the Dalton Trail. Today Haines (pop. 1,847) has a sawmill, a large fishing fleet, and the hotels and other tourist facilities that mark the end of the Marine Highway and the beginning of the land road to interior Alaska. Near the ferry docks, a tank farm marks the end of a six-inch oil pipeline to Fairbanks, built in 1953 and now in dead storage.

Haines has attracted many artists in a variety of media. You will find their work in local galleries and stores. An enthusiastic small theater group performs its own productions.

Bald eagles are a big attraction at the Chilkat Bald Eagle Preserve along the Chilkat River flats between Mile 8 and Mile 31 out of Haines, in fall and winter. The river has warm springs running into it, so it seldom freezes and supports a late fall salmon run, thereby providing the eagles with a dependable food supply. The largest known congregation of bald eagles meets here to fish and spend hours perched in snowy trees along the highway. Over 3,000 have been counted here in a single day! November is the peak month, but you will see many from October through January.

To See and Do

Tour Fort William H. Seward, 5 miles from ferry, just south of town. Walking-tour brochures are available at hotels and the Chamber of Commerce.

Visit the Alaska Indian Arts workshop and totem village (on walking tour). Watch totem carving, and purchase crafts made here.

See the Chilkat Indian dancers in authentic costumes. Chilkat Center for the Arts, performing Mon, Wed., and Sat. at 8 p.m. Adult $7, Child $3.50. Five miles from ferry at Ft. William H. Seward. Performances in Port Chilkoot Tribal House by appointment. Ask at the Visitor Information Center or Chilkat Center for times of other performances.

See melodrama "Lust for Dust or Patience Rewarded" at Chilkat Center for the Arts, Fri. and Sun., 8 p.m. Adult $7, Child $3.50.

Enjoy a salmon bake over alderwood fire, served at the Chilkat Raven tribal house, Port Chilkoot. All you can eat. Beer and wine served. Daily except Thursday, June through August, 5 p.m.–8.p.m. Adult $18.75, Child half price. Information at Hotel Halsingland, 766-2000.

Visit Sheldon Museum, 5 miles from ferry, Main St., in new building. Historic native artifacts, changing exhibits, video and slide shows. Open daily in summer. 766-2366. Hours as posted or ask at Visitor Center, $2 adults over 18.

Walk down to the boat harbor where 65 fishing boats are based, all year, in addition to several hundred during fishing season. Watch fishermen mending nets and get close-up look at the different types of boats and gear used in Alaska.

Watch salmon pass fish weir in the Chilkoot River, below Chilkoot Lake, about 4+ miles north (to the right) of the ferry terminal, June through October.

See Davidson Glacier from Mud Bay Rd., and Rainbow Glacier (hanging) from farther down Mud Bay Rd.

Haines Visitor Center on 2nd Avenue, the place to get answers and information.

Fish in Lynn Canal and Chilkat River for salmon, in Lynn Canal for halibut, and in Chilkoot Lake for trout, Dolly Varden and salmon. Fishing charters available. Haines Visitor Center has a current list.

Watch bald eagles at the 48,000-acre Chilkat Bald Eagle Preserve on the Chilkat River flats along the Haines Highway. Eagles are there October through January, with greatest numbers between Miles 19 and 22 from Haines. Truck traffic along the narrow road is fast, so one should use the pullouts which are good eagle-watching view-points. The eagles will be disturbed and fly away when approached closely, but you can watch easily from the pullouts and get good photos for hours on the same branch, making photography easy. Dress warmly and bring a hot thermos. Rental cars are available in Haines if you don't bring your own. The Haines Visitor Center has a brochure on the eagles.

Hike the trail up Mt. Ripinsky for a grand view down Lynn Canal and over surrounding mountains.

Visit Chilkat State Park on Mud Bay Road. Visitor Center, camping, picnicking, boat launch, dock, trails. Some programs in summer. Dates open according to snow. Great scenery.

See old salmon cannery at Letnikof Cove on Mud Bay Road.

Hike trails on Chilkat Peninsula. Get trail info in the Haines Visitor

Guide, free at the Visitor Info Center. Get "Haines is for Hikers" brochure, with maps, descriptions, and distances for hikes along the shore of the peninsula, on the Chilkat River Flats, and up nearby mountains. In winter, cross-country skiing and snowmobiling are popular on some trails and back roads.

Fly over Glacier Bay and the Juneau Icefields. Air charters are available at Haines Airport.

Tour Haines by bus on longer ferry stops. Most southbound ferries in 1992 stop in Haines at least two hours. Though the dock is five miles from town, there is bus service and time for shopping or a tour if you have boarded at Skagway. Bus meets ferries, in summer only.

Take a walking tour of town including the waterfront park. Get a self-guiding brochure at the Visitor Center.

Enjoy the library with a good Alaska section, newspapers, and restrooms. Browsers welcome.

Go on a guided nature tour with **Alaska Nature Tours**, 766-2876. Tours feature forest and Chilkat River flats. You'll see some eagles any time of year though the greatest concentration is in fall. Daily tours mid-May to mid-September. Winter tours by appointment in the preserve. 3 hour tour, $45, Saturday special $25. 6 hour tour, $80.

Tour Chilkoot Lake with **Chlkoot Lake Tours**, 766-2891, for fishing, wildlife watching, photography.

Rent a bicycle to explore Haines, Port Chilkoot, Chilkat State Park, and ride up to Chilkat Lake on your own. **Sockeye Cycles** in Fort Seward, 766-2869.

Winter visitors enjoy cross-country skiing and snowmobiling on logging and mine roads near Haines. Haines has generally drier snow than Juneau. Check with the **Visitor Center** for dates of winter holidays and snowmobile races.

INFORMATION AVAILABLE at the Chamber of Commerce Building, 2nd and Willard St., downtown, **Haines Visitor Center and Chamber of Commerce**, P.O. Box 518, Haines, AK 99827. 766-2234. 800-458-3579, U.S. including Alaska. 800-478-2268, Canada's 403 area code only. Fax 766-3155.8 a.m.–8 p.m., daily in summer, 8-10 Mondays. Shorter winter hours. U.S. Forest Service and Alaska State Parks have a summer office .

Transportation

FERRY: **Alaska Marine Highway**. Ships run daily in summer. Dock is five miles north of town on Lutak Inlet. 766-2113.

Take a side trip to Skagway with **Haines-Skagway Water Taxi**, 766-3395. Two round trips daily between Haines and Skagway for walk-on passengers only, $29 round trip.

BUS: Runs to and from ferry dock and airport. Stops at all hotels. **Haines Tours & Taxi**, 766-3138, also has tours of Haines and Fort Wm. H. Seward during ferry stops. May-September.

Alaska-Yukon Motorcoaches to Fairbanks, Anchorage, Valdez, McKinley Park. Picks up at Hotel Halsingland, Haines, 766-2435. Anchorage (907) 276-1305. **Alaska Denali Transport** and **Royal Hiway Tours** (has tours to Valdez, via ferry to Columbia Glacier, and on to Anchorage). Visitor Center has info.

Alaskon Express to Tok, Glennallen, Anchorage, Whitehourse. Ferry dock (meets Bellingham ship), and 277 Main St. downtown. Division of Westours. Toll-free in cont. U.S. 800- 544-2206. Runs three times a week, so it's best to call for info.

BUS TOURS (local): **Alaska Sightseeing**, office in Hotel Halsingland, 766-2000. **Haines Streetcar**, 766-2819. **Haines Tour & Taxi**, 766-3138.

TAXI: **Haines Tour & Taxi**, 766-3138. Offers all year transport between town and ferry dock.

CAR RENTALS: **Eagle Nest Car Rental**, Eagle's Nest Motel, 766-2352. **Hertz**, Thunderbird Motel, 766-2131. **Avis**, Halsingland Hotel, 766-2733. **Captain's Choice Motel Car Rental**, 766-3111.

DRIVE-OFF FERRY SERVICE (for cars whose drivers don't accompany them): **Eagle Transport**, 766-2221. If you put your car on the ferry with reservation to Haines, but want to stop off en route without it, these people can drive it off and store it by prior arrangement.

AIR: **LAB Flying Service**, Box 272, Haines, AK 99827, 766-2222. Juneau office: **Wings of Alaska**. Haines office: 766-2030. Juneau office: 789-0790. **Haines Airways**, Box 61, Haines, AK 99827. 766-2646. All have scheduled service to Juneau and Skagway, plus charters.

BAGGAGE STORAGE at hotels for patrons, on day of departure. Also at ferry terminal.

Hotels
Bus stops at all hotels en route to ferry in summer. Sales tax 5% additional. Note that in Haines the line between hotels and bed & breakfasts is blurred. Former officers' quarters in Fort Seward have been converted into hotels, condos and bed & breakfasts with more rooms than is usual in B & B's. I have included all the currently listed ones here. A third of the rooms in Haines are available all year.

Captain's Choice Motel—5 miles, corner 2nd and Dalton. 40 rooms. TV, Showtime, telephone, courtesy coffee, view of Lynn Canal. In-room refrigerators. Rental cars. Courtesy transfers. Box 392, Haines, AK 99827. 766-3111. 800-478-2345 in Alaska and Canada. 800-247-7153 in continetal U.S. Fax 766-3332. Single $82, Double $92, Twin $97, Triple with double beds $102, Executive Suite $127. Pets allowed, some rooms.

Eagles's Nest Motel—5 miles from ferry, 3.5 miles from airport. Haines Highway at Sawmill Rd. Box 250, Haines, AK 99827. 766-2891. Fax 766-2848. 9 rooms, 2 family size, 7 doubles, all with queen-sized beds. Newly remodeled, color TV, Showtime, courtesy coffee. Single $52, Double $59. Family rates. Walking distance to downtown on Hwy. 7. Pets allowed.

Fort Seward Bed & Breakfast—5.5 miles from ferry, in Fort Seward. House # 1 Seward Drive. Mail: Box 5, Haines 99827. 766-2856. Bed and breakfast inn in former officer quarters. Sourdough hotcakes. Single $63, Double $78. Pets and chldren welcome. Open April 15–September 30.

Fort Seward Condos—5.5 miles from ferry in Port Chilkoot. Gregg Enterprises, Box 75, Haines, 766-2425. Converted apartments in officers' quarters at historic Ft. Wm. H. Seward. 1 and 2 bedrooms, some with fireplaces, overlooking bay and mountains, fully equipped with kitchens. $75 per day (2 day min.), $450 per week.

Fort Seward Lodge—5.5 miles from ferry. Box 307, Haines, AK 99827. 766-2009. Ten rooms, courtesy van, Deck with Lynn Canal view. Restaurant featuring seafood. Rooms with private bath, Single $50, Double $55. Shared bath, Single $40, Double $45. Ocean view rooms with kitchenettes $75. Open all year.

Hotel Halsingland—5.5 miles from ferry, 4 miles from airport, in Port Chilkoot, Box 1589, Haines, AK 99827. 766-2000. 800-542-6363 in U.S., 800-478-2525 in Yukon and B.C. Fax 766-2445. 60 rooms. Restaurant, cocktail lounge, salmon bake, gift shop, car rental. Courtesy transportation from ferry. Building was formerly the commanding officer's house in Ft. Wm. H. Seward. Single $70, Double $75. Open Mar. 1-Dec. 1.

Mountain View Motel—5.5 miles from ferry, 151 Mud Bay Rd., Port Chilkoot. Mail: Box 62, Haines, 766-2900. Eight housekeeping units. TV, Showtime. Single $54, Double $59. Open all year. Pets allowed.

Officers Inn—5.5 miles from ferry, in Fort Seward. Box 1589, Haines, AK 99827. 766-2000. 800-542-6363, or in Yukon and B.C. 800-478-2525. 14 rooms in former officer's house, Fort Seward. Views, phones, TV, fireplaces. Private and shared baths. Courtesy transfers. Senior rates. Open in summer and early fall. Reservations coordinated with Hotel Halsingland. Breakfast included. Well behaved pets allowed. Private bath,

Fort Seward and Haines with the Cathedral Range behind.

Single $74, Double $79. Shared bath, Single $40, Double $50.

The Summer Inn—5 miles from ferry in town at 247 Second Ave. Box 1198, Haines, AK 99827. 766-2970. 5 rooms,views, breakfast included. Single $55, Double $65, Triple, $85. Open all year.

Thunderbird Motel—5 miles from ferry, Dalton and 2nd. Mail: Box 589, Haines, AK 99827. 766-2131. 800-327-2556. 20 units (6 have kitchenettes), restaurant and bar around corner on 2nd. Phone, TV. Small pets allowed. Single $58, Double $68, Triple $78.

Youth Hostel—8 miles from ferry, 1.5 miles from post office on Small Tract Rd. **Bear Creek Camp & Hostel**, P.O. Box 1158, Haines, AK 99827. 766-2259. Open April 1 to November 1. Some woodstoves, cooking facilities, tent camping. Dorms. $10 AYH members. $12 non-members. Family cabins. $30/night. Tent space. Ferry shuttle available—call from terminal.

Campgrounds

STATE: **Chilkat State Park**—7 miles, Mud Bay Road. 32 vehicle spaces and 12 hike-in-camper spaces. Boat Launch, dock. Tent pads, picnic tables, fireplaces, restrooms, water. Open dates according to snow. Note that the land just *outside* the entrance is private and camping is not allowed on it.

Chilkoot Lake—5 miles to right of ferry dock on Lutak Road; 10 miles from town. 32 spaces.

Portage Cove—1 mile from town, 7 miles from ferry, on Beach Road.

Limited spaces. Tent campers and picknickers. No RVs.

Mosquito Lake Campground—32 miles from ferry, Mile 27 Haines Highway. 11 spaces.

Note that state campgrounds in Alaska are scenic and have trees and more room between spaces than commercial ones, but have no hookups. They have firepits, tables, water and toilets (sometimes pit rather than flush). An overnight fee of $6 is now charged for all of the above campgrounds, and an annual pass costs $60.

PRIVATE (plus 5% tax): **Port Chilkoot Camper Park**—5.5 miles from ferry, Port Chilkoot. Box 473, Haines AK 99827. (907) 766-2755. All facilities, showers, laundromat. 60 spaces, most with electricity and water. No pull-throughs but spaces are large. Dump station. Showers, laundromat. Full hookups $15, electrical only $12.50, without hookups $10. Tent space $6.75.

Eagle Camper Park—5 miles from ferry, downtown at end of 6th Street. Box 28, Haines 99827. 766-2335. 52 spaces, 30 with full hookups including cable TV, $18/day. 22 with electricity only, $15/day. Tent camping, $12 /2 people. Showers, dump station. Laundry for guests. Good Sam park.

Haines Hitch Up RV Park—5 miles from ferry, Main St. Box 383, Haines AK 99827. 766-2882. 92 spaces, of which 20 are pull-throughs. Full, partial and no hookups. $13–16. Laundromat, showers, restrooms, propane, and gift shop.

Oceanside RV Park—5 miles from ferry, Front and Main near museum. Box 149, Haines, AK 99827. 766-2444. Fax 766-2832. 20 spaces with full hookups including cable TV. Rents boats, offers gold panning tour (you keep what you get). $12. Open march through September.

PARKING is allowed off pavement toward town from dock along first 1/4 mile of road (though not recommended due to chance of vandalism). Overnight parking is done here "all the time".

Facilities

ICE: **Food Center, Alaska Liquor Store, Howser's Supermarket, Pioneer Bar and Liquor Store, Harbor Mini Mart.**

PROPANE: **Eagle Camper Park and Ward's Transportation.**

DIESEL FUEL: **Valley Fuel Service** (50 gal. minimum), **Haines Automotive, 2nd Ave. Ward's Automotive, B & J Auto** (1 mi. Haines Hwy.).

CAR WASH: **Haines Auto Service Center**, 2nd and View Streets. Also **Tom's Self-Serv Car Wash**, Union and Main St.

Staff at left prepares salmon bake served on tables in front of Chilkat Raven tribal house in Fort Seward.

Southbound vehicle owners who wash cars before loading on crowded car deck will save their own clothes and others' from rubbing on dust-covered cars.

DUMP STATION **Chevron**, Haines Hwy. and 3rd St. across from City Hall. $3 or free with 20 gal. gas purchase. **Totem Oil**, Main St. and Haines Hwy. at Y in the road, free dump station.

CLINIC: **Chilkat Valley Medical Center**, 766-2521, South 2nd St., doctors, nurses. Dentist on Main St.

HORSE STALLS & EXERCISE AREA: Three transient box stalls available, more by arrangement. $5/night, negotiable if left clean. Riding area. (907) 766-2476, or 2478 in mornings, or Linda Mattews, (907) 766-2476, or 2478 in mornings, or Linda Matthews, (907) 766-2163 at other hours. Southeast Alaska Fairgrounds at southwest edge of town. For those vanning horses between South Central Alaska and the Lower 48, this is probably the best place en route to give them a break.

LAUNDROMATS: **Port Chilkoot Camper Park**—Port Chilkoot, 10 a.m. to 10 p.m. **Haines Hitch-Up RV Park**— Main St., 766-2882. **Susie Q's**— Main St., across from museum. Have showers.

Boats

Launching facilities at small boat harbor. Fuel available. For charters see Visitor Center or harbor bulletin board. Several charter boats and guides operate in summer and fall. Hunting guides are also available in Haines for deer, goat and bear hunting.

RIVER RAFT TOURS: There are several operators working out of Haines in summer. The following outfitters run trips on the Chilkat, Alsek, Tatshenshini, and other rivers: **Chilkat River Guides**, Box 170, Haines, AK 99827. 776-2409. **Alaska Cross Country Guiding & Rafting**, Box 124, Haines, AK 99827. 776-2040. **Alaska River Expeditions** specializes in raft trips on the Arctic North Slope, and runs 10-day trips on the Tatshenshini River, with trips starting from Haines. 419 K Street, Salt Lake City, UT 84103. (801) 322-0233.

Happenings

Southeast Alaska State Fair at the fairgrounds on the southwest edge of town, August 12–16, 1992, regional fair with crafts, contests, carnival, parade, and horse show. **Bald Eagle Music Festival** with day and evening performances.

Master Anglers Fishing Tournament, August 19–30, 1992.

Octoberfest, celebrating Alaska's purchase from Russia, October 18.

Ask at the Visitor Center about performances and exhibits by local artists, some not scheduled at presstime.

CUSTOMS: U.S. and Canadian customs stations are about 40 miles out of Haines on the Haines Hwy. They are closed from midnight to 8 a.m. and there are no facilities in the area. Requirements for Canadian customs are described at the end of the Prince Rupert section.

Ferry Tale

A bearded sourdough in wool shirt and black felt hat was riding the ferry back to his home on the Haines Highway. "I sit up on my hill looking down on that bend in the road and I can't see what all those folks are in such a hurry for. When I get out on the road with my horse and wagon, we only go 4 miles an hour but you wouldn't believe all the things we see. Wheels, hubcaps,—and you know those wire screens they put over their lights to keep the rocks off? Folks out my way all made rabbit hutches out of 'em."

Views from the Haines Highway on a clear day are magnificaent! Take time to stop at this pull off near Chilkat Pass. The Dalton Trail to the Klondike climbed up the valley here.

UP THE HIGHWAY (THE LAND ONE!)

From Haines it's 775 miles to Anchorage and 653 miles to Fairbanks. The Klondike Highway from Skagway to Whitehorse is partly gravel. Even in summer, you will enjoy the trip more as well as be safer if you don't try to hurry, but drive at reasonable speed, allowing for wildlife around the next bend. At night those animals are hard to see. Drive a reasonable number of hours per day and pull off to enjoy views or rest. Gas stations and mechanical service are a long way apart. Carry a few spares and basic tools as well as the service manual for your car. Screen protection for your headlights and radiator from flying rocks is recommended. So are a tow chain, flares, and extra water and fuel cans (which are best filled after you get off the ferry as they can't be stored on your car on the ship).

In winter all the above precautions apply, plus others. Think of Wyoming in January for driving conditions. Avoid driving in storms which can lead to white-out conditions and at night when unlit moose find the road an easy trail. With short daylight, you will probably drive some hours in the dark, but be careful. The RCMP, Alaska State Troopers and the ferry terminals have latest road conditions. If the weather ahead is awful when you get to Haines, your best bet is to wait a day or more.

If you've driven in Montana in winter, you already know that fuel systems require thought at -25 and below. Gasoline engines require additives to remove water even above freezing. If you fill a diesel car or truck in Seattle with the #2 fuel usually sold there, it will not run at winter temperatures in the Alaskan and Canadian interior. Stations in Haines, Skagway, and Canada do sell #1 diesel for winter use. Using your block heater before you start will help. You should carry a heavy duty extension cord to reach the nearest electrical outlet for it.

Be **sure** your car is in good condition for cold weather driving, with good studded snow tires or chains, plenty of antifreeze, winter oil, and and engine block heater. Carry a flashlight and spare batteries and shovel and something for traction such as sand, kitty litter, burlap sacks, or pieces of expanded metal screen to put under spinning tires. Have plenty of warm clothes and sleeping bags for everyone in the car. Be prepared to spend the night in the car without running the engine for heat and carbon monoxide, and to be able to walk a few miles for help (if it's more than a very few or there are any vehicles coming by, don't walk). Keep your gas tank full as bad conditions can force you to drive miles in low gear. Allow enough time for the drive and take more if needed to keep from driving while tired.

Driving to or from Prince Rupert in winter requires the same planning. In rare winters the road may be intermittently closed or cars led through in convoys due to avalanches on the highway between Smithers and Prince Rupert. Keep your speed down on this scenic 2-lane paved road and be prepared for several well-marked sharp turns the road makes across the railroad tracks. It's easy to forget while negotiating those turns to look for the occasional train as well! If you pull off at scenic points, you'll enjoy one of the more beautiful drives in the world.

The Alaska Highway is still an experience to drive even though most of it is paved and many bends have been straightened. In 1942 its construction in less than a year when it was so desperately needed was an incredible achievement. Near Fort Nelson there are more than 70 tractors under the road bed where they sank in the muskeg and the road was built over them. The road served as a supply route for truck traffic and as a major navigational facility and forced landing strip for planes being ferried to Alaska. It still performs both functions today. On my first flight to Alaska in the 70's I didn't land on it, but took off from it twice when the strips I had landed on were too rough.

In 1992 the fiftieth anniversary of the Alaska Highway is being celebrated in Canada and Alaska, commemorated at communities all along its length. Several RV groups are running caravans to Alaska. Travelers

Reaching Haines on the ferry, a group with motorhomes camps beside Lutak Inlet before heading up Haines Highway.

Sign beside highway leading into Stewart, B.C. warns of leftovers from avalanche control needed to keep the road open in winter.

will see memorials and tapes assembled for the anniversary.

Ferry Tale

Two women headed south on the ferry talked about the Alaska Highway they had driven up, the usual about the holes, gravel, and transport trucks. "And those miles of too-close-together trees. Why we have better trees than that in our backyard!"

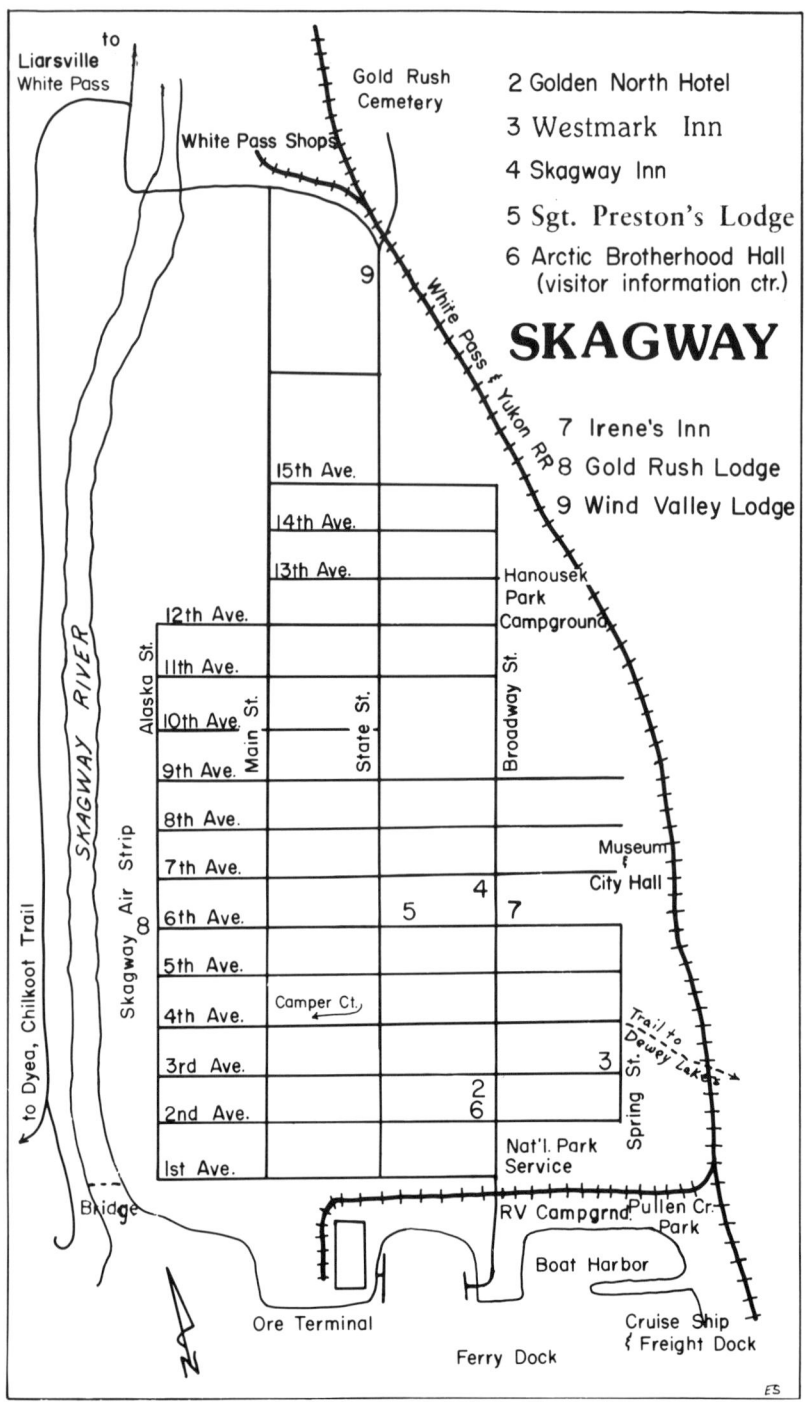

to
Liarsville
White Pass

Gold Rush
Cemetery

White Pass Shops

2 Golden North Hotel

3 Westmark Inn

4 Skagway Inn

5 Sgt. Preston's Lodge

6 Arctic Brotherhood Hall
(visitor information ctr.)

SKAGWAY

9

White Pass & Yukon RR

7 Irene's Inn

8 Gold Rush Lodge

9 Wind Valley Lodge

15th Ave.

14th Ave.

13th Ave.

12th Ave.

11th Ave.

10th Ave.

9th Ave.

8th Ave.

7th Ave.

6th Ave.

5th Ave.

4th Ave.

3rd Ave.

2nd Ave.

1st Ave.

Alaska St.

Main St.

State St.

Broadway St.

Spring St.

SKAGWAY RIVER

Skagway Air Strip

to Dyea, Chilkoot Trail

Hanousek
Park
Campground

Museum
City Hall

Camper Ct.

Trail to Dewey Lakes

5

4

7

8

2
6

3

Nat'l. Park
Service

Bridge

RV Campgrnd

Pullen Cr.
Park

Boat Harbor

Ore Terminal

Ferry Dock

Cruise Ship
& Freight Dock

N

ES

Broadway is lined with restored Gold Rush buildings and wooden sidewalks. Skaguay News Depot sells historic issues of the paper and posters.

SKAGWAY

(Area Code 907, Zip Code 99840)

SKAGWAY (pop. 700) was founded in 1888 when Captain William Moore and his son settled here. They were overrun by the stampede to the Klondike in 1897. Skagway is at the head of the Taiya Inlet, the northern end of the Inside Passage, and the south end of the White Pass Route. Skagway and the ghost town of Dyea both served the Chilkoot Trail, and mushroomed into tent and clapboard cities during the winter of 1897-98. Later, when the White Pass and Yukon Railroad was built , Dyea died and Skagway became the main gateway to the Klondike, over 500 miles to the north. In Skagway, Soapy Smith, the notorious con artist, and his gang were expert at separating prospectors from their money and goods. Today the town lives on its historic past, with a good museum and many original buildings. In 1976 Klondike National Park was established, including the Chilkoot and White Pass trails, and most of Broadway (the main street of Skagway).

The Klondike Highway is open all year over White Pass to Carcross and on to Whitehorse. For 14 miles it climbs to an altitude of 3,290 feet along the route of the Klondike gold seekers. The scenery is fabulous and the road is paved from Skagway to the summit and most of the way to

Whitehorse, 108 miles. You can connect with the Alaska Highway near Whitehorse. There is fishing at lakes along the way if you have the appropriate British Columbia or Yukon fishing license. At stops to enjoy the view, you can also enjoy the tiny alpine tundra flowers at your feet.

There are several good spots to camp or picnic between the summit and Carcross. There are no facilities other than the customs station between Skagway and Carcross. Carcross has a visitor center in the former White Pass and Yukon train depot, restaurants and gasoline. It is about 31 miles from Carcross on to Whitehorse.

Since some Yukon mines reopened, ore concentrate is being hauled to the Skagway terminal by specially built tractor-trailer rigs over 80 feet long. You may meet one per hour. Do not try to pass them. They will pull over at pullouts. Southbound trucks are heavily loaded. They have radios and can call for help for you if you need it.

To See and Do

Explore historic streets and buildings from the Gold Rush days.

Stop at the restored railroad depot on 2nd Avenue and Broadway for exhibits and programs by the National Park Service. Films and talks are given several times daily in summer, as are walking tours of historic features in Skagway. You can get the latest Chilkoot Trail information here. Open daily from mid-May to mid-September.

Visit the museum on 7th Avenue, 1 block east of Broadway. 9-5 daily in May and September, 8-6 in June, July and August. 983-2564. Very entertaining collection of costumes, tools, photos, and other artifacts from the Klonkdike Gold Rush. Donation, $2 adults, $1 for children.

See the "Days of '98 Show" in Eagle's Hall, Broadway and 6th. Adults $12, children $6. Daily mid-May to mid-September, fun gambling starts at 7:45 p.m., the show at 8:30 p.m. Matinee performances and sometimes morning shows on cruise ship days. No gambling at daytime shows. For times see the board in front of the hall. 983-2545. Jim Richards as Soapy Smith should *not* be missed!

In 1992, most ferries stop long enough in Skagway for a walk around town. Some stops are long enough for a drive to Dyea and the Chilkoot trailhead. I'd wait and see what time the ship actually arrives before counting on that if you are riding back on the same ship. The long stops make this a good one-day excursion from Juneau, especially on Mondays and Thursdays in summer.

Ride the **White Pass and Yukon Railroad** on a 3 hour excursion to the summit of White Pass and back. The historic narrow gauge train will run

Not an extra-terrestrial, the cruise ship docked a quarter mile south of town seems to fill Broadway.

daily, May 1 through September 30, 1992, leaving at 8:45 a.m. and 1:15 p.m. Trains may run some days earlier—check with **White Pass & Yukon**, 800-343-7373. Extra trains may run when several cruise ships are in port. Fare adults $72, children 12 and under, $36. Besides enjoying the train experience, you can see much more of the historic route from the train than you can from the highway.

There is scheduled service to Whitehorse in summer, riding the train from Skagway to the summit, leaving at 8:10 a.m. and 12:45 p.m., using a motorcoach between Fraser, B. C. andWhitehorse, arriving at 6:30 p.m. Southbound, the bus leaves Whitehorse at 8:15 a.m., arriving in Skagway at noon. One-way fares, adults $92, Children $46.

A motor rail car provides Chilkoot Trail service mid-June through mid-September from the trail end at Bennett, B.C. to the highway at Fraser. From there hikers can take the train back to Skagway, or a bus north or south. One-way fare Bennett to Fraser $15, Bennett to Skagway, connecting with southbound train at Fraser, $72. For reservations or info, **White Pass & Yukon Route**, Box 435, Skagway, AK 99840. 800-343-7373.

See both bald and golden eagles in the area. Swans sometimes stop near Dyea during migration.

Fish Taiya Inlet, Skagway and Dyea rivers, and Dewey Lakes. Salt water fishing is generally better than lake fishing here. Dolly Varden in May and June, and salmon and halibut have all been caught from shore, dock or skiff very near the ferry dock. Ask the locals and remember to get a license even for salt water fishing.

Visit Dyea, the takeoff point for the Chilkoot Pass. See the remains of buildings, boats, and the slide cemetery (for victims of the avalanche on the Chilkoot Trail in 1898). Any taxi will take you on the 9 miles of gravel road each way.

See the Gold Rush cemetery at the north end of Skagway, with the graves of Soapy Smith and Frank Reid.

Hike up to Dewey Lakes , 1/4 mile, Reid Falls 1/2 mile, and Icy Lake 2 miles. Beautiful views and forest.

Walk over the new footbridge across the Skagway River and follow the trail to Yakutania Point for short, level hike to a good picnic spot. Ambitious hikers can hike the trail from that point up the ridge overlooking Skagway 5.5 miles each way to A.B. Mountain at 5100 ft. Several view points along the way offer good photography and shorter hiking goals.

Backpack the historic and strenuous 33-mile Chilkoot Trail. Information on trail conditions is available from the National Park Service. Additional comments and suggestions on hiking the Chilkoot Trail are in the next chapter.

Go flightseeing by helicopter over Skagway, the Chilkoot and White Passes, and the Juneau Icefield, including a landing on the Icefield. **Temsco Helicopters**, 1st & Broadway, near ferry. Box 434, Skagway, AK 99840. 983-2909. From May through September flies over Chilkoot and White Pass Trails, nearby glaciers with tours from 30 minutes to 1 hour, the latter touring both passes.

Go flightseeing by plane over Icefield, Klondike Trails, Glacier Bay and a lunch tour to see the Chilkat Dancers in Haines. **Skagway Air Service**, Box 357, Skagway, AK 99840. 983-2233.

Take a day bus tour over White Pass to Carcross and back or overnight to Whitehorse. The scenery and history combine to make this a great trip. Enjoy flowers in summer and fall colors in September.

In winter and spring, ski cross-country near White Pass. Dry snow and gentle, rolling country for miles! S

INFORMATION AVAILABLE at the **National Park Service Visitor Center** in the restored railroad depot on 1st Ave., one block to the right at the first intersection. 983-2921 all year. The Park Service has the latest information on Chilkoot trail conditions and U.S. and Canadian regulation of the trail. They have good maps. Open 8 a.m.–8 p.m. in summer.

White Pass and Yukon train rounds the bend approaching Skagway's station.

Skagway Convention and Visitors Bureau, P.O. Box 415, Skagway, AK 99840. 983-2854. Fax 983-2151. In the Arctic Brotherhood Hall at Broadway and 2nd. Open 8:30 a.m.–5 p.m., May 15–Sept. 30. Get information in City Hall in winter. They have a good map of downtown Skagway with a map of nearby hiking trails on the back.

Transportation

FERRY: **Alaska Marine Highway**, 983-2941. daily in summer, 4 times per week in winter. Dock is at south end of Broadway. **Haines-Skagway Water Taxi**, 766-3395. Two round trips daily between Skagway and Haines. Walk-on passengers only. $29 round trip.

BUS: None local. In summer **Atlas Tours**, 983-2402, and **White Pass & Yukon Motorcoaches**, 983-2241, have bus service from Skagway to Whitehorse. In winter, **Sourdough Tours & Taxi**, 983-2523, runs bus several days a week.

TRAIN (& bus): **White Pass & Yukon Route**. Scheduled service to Whitehorse, by train from Skagway to the summit, leaving at 12:45 p.m. and by bus from Fraser, B. C. to Whitehorse, arriving at 6:30 p.m. Southbound, the bus leaves Whitehorse at 8:30 a.m. One-way, Adults $92, Children $46. May 1–Sept. 22.

TAXI: Most hotels have courtesy transportation from the ferry if you ask when you reserve. **Frontier Tours & Taxi** 983-2512, **Pioneer Taxi** 983-2623, **Sourdough Taxi** 983-2523.

TOURS: **Frontier Tours** 983-2512, **Grayline of Alaska** 983-2241, **Pioneer Taxi & Tours** 983-2623, **Skagway Streetcar Company** 983-2908, **Sourdough Taxi & Tours** 983-2523, **Princess Tours** 983-2895. All these operators run tours around Skagway. Some also run to Dyea and to Carcross and Whitehorse.

Sourdough Taxi & Tours 983-2523, runs a variety of tours October through April at reasonable prices. Some are van tours; others include rental car and hotels. Destinations include cross-country skiing areas near White Pass, Carcross, Whitehorse, Atlin, and a circle back to Haines.

BICYCLE RENTAL: **Sourdough Taxi and Tours**, 983-2523,

CAR RENTAL: **Avis**, 983-2247. **Eagles Nest Car Rental**, 983-2523.

AIR: **Skagway Air Service**, Box 357, Skagway, AK 99840. 983-2218. **LAB Flying Service**, 983-2471. **Wings of Alaska**, 983-2442.

ROAD: The Klondike Highway to Carcross, the Alaska Highway (99 miles), and on to Whitehorse (108 miles) is open all year, paved. Just north of Skagway there's an 11.5 mile grade up to White Pass, 3290'. The rest of the way is rolling upland with beautiful, unpopulated scenery. Both U.S. and Canadian Customs are open 24 hours a day all year at Fraser near White Pass.

BAGGAGE STORAGE at hotels, for patrons, on day of departure.

Hotels
(rates plus 8% tax)

Gold Rush Lodge—.5 mile from ferry, 6th and Alaska. Box 514, Skagway, AK 99840. 983-2831. Courtesy van. Queen or double and twin beds, with private bath. Street level, modern. Cable TV. 12 rooms, some non-smoking. Continental breakfast included. Senior rates. Single $65, Double $75. Triple $85. Open all year.

Gramma's Bed & Breakfast—.6 from ferry, 7th and State. Box 315, Skagway, AK 99840. 983-2312. Four rooms. Satellite TV in living room. Hearing impaired telephones. Continental breakfast. Shared bath. Courtesy transportation from ferry and to town (an easy walk). Single $45, Double $50. Triple $60. Open May 1-Sept. 15.

Golden North—.35 mile from ferry, on Broadway and 3rd, Box 431, Skagway, AK 99840. 983-2451 and 983-2294. Fax 983-2755. Has Gold Rush era furnishing. Private and shared baths. Restaurant, lounge, beauty shop, tours. Single $60, Double $70, Twin $75, Triple $80, Quad $85. Open year around. Winter rates.

Irene's Inn—.5 mile from ferry, on Broadway at 6th, Box 380, Skagway, AK 99840. 983-2520. Fax 983-2998. Built in 1899. Rooms upstairs. Restau-

Fishing for Dolly Varden and pink salmon in Pullen Creek Park campground.

rant, bakery. Single $35, Double $50, with shared bath. Single $60, Twin $65, Triple $70, Quad $75 with private bath. May 15-Sept. 30.

Westmark Inn—.4 mile from ferry, 3rd Avenue between Broadway and Spring, Box 515, Skagway, AK 99840. 983-6000. 800-544-0970. Fax 463-3567. Restaurants and cocktail lounge, entertainment. Laundromat. Courtesy van from ferry, airport. Avis car rental. Single $112, Double $126, including breakfast. Children 18 and under free. Annex, Gold Rush, and Backpacker rates in nearby facilities, $49–75, space available. Open mid-May to late September.

Skagway Inn Bed & Breakfast—.5 mile from ferry, on Broadway between 6th and 7th, Box 500, Skagway, AK 99840. 983-2289. Living room. Shared baths. Built 1897, it has friendly Gold Rush atmosphere with rooms named, instead of numbered, with the names of the "girls" who worked here. Continental breakfast "plus" (yogurt, granola, and all homemade breads, muffins). Courtesy pickup at ferry, airport. Single $45, Double $52. Add'l, $7/person. Senior discount. Open May 1–Sept. 15.

Sgt. Preston's Lodge—.6 mile from ferry, on 6th between Broadway and State, Box 538, Skagway, AK 99840. 983-2521. 22 rooms, private and shared baths. Courtesy van. Handicap access. Telephone and cable TV in rooms. Continental breakfast. With private baths, Single $60, Double $70, Triple $75, Quad $80. With shared baths, Single $50, Double $60, Triple $65, Quad $70. Open all year—winter rates. Car and bicycle rentals across street.

Wind Valley Lodge—.8 mile from ferry, 22nd and State Street. Box 354, Skagway, AK 99840. 983-2236. 30 rooms, modern, AAA approved, cable TV. Non-smoker rooms. Handicap accommodations. Laundry, spa for guests. Standard rooms have 2 double beds, bath. Deluxe rooms larger with 2 queen-sized beds, sitting area. Courtesy transportation. Single $59, Double $69. Add'l. $10/person. Children under 6 and cribs free. Open Mar. 15–Nov. 1.

Skagway Home Hostel—.5 from ferry, 3rd between State and Main. Box 231, Skagway, AK 99840. 983-2131. Reservations advised. 10 beds in male and female dormitories. Hot water, cooking facilities. Sleeping bags recommended. No pets, drinking or smoking. 11 p.m. curfew. Check in 5–10 p.m. AYH members get priority on space, $10. Nonmembers $15. Open all year, but reservations required Sept. 1–May 1.

Trailer Parks

Hoover's Camper Court—1/2 mile, 4th Ave., between State and Main, Box 304, Skagway. 983-2454. 18 spaces with hookups. $10 water, sewer, electricity. Hot showers. Propane. Dump station. Open April through October with full or partial facilities. One space available in winter.

Campgrounds

Hanousek Park—.9 mile from ferry, Broadway at 14th. 12 spaces with water and electrical hookups, $15. 50 tent sites, $8. Firepits, tables, water, restrooms with hot showers, dump station. Open May 1-Sept. 30.

Pullen Creek Park & RV Campground—.2 mile from ferry, to right of Broadway. New city-owned campground. All spaces with hookups. Park has a creek, pond, picnic shelter. $8 without hookups. $15 with water and electricity. Bathhouse with showers. Central dump station. Open May 1-Sept. 30.

You should call ahead to reserve space at the campgrounds, especially on Sunday and Monday nights with the *Columbia* from Bellingham arriving on Monday. 983-2768.Box 324, Skagway, AK 99840.

Facilities

LAUNDROMAT: **Service Unlimited**, 2nd and State.

DUMP STATION: **Pullen Creek Park** and **Hoover's Chevron**, 4th Ave. between State and Main.

PROPANE: **Hoover's Chevron**, 4th Ave., between State and Main.

DIESEL: **Service Unlimited**, International Chevron. 2nd and State Streets. Also car wash. (If you use it southbound, you'll save your clothes & paint when you slide between your car and the next on the car deck.)

Cruise ship, *Star Princess*, over 1500 passengers, backs away from the Skagway dock with help from a tug.

ICE: **Fairway Supermarket** and all liquor stores.

CLINIC: **Dahl Clinic.** 11th Ave., between State and Main. 9–5 weekdays, 983-2255. After hours, 983-2418.

PETS: Veterinarian is **Judy Selmer**, Broadway & 7th. 983-2313. On sabbatical April 1992–April 1993.

Boats

Charters for fishing and tours available. Information at **National Park Service** and **Skagway Convention & Visitors Bureau.** Moorage and fuel at harbor.

Westours at the Westmark Inn, 983-2241, has a 2 hour scenic and historic boat tour.

Happenings

Skagway Windfest, March. Games, races, contests with Klondike theme—Ore Truck Pull, Chainsaw Toss, Chili cookoff, etc. Winter festival. 983-2775.

Buckwheat Ski Classic, late March. Cross country ski races on groomed course near White Pass and mountain lakes. Call 983-2544 or 983-2234.

July 4 Parade and Celebration. Tradition started when Soapy Smith led the parade as grand marshall on a white horse in 1898, 4 days before he was shot. Full day and evening of games and contests followed by fireworks. 983-2297.

Soapy's Wake, July 8, 1992. Soapy's descendants provide champagne for the occasion, which includes a ceremony and toast at the Gold Rush Cemetary with the cast of the Days of 98 show as well as locals and visitors. 983-2545.

Flower Show and Gold Rush Garden Club Awards, August 16–18, 1992. Features Skagway's gardens at their peak in the long summer days as well as floral displays by local businesses. Tea and cookies. 983-2365.

Dyea Dash, August 22, 1992. Fun run for your choice of 3 distances on Dyea Road serves as warmup for Klondike Road Relay. 1992 event will benefit Cancer Society. 983-2354, 983-2210.

Klondike Trail of '98 Road Relay, Skagway to Whitehorse. Sept. 11–12, 1992. 10-person teams from all over the western US and Canada start Friday at midnight from the Skagway waterfront and race 110 miloes up the highway and over White Pass to Whitehorse, finishing Saturday afternoon in time for dinner and dance that night. The race has grown until now there's a 70 team limit. Teams come from all over North America to join the locals. For info, call (403) 668-3331 in Whitehorse.

Eagles Christmas Party, December 24, 1992. Town Christmas program with band and choir. Presents for town children. 983-2234.

Southbound cars and RVs lined up according to where they will unloadwait for the ferry at the Skagway terminal.

THE CHILKOOT PASS

Gold was discovered in creeks running into the Yukon's Klondike River in August 1896. As word spread through the north country, prospectors for many hundreds of miles around converged on the camp that became Dawson City. They staked claims, struggled and starved with bottles of gold nuggets on the shelf (there was gold but not enough food for so many people in the Yukon that winter). Finally in July 1897 the Portland arrived in Seattle with a load of gold, and the rush was on, world-wide.

Despite its difficulties, the Chilkoot Pass proved to be the quickest and one of the easiest routes to the Klondike. During the winter of 1897-98 thousands struggled over the pass, not once but many times as they shuttled back and forth moving the ton of supplies the Mounties now required for entry to the Yukon (to avoid a repetition of the starving times). By spring, when the ice went out on the river, over 20,000 miners waited on the shores of Lakes Lindeman and Bennett with hand-built boats to float the last 500 miles. They arrived to find all likely land and much unlikely area already staked. Few got any gold, but for all the trip was the most memorable time of their lives.

Today the trail is included in national parks on both sides of the border and maintained by U.S. and Canadian personnel. Many artifacts remain, and must be left as they lie. Along the trail are remains of wagons, boots, harnesses, stoves, and sleds once pulled by miners. There are metal pictures of views as they were then from the places you are standing now. The Chilkoot Trail is much more than a rugged 33-mile backpack trip. Even in summer it's a walk for several days through the world's most scenic historical museum.

To enjoy this trip requires some planning. The trail goes from sea level at Dyea to 3739 ft. (Parks Canada says 3502!) at the summit, mostly from mile 13.5 to mile 16.5 (which is very hard on legs if you start from the north end and go in reverse), and back to 2153 ft. at Lake Bennett. July is the most popular month, as much of the winter's snow is gone and the wildflowers are lovely. The trip takes three to five days for most people.

You still can expect wind and rain any time. In the pass this can be miserable and force you to concentrate on the trail markers so as not to lose the trail. The trail is often muddy, crosses streams, has several miles of snow at any season and several miles of loose rock near the U.S. side of the pass.

On the Canadian side avalanches sometimes run across the trail even in mid-summer. Canadian wardens you'll meet near the pass have good advice on snow and weather conditions. For the latest information on trail conditions you should see the **National Park Service** in Skagway, which can give you a useful trail profile and the Canadian number to call for customs clearance. Topographic maps are available at the **Skagway Sports Emporium** on Fourth Avenue.

Adequate clothing and boots well broken-in are critical. The shelters are widely separated and nowhere near the pass. Good rain gear that's windproof is essential—rain pants and parka or cagoule. Ponchos don't work in wind, and the new breathable synthetics haven't proven waterproof in this climate for anyone I know. Pants must be wool or polyester fleece. (Synthetic *inner* layers and insulation do work well in this climate and dry quickly in camp.) Damp cotton pants lose heat, even under rain pants, faster than if you were undressed. Wearing them here leaves your whole safety margin to the luck of the weather and says some things about your judgment you wouldn't want to advertise. A wool cap and water repellent gloves that dry quickly are essential. Breathable gaiters are *very* good for keeping mud and snow out of boots, and keeping pants dry.

Camping is only approved in designated spots. Wood is scarce and you are advised to bring a stove and fuel for cooking. Shelters are only for drying out—not for camping in. You should also bring 50 feet of light rope for hauling your pack up out of bears' reach on the horizontal poles provided at most campsites. Water, especially from lakes with campsites, should be boiled or treated with water tablets.

Deep Lake is the prettiest campsite on the trail but is located so it doesn't fit many people's schedules. The flowers here are lovely in July, and you can easily spend an afternoon discovering artifacts hidden by the brush. Happy Camp is *not* in the first trees you come to on the Canadian side, and the "four miles" the map says it is from the summit are a sadistic underestimate. But this is a great trip and one I want to do again!

A **White Pass & Yukon** rail motorcar leaves Bennett daily from mid-June to mid-September at 8:30 a.m. and 1:15 p.m. for the 45 minute ride to Fraser where you meet the southbound train or take a bus to Whitehorse or Skagway. Fare from Bennett to Skagway is $72, Bennett to Fraser only, $15. Call (800) 343-7373 or (907) 983-2217 for dates and conditions.

White Pass & Yukon controls the track right of way and is concerned about liability for people walking tracks on which several vehicles a day run. They have posted it and are prepared to be firm with anyone they find on their right of way. This unfortunately limits access (or some of the pleasure of it) to a national park. Parks Canada is working on restoring a section of the historic trail which may solve the problem. The alternate trail may not yet be available. It's a good question to ask the park offices on either side of the border.

If you don't ride the rail car, your choices are: 1) skip Bennett and leave the trail at a fork just beyond Bare Loon Lake at about Mile 30 for a 5 mile walk out along the train tracks to a place on the road called Log Cabin where there's no longer a cabin, to meet the bus (get schedule in Skagway) or 2) walk on the trail all the way to Bennett and then 8 miles back along the tracks to Log Cabin, at least getting to see the whole historical story.

From Log Cabin on the Klondike Highway you can catch the bus going either north or south, to Whitehorse or back to Skagway.

Suggestion: If you don't want to climb the pass, but want an interesting trip, you could leave the highway at Log Cabin and hike into Bennett or Lake Lindeman for a few days in beautiful, rolling upland with flowers and history. I highly recommend this trip as the weather is drier on this side of the mountains, the terrain is gentle, you start from over 2000 ft. above sea level, and you can do as much or as little as you like. Beginning backpackers and less-conditioned people could enjoy this variation no matter how the weather turned out.

Seeing the award-winning film "City of Gold" narrated by Pierre Berton and reading his book *Klondike Fever* (US edition) or, as it's titled in Canada, *Klondike*, will make the trip mean more, I think. The film is shown sometimes on the ferries and in Skagway. Berton's father went over the pass, and he grew up in Dawson. With that preparation, a friend and I panted up the pass on a sunny July day trying to imagine spending weeks on it in mid-winter and marvelled "they did all this for *gold?*"

For additional Information, write or call Area Superintendent, Yukon National Historic Sites, Box 5540, Whitehorse, Yukon Territory YIA 5H4 Canada. Phone (403) 668-2116. In Skagway you can write or call Superintendent, Klondike Gold Rush N. H. P., Box 517, Skagway 99840. (907) 983-2921.

SMALLER PORTS
(Served by the *Aurora*, and *LeConte*, but not by the larger ferries)

METLAKATLA
(Area Code 907, Zip Code 99926)

METLAKATLA (pop. 1100) was established in 1887 when Father Duncan moved his religious community of Tsimshian Indians from Canada to Annette Island. The island remains an Indian reservation, by vote, after the native claims settlement. A neat, well-planned community, Metlakatla depends on timber and fishing, with both a cannery and a sawmill in town. The eastern half of the island is mountains with lakes and waterfalls, while the western half, where the town and 7500 ft. airport are, is flat.

To See and Do

See Father Duncan's Cottage, open 10-5, Mon.- Fri. Weekends by request. Restored as a museum. Curator, 886-6926.

See cannery operating in season.

See Duncan Memorial Church, replica of the original burned in 1948.

See the longhouse, used for tribal ceremonies. Tsimshian crafts displayed and for sale.

Beachcomb, picnic, hike almost anywhere on island. Walk out road west, past cemetery is popular. Pt. Davidson, 10 miles by gravel road, is good picnic and bird watching area. Purple Lake Trail, 3 miles, is steep and rugged, but beautiful.

Bring bicycle on ferry for tour of island roads, trip to Pt. Davidson. Call Community Services Dept., Bonnie G. Scudero, or Stanley Patterson, 886-1216 for info.

Founder's Day, Aug. 7, celebrates arrival of Father Duncan and his followers in 1887. Tribal dancers, community lunch, special events.

See operating fish hatchery at south end of the island.

Walk trails such as Yellow Hill Viewpoint Trail, 2 miles south of town, and Skaters Lake Trail (1/2 mile long), 1/4 mile from town toward airport.

Facilities

ACCOMMODATIONS: **Metlakatla Hotel and Suites,** Box 670, Metlakatla, AK 99926. 886-3456. 7 rooms, 2 with kitchenttes, 1 withjacuzzi. All rooms have cable TV, refrigerators, original art work. Restaurant. Single/Double $95. Winter rates. Open all year.

AIR SERVICE: **Taquan Air Service,** charter and regular service to Ketchikan. Box 600, Metlakatla. Jerry Scudero. 886-6868, 6888.

CAR RENTAL: **Rent-A-Dent** in Metlakatla. Toll-free reservation from U.S. outside Washington, 800-426-5243. Metlakatla, 886-4622.

BUS SERVICE: None public.

GROCERY STORES: 1 supermarket, 1 minimart.

SWIMMING POOL, with sauna and fitness room, open to public at Lepquinum Recreation Center.

BOATS: Visiting boats and vehicles can get fuel at Guthries' on dock, tie up. A new breakwater and small boat harbor are completed.

FERRY: Ferry service is almost daily, 1.5 hours from Ketchikan on *Aurora.* The ferry dock is 1 mile from downtown.

INFORMATION AVAILABLE at the Council Annette Islands Reserve, Box 8, Metlakatla, AK 99926. 886-4441. Fax 886-7997.

Note: Metlakatla is legally dry. There is no place to buy alcohol, and it cannot legally be brought to the island.

A log barge loads near Hyder to haul logs to a mill. The one-man tug or "boom boat" at the left corner of the barge gives an idea of its size.

HYDER
(Area code 604, Zip code 99923)

Hyder is a village of 90 people at the head of the Portland Canal, a long scenic inlet George Vancouver followed in hopes it would be the Northwest Passage. Adjacent is Stewart, B.C. with about 1000 people. The Alaska ferry makes one trip a week from Ketchikan, actually docking in Stewart. You can drive from the Cassiar Road to the ferry and board with a vehicle up to 25' long. Or you can ride one way on the ferry from Ketchikan and fly the other way on the mail plane. The ferry terminal in Ketchikan can tell you which air taxi has the run.

Hyder and Stewart have both seen bigger days in their scenic fiord, surrounded by cliffs leading up to icefields and glaciers above. Both were busy mining towns—Hyder had over 10,000 people. More recently Stewart was the base for the Grand Duc copper mine until the fall of copper prices closed it. The Premier and Big Missouri gold mines near Hyder have rebuilt bunkhouses and other buildings and have reopened. Anything you can't find in Hyder you probably can in Stewart. The latter has several motels and restaurants and an air strip. Hyder children go to school in Stewart.

Note that Hyder's phone area code is British Columbia's 604, but the zip code is a U.S. code.

To See and Do

Walk around the quiet dirt streets, the banks of the Salmon River or the Portland Canal and enjoy the scenery.

Fish in Salmon River or Portland Canal. If you have a boat, set a crab or shrimp pot in Portland Canal.

Watch bears fishing and salmon spawning at Fish Creek, 5 miles north of Hyder.

As this is a mineralized area, rockhounds can enjoy flashy mineral specimens from roadside or abandoned slag heaps at mines.

Pick berries and enjoy summer flowers everywhere.

At your own risk in summer, with a good car or pickup and plenty of gas, you can drive *very* carefully up the road from Hyder toward the Grand Duc Mine for great scenery and glacial views.

Help the residents celebrate International Days, July 1 through the 4th. The Canadians start on the 1st with Canada Day and the holiday runs through the U.S. Independence Day, including games, fireworks, and a bed race from Hyder to Stewart.

Get Hyderized. Anyone can tell you how. (hint: with 3 bars, open until 5 a.m. 7 days a week, it's easy.)

Facilities

BUS (also tours): **Seaport Limousine** in Stewart, 636-2622.

AIR: **Taquan Air,** agent Sue Hickman, 636-9150.

DIESEL, GAS: **Yankee Trader** in Hyder, 636-9143. **Shell** in Stewart, 636-2344.

PROPANE/ICE: **Granmac**, Stewart, 636-2402.

GROCERIES: **Dean's**, in Stewart, 636-2422. Laundromat in Stewart.

HOSPITAL: **Stewart General Hospital**, 11th Ave., 636-2221.

BOAT MOORAGE and launching: Hyder 636-9148.

BOAT CHARTERS: several, both in Hyder and Stewart. Some of the best fishing in Alaska (a good place for a crab or shrimp pot, too).

ACCOMMODATIONS: **Sealaska Inn,** 1/2 mile from ferry dock, in middle of Hyder. Hyder, AK 99923. (604) 636-9001. 10 rooms, queen-size beds. Restaurant, bar. Single or Double, $40.

Grand View Inn, 1 mile from ferry. P.O. Box 49, Hyder, AK 99923. (604) 636-9174. New hotel with 10 rooms, TV available. $45, Double $50.

INFORMATION: **Hyder Community Center**, Box 149, Hyder, AK 99923. (604) 636-9148.

Salmon River Glacier from the Grand Duc Mine Road above Hyder.

PRINCE OF WALES ISLAND, CRAIG, KLAWOCK
(Area Code 907, Zip Codes Craig 99921, Klawock 99925, Hydaburg 99922)

PRINCE OF WALES, 45 miles west of Ketchikan, is the largest island in Southeastern Alaska with over 1000 miles of shoreline. It's served by ferry to Hollis, daily in summer, several times weekly in winter. From there a paved road reaches Craig, 35 miles, pop. 1535, and Klawock, pop. 897, 7 miles from Craig and 28 miles from Hollis. Gravel roads go to the native fishing village of Hydaburg and north to the big logging camp of Thorne Bay. Gravel roads now reach the north island logging camps of Whale Pass and Coffman Cove. Pt. Baker, also on the island, is reachable only by air and boat.

There is excellent fishing in many places, both fresh and saltwater. The west coast has many islands with sheltered coastline—a good place for boat touring and camping. Fishing and logging are the main activities on the island. There is abundant wildlife, including many black bears and eagles, even wolves.

To See and Do

Visit totem park at Klawock, 21 totems.

See the new fish hatchery in Klawock.

Watching birds and wildlife is rewarding here—and there's lots to photograph. Eagles are everywhere. A wolf trotted across the road in front of us.

Fish both fresh and salt water and hunt, many places, in season.

Enjoy July 4th celebrations in Craig and Klawock—logging contests, games, fireworks.

Big king salmon here. Fishing derby.

Kayak between islands in many protected bays. Bird and whale watching are great, especially on west coast.

Camp dry in Forest Service cabins, most reached by boat or floatplane.

Walk the scenic bike path in Craig and **One Duck Trail** (sign on the Hydaburg Rd. 2 miles south of its start on the Craig Hollis Rd.) to timberline and shelter.

Bring a mountain bike and explore the road system, camping at lakes and bays. Be careful with logging truck traffic and black bears in camp.

Watch gravel beaches and road shoulders for interesting rocks. Prince of Wales Island has a great variety, including the marble used for the pillars in front of the state capitol.

Totems in Klawock park overlook the harbor.

Facilities

FERRY: **Alaska Marine Hwy.** from Ketchikan to Hollis (where the road ends and there's a small terminal building open for ferry arrivals. Note that traffic has increased greatly in the past few years between Ketchikan and Prince of Wales Island. If you're taking a vehicle any time of year, you should have reservations. Hollis terminal, 530-7115. Craig, 826-3432.

ROADS: Most extensive road system, 2000 miles, in Southeastern Alaska, mostly gravel, though some in central part of island are now paved. Vehicles going to northern area should carry extra fuel and two spare tires. Watch for logging trucks. Hollis, a former logging camp, has no facilities. The first person with a mobile coffee/sandwich van here can probably retire early.

AIRPORT: State-maintained airport at Klawock is 5000' paved. Free tiedowns. Unicom 122.8. Attended irregularly. No phone, fuel, facilities.

ACCOMMODATIONS: **Haida Way Lodge**, downtown Craig, 35 miles from Hollis. On Front St., Box 90, Craig, AK 99921. 826-3268. 25 units. TV, coffee, phones. Open all year, Single/Double $85.

Fireweed Lodge-Riptide Outfitters, 28 miles from Hollis. On Craig-Hollis Hwy., Box 116, Klawock, AK 99925. 755-2930. Open all year. Boats, canoes, ocean fishing charters, island touring, hunting outfitters. 18 rooms with private bath. Family style dining. Budget rental cars. $75 per person plus meals.

Prince of Wales Lodge, 28 miles from Hollis, on Big Salt Rd. Box 72, Klawock, AK 99925. 755-2227. Since the lodge building burned, guests are housed in 3 bedroom apartments with room for 12 fishing guests. Operates April through September, with fishing packages and day charters. 3-day fishing package including air transportation from Ketchikan, room and meals, guide, boat, and gear for saltwater fishing is $1625. Apartments are open year around, $85, $20 each additional person. Has brochure. Rental cars and pickups available.

Ruth Ann's Hotel, 31 miles from Hollis. P.O. Box 145, Craig, AK 99921. (907) 826-3378. Restaurant and lounge. Rooms $65 and up.

Lighthouse Bed & Breakfast, (summer only), Box 77, Craig, AK 99921. 826-3606.

SPORTS EQUIPMENT (and resort package): **Log Cabin Campground & Resort.** 28 miles from ferry. Box 54, Klawock, AK 99925. 755-2205. 800-544-2205. Has bicycles, tents, fishing equipment, showers, boats for rent separately or as package. Fishing and adventure packages, include halibut and salmon charters, gold panning, backpacking and canoeing, beach cabins or log house, free transportation to and from ferry. Fishing packages include transportation from Ketchikan, boat and gear, beach cabins with shared kitchen. Daily rate for cabins is $35 for 2 people. Log house, $100 for 2, plus $10 per person additional up to 5.

The cabins and campground are among big trees facing gravel beach and boat dock. There are so many eagles fishing nearby and perched in the trees overhead that you may wish our national bird wasn't such a chatterbox at 4 a.m.! Photography with still cameras and camcorders is easy here, though 200 and 400 mm lenses are helpful. Campground has some spaces with hookups, $20 per vehicle and two people. Tent space, $5 per person. Kitchen and showers in adjacent building.

TAXI: **Jackson Cab**, 755-2557, Klawock. In Craig, **Chief Wiah Cab**, 826-3375, and **Call Me A Cab**, 826-3994.

BUS SERVICE: to ferry **Prince of Wales Transporter**, P. O. Box 228, Klawock, AK 99925. 755-2348. Fares from Hollis to Klawock, $20 if you're

Two young eagles perch in spruce tree above Log Cabin campground.

Bald eagles flock like chickens to eat fish scrap below the fish cleaning shed at Prince of Wales Lodge.

only passenger, $16 ea. for two or more. To Craig, $22 for one, $17 ea. for more. Senior and student rates. Special inland runs on the island as well as to ferry.

CAR RENTAL: **Allstar Rent-a-Car**, Klawock. 755-2524. **Prince of Wales Lodge** and **Fireweed Lodge** have rental cars and pickups.

GROCERY STORES: two in Craig, generally open 9 a.m. to 7 p.m., supermarket, beauty shop, clothing stores. Klawock has a convenience store and a general store. Thorne Bay, Coffman Cove, Whale Pass and Hydaburg have small grocery stores.

RESTAURANTS: four in Craig—**Haida Way Lodge**, one across the street from Ruth Ann's Hotel, a pizza place, and a Mexican restaurant. **Dave's Diner** and **Fireweed Lodge** in Klawock.

LAUNDROMATS: In Craig, **T.L.C. Laundry & Rooms**, 826-2966, has laundromat and bunkhouse rooms above with shared bath. $30–45. Weekly rates. One in Klawock near road from Hollis.

GAS STATIONS in Craig, Klawock, Thorne Bay. Note that there is no gas anywhere else on the island and miles of gravel road can use a lot of it. Fill up any time you pass a station. Auto parts store in Craig.

PROPANE and DIESEL: **Black Bear** in Klawock. For propane only, **Klawock Fuels** in Klawock, **Island Propane** in Craig.

ICE: all grocery stores, liquor stores in Craig and Thorne Bay.

HEALTH CLINIC: Craig, with doctor and physician's assistant. Open 10–4, M–F. Radio contact with hospital in Ketchikan. 826-3257, after hours 826-3330. For emergency in Craig, dial 911.

BOAT FUEL: Craig, Klawock, and Thorne Bay (as a convenience here). Boat rentals at Thorne Bay. Launch ramp, Craig, at City Center (North Cove).

TOURS: **Adventure Outdoors** offers small group van tours using ferries and including 4 days on the island for fishing and sightseeing. Box 4461, Rolling Bay, WA 98061. (206) 842-3189.

Kayak rental, tours, fishing charters: **S. E. A. Coastal Adventures**, Box 268, Craig, AK 99921. 826-3425.

Fishing charters, sightseeing: **Duke's Charter Service**, P.O. Box 84, Craig, 99921. 826-3809. **Craig Charters**, Box 495, Craig, AK 99921. 826-2939. **Catch-A-King Charters**, Craig. 826-2938.

CHARTER AIR SERVICE from Ketchikan by any of the operators there. **Taquan Air**, 826-8800, and **Ketchikan Air Service**, 826-3333, have scheduled service, allowing you to pay by the seat instead of for the whole plane.

INFORMATION AVAILABLE at City Hall, **City of Craig**, P.O. Box 23, Craig, AK 99921. 826-3275. Fax 826-3278. **U.S. Forest Service**, Box 500, Craig, AK 99921. 826-3271. You can get the "Prince of Wales Road Guide" for $2 from the Forest Service office here or in Ketchikan. **City of Klawock**, P.O. Box 113, Klawock, AK 99925. 755-2261.

Deck hands on a purse seiner in Craig get ready for salmon open season the next day.

Hand troller returns to Klawock harbor. This method of fishing works well in protected waters and doesn't require a large investment.

Expressive weathered totem in Hydaburg totem park.

HYDABURG

Hydaburg is a village of 464 people, mostly native American Haidas, on the south shore of Prince of Wales Island. Until the gravel road was cut through from the Craig-Hollis Highway in 1983, it could only be reached by boat and plane. There is excellent fishing and kayaking here as well as a totem park with 15 totems carved during the 1930's. The road to Hydaburg is scenic with good berry picking in season (blueberries and red huckleberries) and fishing in several streams.

Villagers fish for salmon and halibut. Some work in logging, and most fish and hunt for part of their food. They appreciate your sensitivity to their culture.

Kayakers and campers with skiffs will find more miles of sheltered water and bay shoreline reachable (without being exposed to open water) from here than from any other town in Southeastern Alaska. It's a great starting point for many trips—exploring the shores and deep bays of Prince of Wales, Long, and Dall Islands. Part of this land is included in the 91,000 acre South Prince of Wales Wilderness Area.

Near Hydaburg, freshly cut logs await tow to mill or log freighter.

Facilities

BUS: from Hollis ferry terminal to Hydaburg 36 miles, about an hour.

AIR: **Taquan Air,** 285-8800, from Ketchikan.

PROPANE: **Island Fuel,** 285-3425 and **Haida Oil,** 285-3283, which also has diesel and boat fuel.

GROCERIES: **Do Drop In,** a general store.

CLINIC: on Main Street with limited first aid. 285-3462.

BOAT MOORAGE: City Harbor, 285-3761.

ACCOMMODATIONS: There are no hotels but the following people will take boarders. **Fran Sanderson,** Box 329, Hydaburg, AK 99922. 285-3135. Mrs. Sanderson teaches native food preparation classes and caters parties with native foods. Interested guests could learn a lot! **Marlene Edenshaw,** Box 41, Hydaburg, AK 99922. 285-3254. On waterfront and can provide meals. $65 includes continental breakfast.

INFORMATION AVAILABLE: **City of Hydaburg,** Box 49, Hydaburg, AK 99922. 285-3761, 3793, and 3954.

KAKE
(Area Code 907, Zip Code 99830)

KAKE (pop. 861) is a Tlingit Indian fishing village on Kupreanof Island, west of Petersburg. It is scenic, has some gravel logging roads, excellent fishing, and is home of the world's tallest one-piece totem pole, 132 feet tall, centerpiece of the Alaska pavilion at the 1970 world's Fair in Japan. Ferry dock 1.5 miles from center of town.

To See and Do
Fish anywhere, even at the ferry dock, for halibut, salmon, sole. Rainbow trout in streams.

Hike, camp, beachcomb. Logging roads provide some trails and ski touring in winter. Road south leads short distance to Boot Lake picnic area, then on to Hamilton Bay, 20 miles.

See the totem pole above town.

Canoe or kayak in bay between Kupreanof and Kuiu Islands. Many inlets and small islands. Several Forest Service cabins.

Facilities
ACCOMMODATIONS (plus 5% tax): **New Town Inn**, P.O. Box 222, Kake. 785-3472, 785-3885. 1 mile from dock. Has 15 beds, sometimes full during summer. Meals family style, for hotel guests. Single $52, Double $79.

Nuggett Inn, 785-6469. 3 rooms—2 singles and a double. $38.

RESTAURANT: **Nuggett Inn**.

GROCERY STORES, 2. **SOS Value-Mart**, 785-785-6444, general store with Alaska souvenirs and postcards.

BOAT FUEL available at Kake cannery dock, launch ramp. No known charters or rentals.

PICNIC AREA at Portage Area, 1.5 miles, to right of dock, no facilities.

TAXI: **Timber Wolf Cab**, 785-3906. **Yukon Cab**, 785-3712, CB Channel 23.

FERRY SERVICE from Petersburg, Sitka, and Juneau several times weekly, *M/V LeConte*.

AIR SERVICE: **LAB**, 785-6435. **Wings of Alaska**, 785-6466 from Juneau. **Bellair**, 785-6411 from Sitka and Juneau. AIRSTRIP: Gravel, 4000'. No facilities. 100 octane fuel is available at seaplane base on waterfront.

CLINIC: **City of Kake Health Clinic**, 785-3333.

INFORMATION: There is no Chamber of Commerce and Kake does not have brochures available. **Petersburg Chamber of Commerce** or **U.S. Forest Service** in Petersburg may have information. **Kake City Hall**, 785-3804. Box 500, Kake 99830.

ANGOON
(Area Code 907, Zip Code 99820)

ANGOON (pop.639), is the only settlement on Admiralty Island. It is a Tlingit fishing village at the mouth of Mitchell Bay, a narrow-mouthed saltwater "chuck" featuring incredible currents at the tide change. This is also the end of the Cross-Admiralty canoe route, a system of cabins, trails, lakes and creeks, connecting the east and west sides of Admiralty Island. There is fishing in season for salmon, trout, herring and halibut. Most of this island has been declared a national monument. Check with U.S. Forest Service in Juneau, 789-3111. Wildlife watching is good—but note that this island has brown bears, an estimated average of one per square mile, who may regard a piece of stream or lakeshore as theirs.

To See and Do

Fish, hike, beachcomb, canoe. Be careful of tides and rough water in Chatham Strait that can develop quickly. Weather can change rapidly.

See **Historical Center** with new totems, artifacts, historical photos.

Facilities

FERRY SERVICE: Several times weekly from Juneau and Sitka.

CHARTER PLANE SERVICE from Juneau and Sitka. **Bellair Service,** 788-3641 from Sitka, six days a week. **Wings of Alaska,** 788-3530. **LAB.** 788-3500.

ACCOMMODATIONS: **Kootznahoo Inlet Lodge,** Box 134, Angoon, 788-3501. At plane float, 2 miles from dock. 10 units, 3 with kitchen. Restaurant. TV in rooms. Single $66, Double $75, Triple $88. Laundry facilities. Skiff charters, $50-$150/day. Bring own fishing gear. Kitchenettes $15 extra.

Raven Beaver Lodge, c/o Richard George, Manager, Box 116, Angoon, 99820. 788-3561. Three miles from dock. Baggage storage until checkout. All rooms have cooking facilities. Single $55. Add'l, $12/person.

Favorite Bay Inn Bed and Breakfast, Box 101, Angoon, 99820. 788-3123. Overlooks Favorite Bay, walking distance from village. 4 guest rooms, 2 baths, family rooms, library, deck. Courtesy transportation from ferry dock and seaplane terminal. Boat, canoe, and kayak rentals, salmon, halibut and trout fishing, guided wildlife trips. Single $49, Double $89, including breakfast. Other meals available at Whaler's Cove Lodge, same ownership. Open all year.

Whaler's Cove Lodge, on Kilisnoo Harbor, 3 miles south of Angoon,

185

on island across from ferry dock. Box 101, Angoon, 99820. 788-3123. Sportfishing for all saltwater fish, plus trout and steelhead. Fishing packages are all-inclusive: round trip air fare from Juneau or Sitka, meals, boat, tackle, and guide, fish processing. Low season rates early summer. High season 3 day package $1995. Open mid-May–mid-September.

GROCERY STORES: Two. **Seaside** and **Angoon Trading Company.**

BOAT FUEL at **Angoon Standard Oil.**

BOAT RENTALS, **Alaska Discovery** through Dick Powers, 788-3123.

CRAFTS: The villagers make and sell blankets, moccasins, and other beaded items at their homes. Also **Ramona's Restaurant and Gift Shop.**

Angoon is a dry community so alcohol cannot be legally obtained locally.

LAUNDRY FACILITIES at hotels, coin operated. Public laundry at Angoon Community Association.

TAXI: **Central Taxi,** 788-3994.

ICE: at the grocery stores.

INFORMATION AVAILABLE at the **Angoon City Office,** 788-3653 and 788-3663. P.O. Box 189, Angoon, AK 99820. Or at **U.S. Nat'l. Monument Office,** Community Services Building, 788-3166.

TENAKEE SPRINGS
(Area Code 907, Zip Code 99841)

TENAKEE SPRINGS (pop. 141) is a settlement near Tenakee Hot Springs on Chichagof Island. It is scenic, quiet, and marks one end of a good canoe route from Hoonah. Main street is a path. The only "cars" in town are the oil truck and fire truck. Hot springs feed the bath house adjacent to the dock and Main Street. The ferry dock is in the center of town. There are 16 miles of excellent footpath along the shoreline, extending 8 miles east and west of town.

Tenakee is an idyllic place to get "unhurried" for a few days. Watching the seals out at the reef, fishing boats coming and going, the eagle on the piling in front of your lodge, salmon spawning in Indian River, and soaking yourself in the hot spring while visiting with the local people is a fine break even in the middle of a tourist trip through the rest of Alaska.

If you're staying over, particularly on weekdays when the cafes keep shorter hours, you may have to plan eating times. Dinner after 4 p.m. means cooking it yourself if you have housekeeping facilities or are camping, or making reservations earlier with the Blue Moon Cafe. for the

Cabin made of hand-hewn logs on Tenakee waterfront.

time you want to eat. On weekends the Tenakee Tavern is open and everybody keeps longer hours.

To See and Do

Fish, hike, canoe. Salmon, halibut, trout. Set a pot for crab or shrimp.

Enjoy hot mineral springs in Tenakee Bathhouse, next to ferry dock. Donations accepted to help maintain building.

Facilities

ACCOMMODATIONS: **Snyder Mercantile Co.**, P.O. Box 505, Tenakee Springs, 99841. 736-2205. Cottages for rent, with cooking facilities. Supplies available at Snyder's General Store. Near ferry dock and plane float. Cottages from $30/day, weekly rates. Cabins sleep 2 to 6. Ask for one of the modern ones with deck just east of the store. Reservations a must. Full info on services and ferry and plane schedules provided when booking reservations.

Tenakee Inn and Tavern, 2 blocks from ferry and hot springs. Mailing address: 167 S. Franklin, Juneau, AK 99801. 736-2241 and 736-9238. Fax 463-3775. Bar, restaurant, housekeeping units in modern Victorian style building on waterfront. Upstairs rooms have balconies. Fishing charters. Single $45–60, Add'l $10/person. Bunkhouse accommodations, $15–20 per person.

CAMPGROUND at Indian River, 2 miles east of town. No facilities. Brown bears sometimes, especially during salmons spawning in the river(I wouldn't camp here then). Be careful with food and garbage and don't argue with the bears.

RESTAURANTS: **Blue Moon Cafe** next to dock. **Tenakee Inn and Tavern,** beverages and pool tables.

GROCERY STORE adjacent to dock, open 9 a.m.– 5 p.m. Mon.– Sat.

PUBLIC PHONE in booth near store and bath house. Available 24 hours/day. Phone is coinless. Accepts collect, credit card or 3rd party calls only. Also a public coin phone at the boat harbor.

BOAT FUEL and tie space available. A Juneau friend cautions boaters to tie near cafe carefully. He moored a skiff to the dock and failed to allow for its tidal swing. When he used the open-bottom restroom at the back of the cafe, he thought a skiff underneath looked familiar. It was!

FERRY SERVICE: *LeConte* northbound from Sitka, Friday night and Tuesday night. Southbound from Juneau, Thursday afternoon and returning Saturday morning, this is a nice excursion with about 24 hours in Tenakee. People in Tenakee have become sensitive to gawkers with cameras tramping through their yards, etc. Please be considerate.

SCHEDULED AIR SERVICE: operators in Juneau and Sitka. **Wings of Alaska,** 736-2247, has daily flights from Juneau. **Bellair** has scheduled flights from Sitka.

INFORMATION AVAILABLE, **Snyder Mercantile Co.** P.O. Box 505, Tenakee Springs, AK 99841. 736-2205.

HOONAH
(Area Code 907, Zip Code 99829)

HOONAH (pop. 1000) is the site of a very old Tlingit settlement on Port Frederick, a good natural harbor that remained ice-free during the last glacial advance that filled Glacier Bay only 200 years ago. Commercial fishing, subsistence hunting and fishing, and logging are the main activities. It has frequent ferry service from Juneau and Sitka. On the north shore of Chichagof Island, it is at one end of the canoe route to Tenakee Springs, about 40 miles including a portage from Port Frederick to Tenakee Inlet.

To See and Do

Walk around the scenic village with its beautiful views across Port Frederick.

Hike Spasski Trail, 3.5 miles, east of town.

Walk the road to the left of the ferry dock, northwest, past the old Indian cemetery to the picturesque cannery at its end—about 15 minutes each way. Fishing is good for Dolly Varden from the point.

The beach north of cannery has a fascinating variety of banded pebbles and rocks, including jasper. Wave-worn now, they were carried miles by the glaciers that shaped Glacier Bay.

Fish for salmon, trout, halibut.

Facilities
(rates plus 3% tax)

ACCOMMODATIONS: **Hoonah Lodge**, Box 320, Hoonah, AK 99829. 945-3636. 24 rooms newly remodelled, dining room, lounge, TV. Fishing and hunting charters can be arranged. Single $60, Double $75, Triple $90.

Bed & Breakfasts: **Alaska Bed & Breakfast Association**, 586-2959. **Mary's Rentals**, 945-3264. **Tina's Room Rentals**, 945-3442, 2–9 p.m.

RESTAURANTS: **Mary's Inn**, 945-3228. This restaurant is part of a non-profit vocational program for young people and serves good food, too. **Spanky's Pizza & Deli**, 945-3453.

CAMP: Check with harbormaster, Paul Dybdahl for acceptable place. 945-3670.

HARBOR FACILITIES: Transient floats inner harbor, under 40 ft. $2/night, over 40 ft. $4/night. 24 hours on outer harbor float, free, telephone, showers and coin-op laundry. Paul Dybdahl, harbormaster, 945-3670.

GROCERY STORES: There are 3, including a coop, and a variety store.

LAUNDROMAT: **Grandma's Washeteria**.

BUS: none. TAXI: none.

FERRY SERVICE: dock about 1 mile from center of town, 945-3292.

AIRPORT: 3600 ft. runway, gravel, lighted, soon to be paved. Scheduled air service from Juneau, **LAB Flying Service**, 945-3661. **Wings of Alaska**, 945-3275.

BOAT FUEL: **Union** and **Standard** available. Tie-up space.

REGISTERED HUNTING GUIDE SERVICE: **Ken Schoonover**, P.O. Box 13 Hoonah, AK 99829. 945-3223.

BOAT CHARTERS: **Double Eagle Charters**, c/o Ernest Jack, Box 94,

Hoonah, AK 99829. 945-3253. Sport fishing for up to 6 passengers. Gear and bait provided. **Floyd Peterson, F.I.S.H.E.S.**, Box 245, Hoonah, AK 99829. 945-3327. Brochures available. **Icy Lady Charters**, c/o Mark Quam, Box 387, Hoonah, AK 99829. 945-3525. Fishing and sightseeing for up to 6 passengers, day trips, overnights. **Hoonah Charters**, 945-3334. **Icy Straits**, 945-3212 and 945-3234. **Nordic Raven Charters**, 945-3695.

CLINIC: City of Hoonah Health Clinic, 945-3386.

INFORMATION AVAILABLE, City Hall M–F, 945-3663, 945-3664. Fax 945-3445. City Clerk. **City of Hoonah**, Box 360, Hoonah, AK 99829. **U.S. Forest Service Hoonah District Office**, Box 135, Hoonah, AK 99829. 945-3664. Has "Hoonah Area Road Guide" for $1.

Happenings

Kid's Trout Derby, end of April and first week of May.

Kids' Field Day, third week of May, end of school games, races. Fishing contest.

4th of July—Parade and booths with games and food.

PELICAN
(Area Code 907, Zip Code 99832)

PELICAN, pop. 297, is a tiny fishing village with a cold storage plant on Lisianski Inlet, a scenic fiord on the northwest corner of Chichagof Island. Ferry service is twice a month all year, and the ferry stays 2 hours, but that is time to get off (and plan to fly back to Juneau) or walk up the one-lane boardwalk main street to the far end of town. Sometimes fish and crab can be bought from the cold storage plant. It is a bustling place during fishing season or on 4th of July, the big annual date in town. The round trip on the ferry makes a good one day excursion from Juneau, stopping at Hoonah both ways in summer.

To See and Do

Walk around town, including fishing harbor with lots of boats and gear, surrounded by spectacular scenery in the fiord. Few places in America have this lifestyle in the 20th century.

Fish anywhere. Peak seasons: King salmon in April, May, June. Coho salmon in July, August. All summer, trout and halibut.

Kayak scenic West Chichagof Island (West Chichagof-Yakobi Wilderness) if you've solved the problem of how to return to Juneau or can stay until the ferry's next trip. Some experienced paddlers go from Pelican to Sitka, a multo-day trip for experienced sea kayakers.

Facilities

ACCOMMODATIONS: **Rosie's Bar & Grill**, 100 yards from ferry dock, has 4 rooms for rent. Box 754, Pelican, AK 99832. 735-2265. Adjacent to Rosie's. Gift shop and museum. Open all year. Single/Double $65.

Lisianski Lodge, Box 776, Pelican 99832. 735-2266. Cabin and charter boat just outside Pelican. Beach cabin for 5 and lodge rooms for 8, bed and breakfast. Steam bath. Can furnish all meals. Complimentary packing of your fish. $100/day room and board, $280/day for room and board plus guide and boat. Guided hikes, $50/day. Whale watching.

Harbor Bed & Breakfast, at top of fishing boat harbor ramp.Box 744, Pelican, AK 99832. 735-2261 or 522-8502 in Anchorage. Laundromat. $65. Rents sea kayaks.

CAMPING: Ask the locals. Very little level ground in area. The flats across the creek south of town flood at high tide.

GROCERY STORE: 1 general store.

RESTAURANT: 1 restaurant and 2 bar & grills.

BOAT FUEL at Chevron in center of town.

LAUNDROMAT: downtown.

SCHEDULED AIR SERVICE: available from Juneau and Sitka. **Wings of Alaska**, 735-2284, 6 days a week, from Juneau. **Bellair**, 747-8636, from Sitka, Tues., Thurs., Sat. **Glacier Bay Airways**, 735-2336.

INFORMATION AVAILABLE: **City of Pelican**, Box 757, Pelican 99832. 735-2202. Fax 735-2258.

A brown bear strolls in her meadow—not ours!

191

HAVING FUN, WITHOUT ACCIDENT,
OFF THE BEATEN TRACK

Southeastern Alaska is a big area with few people and lots of cool, wet weather, poor visibility, and miles of **very cold** water. One quickly develops respect for prehistoric Indians who roamed these forests and paddled open canoes as far as Portland, Oregon. They must have been very good at staying dry, or very stoic about being cold and wet.

Judgment and planning are everything, whether you're hiking, boating, or flying. Any time you move into a new climate and an unfamiliar area, you have a new set of nature's rules to learn, and in Alaska, nature can be very quick and violent.

Weather, tides, and currents change rapidly here. When 20 vertical feet of water go somewhere every 6 hours, the currents in narrow places, especially mouths of wider bays, can quickly get over 8 knots. Winds and downdrafts in mountain passes can do the same thing. Visibility can drop rapidly, a long way from harbor, airport, or campsite.

Clothing should include the rain gear and warm woolens you'll need if it gets cold and wet. If it's warm now, you can wear light clothing, but have the other with you. Passengers who fly with me wear a lifejacket or floatcoat flying over water, and wear or bring boots, parka, etc. for flying over the icefield. If a boat sinks or capsizes, what will you have with you on the beach? Down is useless when wet—wool and fiberfill retain some warmth. Wet blue jeans are deadly. Surplus stores and the Salvation Army have inexpensive wool pants.

Shelter. Some light emergency shelter should be in your boat, plane or pack, adequate for overnight in rain on wet ground. A tube tent fastened to your floatcoat or lifejacket, so it and you reach shore together, is a good idea.

Fire starter or stove can be useful, though it's best not to count on being able to burn wet wood. Large clear plastic playing dice make excellent fire starter that doesn't crumble in a pocket. Bring an ample supply of starter and dry matches. Practice starting fires in wet conditions if you haven't done it before. Spruce sap or gum pulled off tree trunks was used by Indians as fire starter.

Insect repellent is a must. Besides the standard ones in every drugstore, you may want to try diluted Avon "Skin So Soft" bath oil which is effective and easier on your skin. It works for black flies as well as mosquitoes, though you'll need to replace it more often for the latter. In a pinch you can use the native solution—rubbing your skin with the inner bark from alder trees.

Distress signals and extra food are musts. People are hard to see in this big country, and it helps to make it easier for those looking for you. Pocket flares or a strobe are good and don't weigh much. Carry a copy of the air-to-ground emergency signals. Waving OK to a plane or helicopter could send him off when you need him.

Let someone know where you're going, and don't go alone. The smaller the area anyone has to search for you, the sooner you'll be in where it's dry and warm. Do let people know when you've returned. Stay together.

Bears need respect if we're to coexist. Brown bears, especially, can claim a territory or fishing stream as theirs. Keep food and food smells away from camp and out of your pockets. Burn all garbage. Make some noise anywhere you go. Bears are apparently attracted to human menstrual odors. Ask local people about recent bear sightings. Anything a bear takes is now *his*.

Turn back if weather or sea get bad. Check weather before going, and then watch it. Listen for reports if you have radio. Weather can change very rapidly here.

Don't have to get there, or back today. Hole up and wait it out. Bring what you'll need to do that.

Learn the area as soon as possible, carry charts and ask the locals a lot of questions. Many aviation radio repeaters have been installed in Southeastern Alaska. With current charts, you can talk to Flight Service Stations in Ketchikan, Sitka, or Juneau from most areas even if you're below hilltops.

For pilots and boaters: In air or water, know the rules of the road and obey. Know your equipment and your ability. Always have an alternative goal—not easy when bays or airports are far apart. Don't overload— always have a margin. Carry adequate personal flotation gear, and wear it when the sea is rough. Watch for partly submerged logs and ice.

Work up to bigger things; don't just jump in. A hiker on his first backpack trip ever, on Chilkoot Pass, complained to the ranger about the steep trail. "But didn't the pictures in town show you it would be steep?" "Oh, I thought with all the people going over, it would have worn down some."

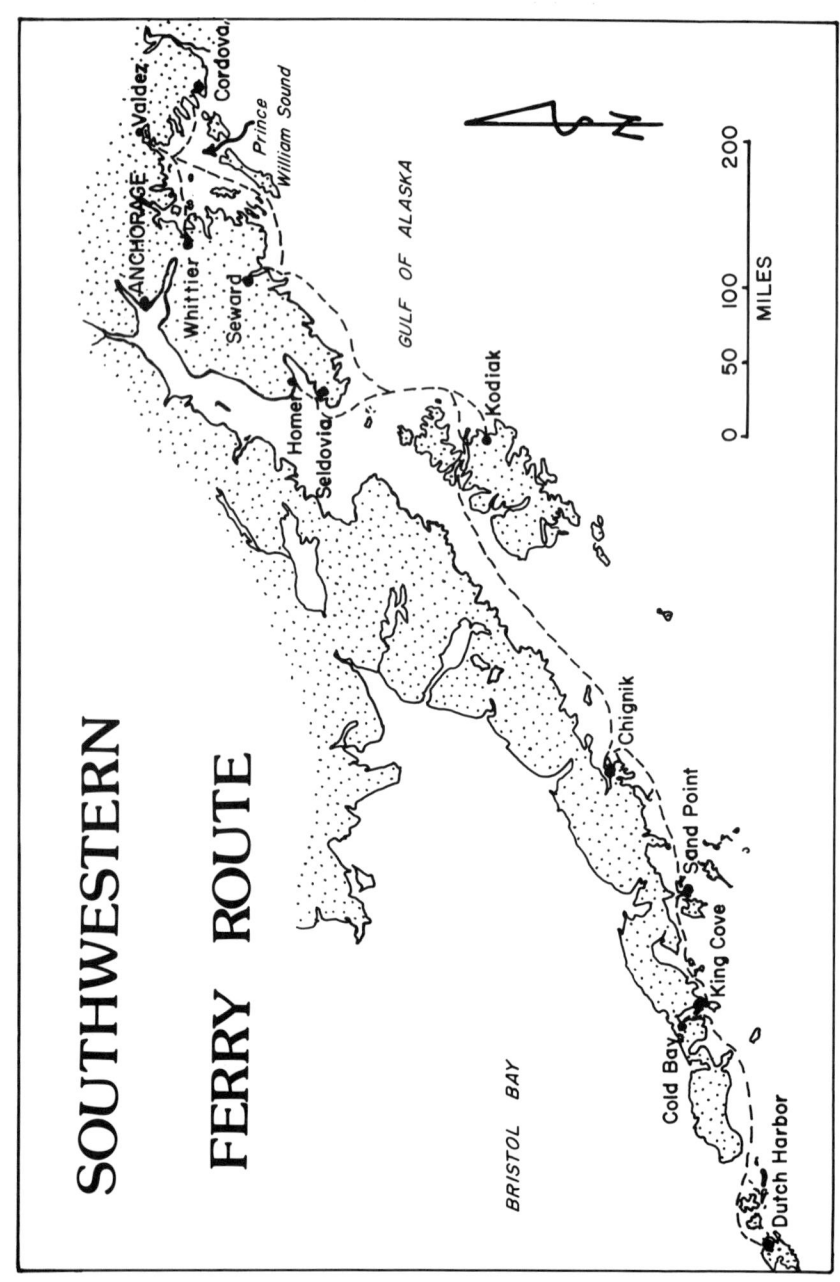

SOUTHWESTERN
FERRY ROUTE

The view over Kachemak Bay to glaciers and mountains, from the hill above Homer.

THE SOUTHWESTERN FERRY SYSTEM

The two ferries, *Bartlett* and *Tustamena,* make up the Southwest System, also part of the Alaska Marine Highway. Their routes don't connect with the Southeastern System, though the *Tustamena* makes several stops in Southeastern Alaska on her run south for winter maintenance. The *Bartlett* serves Prince William Sound with stops at Whittier, Valdez, and Cordova. The *Tustamena* serves Seward, Seldovia, Homer, Kodiak, Port Lions, Valdez, and Cordova, and has several trips annually out the Aleutian Chain with stops both ways at Kodiak, Chignik, Sand Point, King Cove, Cold Bay, and Dutch Harbor. Reservations are needed, even for walk-on passengers on all these runs, especially in summer.

The *Bartlett's* trips in Prince William Sound are beautifully scenic and make a fine excursion from Anchorage, using the Alaska Railroad to reach the ferry at Whittier, which doesn't have road access. You can also drive to or from Valdez, which has bus service as well. Cordova doesn't have road connections with the rest of Alaska, though it has daily service from Anchorage and Juneau with **Alaska Airlines**. The nearby Copper River Delta is one of the world's important migratory waterfowl rest areas and has nesting swans.

The *Bartlett* turns into the fiord and cruises 3 miles from Columbia Glacier on its summer trips between Valdez and Whittier. The officers announce sea otters and seals on the ice. As the huge front of the glacier is very active, you're sure to see pieces "calve off" into the bay. Recently Alaska's governor bowed to several tour boat companies and limited the *Bartlett* from going closer as she formerly did. Note that on direct trips between Cordova and Whittier, the route crosses Prince William Sound without going near the glacier.

On weekends there is also a Forest Service naturalist on board helping you spot wildlife. Whether you ride the ferry or one of the cruise boats between Valdez and Whittier, this is a fine trip.

In summer, the *Tustamena* stops 3 miles from the Columbia Glacier on her weekend trips between Seward and Valdez, allowing some who aren't going to Whittier a glacier view. This is an unhurried and uncrowded trip on which you may be able to get a stateroom.

The *Tustamena's* runs to Kodiak Island are an experience. These are not protected "inside" waters, and the 10 hour trip is locally known as the "Dramamine Run". In summer it may be quite calm with many puffins flying by, sea otters, whales, and bird rookeries on the Barren Islands. If you want the experience or want to get your car to Kodiak, you can enjoy a real ocean trip. For the runs out the Chain you definitely need reservations. The *Tustamena* has some staterooms, but the *Bartlett* has none.

If you're going on the summer trips out the Chain, most direct access is from Homer. If you get on the ferry at Seward, the ship goes to Kodiak and back to Homer and returns to Kodiak before going west. You can stay on for several crossings of the Gulf, paying for the additional distance, or you can stop over in Kodiak. For trips west or to Kodiak, you could go one way on the ferry and fly to or from Anchorage the other way.

Kodiak has famous scenery, sportfishing for halibut and salmon, and hunting for bear and deer. It is the site of the first permanent Russian settlement in Alaska and has a fine museum in the Russian-built Erskine House a block from the ferry dock. The harbor is home to one of Alaska's largest fishing fleets and charter boats for fishing, hunting, and trips to bird rookeries. The bird, otter, and whalewatching alone would be worth the trip, whether you go by sea or air. Seniors have noted that the senior travel privilege on the Tustamena (space available) makes this an inexpensive trip from Seward or Homer.

The towns on the Alaska Peninsula and the Aleutian Chain are famous for birdwatching during migration, as is the Copper River Delta near Cordova. Whole species of waterfowl pass through here, stopping off to rest and feed at eelgrass beds in Izembek Lagoon near Cold Bay. The

Copper River Delta is a nesting area for waterfowl including swans.

Homer and Seward are popular destinations for travelers, especially RV campers. Both towns have hotels, bed & breakfasts (several on small farms east of Homer), campgrounds, fishing charter boats, and bicycle and kayak rentals. Nearby are state parks, wilderness areas, U.S. Forest Service cabins, glaciers and hiking trails.

In recent winters the *Tustamena* has made several trips between Seward and Juneau, offering an alternative to winter driving up the highway. A smooth ride isn't guaranteed across the Gulf of Alaska in winter! These trips are reserved far in advance.

The Southwest ferries both have solariums and dining rooms with service, but neither has an elevator. The *Bartlett* doesn't have rental blankets or pillows as most of its runs are in daylight. It also doesn't have a baggage cart. For another dimension to Alaska and unbeatable scenery, why not try the marine buses of the Southwest?

You can make reservations and buy tickets at any ferry terminal in Southwest Alaska, in Anchorage, or by calling the **Juneau** main office, (800) 642-0066 or (907) 465-3941. Other terminal numbers are: **Anchorage,** 272-4482, **Cordova,** 424-7333, **Homer,** 235-8449, **Kodiak,** 486-3800, **Seldovia,** 234-7868, **Seward,** 224-5485, and **Valdez,** 835-4436.

INFORMATION AVAILABLE: **Cordova Chamber of Commerce,** 424-7260, **Homer Visitor Center,** 235-7740, **Kodiak Island Visitor Center,** 486-4782, **Kodiak National Wildlife Refuge,** 487-2600, **Seward Chamber of Commerce** 224-3094, **Valdez Visitor Center** 835-45836, **Chugach National Forest** 271-2500 (for trail and Forest Service cabin info).

Motorhomes from all over the United States and Canada stop at "the end of the road" on Homer Spit's city-owned campground.

M/V Tustamena

AUGUST EASTBOUND

LEAVE SELDOVIA	LEAVE HOMER	LEAVE PORT LIONS	ARRIVE KODIAK	LEAVE SEWARD	ARRIVE VALDEZ
			Lv. W5 3:00P	TH6 10:00A	TH6 9:00P
SU9 5:30A	SU9 8:30A		SU9 8:30P		
	M10 1:30P	M10 11:30P	T11 1:30A		
T11 8:00P	T11 11:00P		Lv. W12 3:00P	TH13 10:00A	TH13 9:00P
SU16 5:30A	SU16 8:30A		SU16 8:30P		
	M17 1:30P	M17 11:30P	T18 1:30A		
T18 8:00P	T18 11:00P		Lv. W19 3:00P	TH20 10:00A	TH20 9:00P
SU23 5:30A	SU23 8:30A		SU23 8:30P		
	M24 1:30P	M24 11:30P	T25 1:30A		
T25 8:00P	T25 11:00P		W26 11:00A		
TH27 9:00A	TH27 3:00P	F28 1:15A	Lv. F28 8:00A	*** TO CHAIN TRIP #4 ***	

AUGUST WESTBOUND

LEAVE VALDEZ	LEAVE SEWARD	LEAVE KODIAK	LEAVE PORT LIONS	LEAVE HOMER	ARRIVE SELDOVIA
*** FROM CHAIN TRIP #4		Ar. W5 3:30A			
F7 7:00A	F7 8:00P	S8 12:30P	S8 3:00P	SU9 2:30A	SU9 4:00A
		SU9 11:30P	Ar.	M10 11:30A	
		T11 3:30A		T11 5:00P	T11 6:30P
F14 7:00A	F14 8:00P	S15 12:30P	S15 3:00P	SU16 2:30A	SU16 4:00A
		SU16 11:30P	Ar.	M17 11:30A	
		T18 3:30A		T18 5:00P	T18 6:30P
F21 7:00A	F21 8:00P	S22 12:30P	S22 3:00P	SU23 2:30A	SU23 4:00A
		SU23 11:30P	Ar.	M24 11:30A	
		T25 3:30A		T25 5:00P	T25 6:30P
		W26 3:00P	W26 5:30P	TH27 5:45A	TH27 7:15A
*** FROM CHAIN TRIP #4		Ar. W2 3:30A			

The *Tustamena* aproaches its Homer dock.

M/V Tustamena
ALEUTIAN CHAIN TRIPS

CHAIN TRIP	#4 JUL 3-JUL 8	JUL 31-AUG 5	AUG 28-SEP 2	SEP 11-SEP 16	
FRI	LV	KODIAK	8:00AM	SUN LV	DUTCH HARBOR	7:00PM
SAT	LV	CHIGNIK	5:00AM	MON LV	COLD BAY	10:45AM
SAT	LV	SAND POINT	3:15PM	MON LV	KING COVE	1:30PM
SAT	LV	KING COVE	11:00PM	MON LV	SAND POINT	9:30PM
SUN	LV	COLD BAY	2:00AM	TUE LV	CHIGNIK	8:30AM
SUN	AR	DUTCH HARBOR	4:15PM	WED AR	KODIAK	3:30AM

SEPTEMBER EASTBOUND

LEAVE SELDOVIA		LEAVE HOMER		LEAVE PORT LIONS		ARRIVE KODIAK		LEAVE SEWARD		ARRIVE VALDEZ	
					Lv.	W2	3:00P	TH3	10:00A	TH3	9:00P
SU6	5:30A	SU6	8:30A			SU6	8:30P				
		M7	1:30P	M7	11:30P	T8	1:30A				
T8	8:00P	T8	11:00P		Lv.	W9	11:00A				
TH10	9:00A	TH10	3:00P	F11	1:15A Lv. F11		8:00A	*** TO CHAIN TRIP #4 ***			
					Lv.	W16	3:00P	TH17	10:00A	TH17	9:00P

SEPTEMBER WESTBOUND

LEAVE VALDEZ		LEAVE SEWARD		LEAVE KODIAK		LEAVE PORT LIONS		LEAVE HOMER		ARRIVE SELDOVIA	
*** FROM CHAIN TRIP #4		Ar.	W2	3:30A							
F4	7:00A	F4	8:00P	S5	12:30P	S5	3:00P	SU6	2:30A	SU6	4:00A
				SU6	11:30P		Ar.	M7	11:30A		
				T8	3:30A			T8	5:00P	T8	6:30P
				W9	3:00P	W9	5:30P	TH10	5:45A	TH10	7:15A
*** FROM CHAIN TRIP #4		Ar.	W16	3:30A							

SEP 17 - SEP 30

THU	SEP 17	LV VALDEZ	10:00PM	MON	SEP 21	LV SEWARD	6:30AM
		AR CORDOVA	3:45AM			LV KODIAK	10:15PM
				TUE	SEP 22	LV PORT LIONS	1:00AM
FRI	SEP 18	LV CORDOVA	3:00PM			LV HOMER	12:45PM
		AR VALDEZ	8:45PM			AR SELDOVIA	2:15PM
SAT	SEP 19	LV VALDEZ	8:30AM	TUE	SEP 22	LV SELDOVIA	3:45PM
		AR CORDOVA	2:15PM			LV HOMER	7:15PM
				WED	SEP 23	LV PORT LIONS	5:30AM
SAT	SEP 19	LV CORDOVA	10:00PM			LV KODIAK	10:30AM
SUN	SEP 20	LV VALDEZ	8:00AM			AR SEWARD	11:45PM
		AR SEWARD	7:00PM				
THU	SEP 24	LV SEWARD	8:00AM	MON	SEP 28	LV SEWARD	6:30AM
		LV CORDOVA	9:15PM			LV KODIAK	10:15PM
FRI	SEP 25	AR VALDEZ	3:00AM	TUE	SEP 29	LV PORT LIONS	1:00AM
						LV HOMER	12:45PM
FRI	SEP 25	LV VALDEZ	5:00AM			AR SELDOVIA	2:15PM
		AR CORDOVA	10:45AM				
				TUE	SEP 29	LV SELDOVIA	3:45PM
FRI	SEP 25	LV CORDOVA	10:15PM			LV HOMER	7:15PM
SAT	SEP 26	AR VALDEZ	4:00AM	WED	SEP 30	LV PORT LIONS	5:30AM
						LV KODIAK	10:30AM
SAT	SEP 26	LV VALDEZ	10:00PM			AR SEWARD	11:45PM
SUN	SEP 27	LV CORDOVA	8:00AM				
		AR SEWARD	7:00PM				

M/V E. L. Bartlett

M/V BARTLETT SCHEDULE
MAY 11, 1992 THROUGH SEPTEMBER 15, 1992

MON	LV CORDOVA	6:30AM	FRI	LV CORDOVA	6:30AM
	AR WHITTIER	1:30PM		AR WHITTIER	1:30PM
MON	LV WHITTIER	2:45PM	FRI	LV WHITTIER	2:45PM
	AR CORDOVA	9:45PM		AR CORDOVA	9:45PM
TUE	LV CORDOVA	12:30AM	SAT	LV CORDOVA	12:30AM
	LV VALDEZ	7:15AM		LV VALDEZ	7:15AM
	AR WHITTIER	2:00PM		AR WHITTIER	2:00PM
TUE	LV WHITTIER	2:45PM	SAT	LV WHITTIER	2:45PM
WED	LV VALDEZ	12:30AM		AR VALDEZ	9:30PM
	AR CORDOVA	6:00AM	SUN	LV VALDEZ	7:15AM
THU	LV CORDOVA	12:30AM		AR WHITTIER	2:00PM
	LV VALDEZ	7:15AM	SUN	LV WHITTIER	2:45PM
	AR WHITTIER	2:00PM		LV VALDEZ	11:45PM
THU	LV WHITTIER	2:45PM	MON	AR CORDOVA	5:15AM
	LV VALDEZ	11:45PM			
FRI	AR CORDOVA	5:15AM			

**PRINCE WILLIAM SOUND ROYAL FLUSH REGATTA ALTERNATE SAILING MAY 16-WHITTIER

**SAT MAY 16	LV CORDOVA	12:30AM	SAT	MAY 16	LV WHITTIER	9:00AM
	AR WHITTIER	7:30AM			AR VALDEZ	6:00PM

DAILY SERVICE BETWEEN VALDEZ-WHITTIER AND RETURN
FROM SEPTEMBER 16, THROUGH SEPTEMBER 22, 1992

	LV VALDEZ	7:15AM	————	AR WHITTIER	2:00PM
	LV WHITTIER	2:45PM	————	AR VALDEZ	9:30PM

The M/V BARTLETT will accept vehicles to a maximum length of 60 feet and a gross weight of 35 tons.

Railway connections required between Portage and Whittier for all Whittier departures and arrivals. Contact the Alaska Railroad at 800-544-0552 (outside Alaska) or (907) 265-2623 for schedules and fares.

SENIOR CITIZENS PASS - HANDICAPPED PERSONS PASS travel will not be allowed on the M/V BARTLETT or M/V TUSTUMENA during May 1 -September 30 period on sailings between Whittier and Valdez or Seward and Valdez

The Columbia Glacier.

THE AUTHOR

ELLEN SEARBY worked on the Alaska ferries as a shipboard naturalist for the U.S. Forest Service during the summers of 1975-77. From 1978 to 1990 she worked as part of the ferry crew. Answering questions for many thousands of passengers, she learned what the Inside Passage traveler wanted and needed to know—and wrote it in this book.

She worked several winters as a research analyst in Alaska's coastal management office. With a B.A. in biology and an M.A. in geography from Stanford, a long-time interest in mountaineering ("I climbed with a lot of good people on their days off"). and a commercial pilot's license (she flies a 1948 Luscombe), she finds the Inside Passage a challenging place to be. In her spare time she started SEADOGS, the Southeastern Alaska search and avalanche dog team.

She did the research, wrote, and published three editions of *The Costa Rica Traveler*, and edited and published the *Vancouver Island Traveler* by Linda Daniel. She is married to Henry Jori, a retired forestry pilot. In 1990 she retired to full-time travel writing and publishing on the family farm in the California redwoods.

INDEX

Windham Bay Press

Guidebooks for independent travelers who want to **See More and Spend Less!** Great photos! Clear maps. Fun to read! Easy to use! Perfect gifts.

The Costa Rica Traveler, Getting Around in Costa Rica by Ellen Searby. 3rd edition, 1991. Update 1992.

Tells all you need to know to explore a warm and friendly spot in the Central American sun—how to get there, what to bring, how to explore on your own, when you'll see more with a naturalist guide. Lists nature lodges plus 300 hotels personally inspected, with their prices and facilities (even whether the desk staff speaks English)!

The Costa Rica Traveler tells where you'll find wildlife and where to go for the particular birds, monkeys, or sea turtles you want to see. A calendar shows fishing seasons, turtle and bird nesting, Costa Rican holidays, and other special activities you may want to plan for.

If you're thinking of retiring in Costa Rica, investing or volunteering there, **The Costa Rica Traveler** has tips, addresses and phone numbers *you need.*

Publishers Weekly Travel Bestseller for warm destinations in 1990, 1991, and 1992!

Readers and reviewers say: "I've been going to Costa Rica for 18 years, but your book is the best!"

"The Costa Rica Traveler, by Ellen Searby, veteran travel writer with a demanding eye for value and frequently updates her excellent guide, which carefully rates hotels and takes you off the beaten track." *The Tico Times,*

"For the armchair traveler, this book is a great read. For the Costa Rica bound—it's a must!"*Marlin Magazine*

Tropical Beaches And So Much More!

ISBN 0-942297-04-0. 304 pages, maps, over 100 photos. US$14.95

Costa Rica Road Map

Most complete map of Costa Rica we have seen, newly published in Canada, text in English.

• 8 miles to the inch.

• Shows all beaches, mountains, parks, and biological reserves.

• Shows all roads where you can drive even a 4-wheel drive, and all towns big and tiny.

• Shows which towns have service stations!

• Colors and type show mountain ranges and an incredible amount of information clearly.

• Map is about 30 x 30 inches, easy to handle in car or bus.

• **Essential for planning your trip and for exploring Costa Rica by car or bus.** Fine for slide and VCR shows when you come back. $7.95.

A Guide To The Birds of Costa Rica, By Stiles and Skutch

- The *only* complete bird guide to Costa Rica—includes 52 pages color.
- Makes bird identification easy—most of the time!
- Highly readable, durable for years of field use, paperback.
- Essential for any birder in Costa Rica!

Published by Cornell University Press. US $34.95.
(Plus shipping. See schedule on order blank.)

Special Costa Rica Set—everything the birder needs but his binoculars!

- The Costa Rica Traveler, 3rd edition
- Costa Rica Road Map
- A Guide to Birds of Costa Rica

One copy of each of the above sent together to same address. US$57.00.
See very special shipping rate for the set—save $4 to $8.

The Vancouver Island Traveler, Guide to the Freshest, Friendliest Place on Earth, by Linda Daniel. All New 2nd Edition!

Cool and forested from nature, but warm and friendly from its welcoming people, Vancouver Island offers you sightseeing and shopping in Victoria, world class fishing, golfing beside the shore, sea kayaking, beach and mountain hiking, caving, diving, bicycling, camping beside lakes and ocean, and simply relaxing!

Canada's Vancouver Island is just a short ferry or plane ride from Seattle or Vancouver. The perfect place to travel with children, it's clean and has lots for them to do. Distances are short so you don't have to keep them for long in car or RV.

The Vancouver Island Traveler gives you all the information you need to plan an exciting or relaxing getaway trip doing what you like best. Hotels, hostels, campgrounds and restaurants are listed, with Daniel's recommendations, even her choices for tea shops in Victoria!

"Finally a detailed guide book" for the island. *The Province,* Vancouver, B.C.
Safe, Friendly, Nearby!
ISBN 0-942297-05-9. 224 pages, maps, over 90 great photos, US$12.95.

Alaska's Inside Passage Traveler, See More, Spend Less. 14th edition. By Ellen Searby

Alaska's Inside Passage Traveler is the authority for using one of the world's last great travel bargains, the Alaska ferry fleet.

Ferries go through "narrows" close to both shores where you can see wildlife on the beach and eagles in their nests. Ferries stop at all the ports, rather than selected ones. Best of all, you can get off at any port, stay as long as you wish, and catch another ship.

You can bring your car or RV, a bicycle, or a kayak. You can reserve a stateroom, or sleep inexpensively on the solarium deck or in reclining chair lounges.

Alaska's Inside Passage Traveler tells all you need to know to make the most of the ferries to see the Inside Passage and its towns. Hotels, hostels and campgrounds are listed with their rates. Searby gives suggestions for traveling with chldren or pets, driving an RV in Southeast Alaska and on the ferry, senior rates, and enjoying the northern wilderness safely.

Author Ellen Searby worked 15 years on the ferries, first as a U.S. Forest Service naturalist and then as a member of the crew.

Readers and reviewers say: "This is the insider's guide to the Inside Passage. If Searby doesn't know it, no one does."

"A must for Alaska travelers." "These books are absolutely the most informative and worth-while." "The book is just what we were hoping for." ISBN 0-942297-06-7. 208 p., maps, 90+ photos. US$12.95

Zip Close Bubble Bags!

Save your gear in rainforest or desert! Keep your cameras, lenses, and binoculars clean and dry in the field! Pad such fragile and valuable items from each other in your day pack while you hike, kayak, cycle, or even ride a trotting horse!

No More Rattles in Your Pack!

Author Ellen Searby brings her cameras home in good shape from months of field use by keeping each in a separate bag in her pack. "It's great to be able to reach in and grab one for a quick shot of a monkey, leaving the others in their bags. I give the bags to my naturalist friends, too."

Heavy duty inner and outer layers of plastic with a layer of airtight bubbles between. Washable, reusable many trips. Roomy 10x12" holds camera or binoculars. #G-1, $2.50 each.

All of the books listed here are available in bookstores, especially those specializing in travel. Stores can order them for you or you can order from

Windham Bay Press
Box 1198
Occidental, CA 95465 U.S.A.
(707) 823-7150

You are welcome to send for our latest catalog.

We hope you have a wonderful trip and look forward to your next one!

Our books are available from stores throughout North America, or order from Windham Bay Press.

Order Form (all prices in US $)
Windham Bay Press, Box 1198, Occidental, CA 95465 U.S.A.
Phone & Fax: (707) 823-7150

Qty.	Item	Price	Amount
_____	Costa Rica Traveler, 3rd ed.	14.95	_____
_____	Costa Rica Road Map	7.95	_____
_____	Guide to the Birds of Costa Rica	34.95	_____
_____	Special Costa Rica Set (all of above)	57.00	_____
_____	Alaska's Inside Passage Traveler	12.95	_____
_____	Vancouver Island Traveler	12.95	_____
_____	Zip Close Bubble Bag	2.50	_____

Subtotal $ _____

Sales tax 7 1/2% on orders for CA addresses $ _____

Shipping, see schedule below: $ _____

(**Books**—Traveler guides: US surface $1.50 first book, .50 ea. add'l. Air $3 first book, .50 ea. add'l. book. Canada surface $2.50, Air $4. Air to Latin America $5, Europe, $7, Asia $10. **Birds of Costa Rica**—US surface $2, Air $4.25. Canada surface $2.25, air $5.25. Latin America, $8.50. Europe $15. All others $19. **Maps & Bags**—U.S., $1 ea. Canada $1.25 ea., All other countries $2 ea. **Costa Rica Set** U.S. surface FREE, air $4. Canada Surface $1.50, air $4.)

Total $ _____

(Please enclose check payable though US bank or US or Canadian postal money order in US $.)

Ordered by

Address

Ship to (if different address)

Prices and postage rates good through December 31, 1992. After that date, please request new catalog.